X

THE PEACE OF BLUE

UNIVERSITY PRESS OF FLORIDA

Florida A&M University, Tallahassee
Florida Atlantic University, Boca Raton
Florida Gulf Coast University, Ft. Myers
Florida International University, Miami
Florida State University, Tallahassee
New College of Florida, Sarasota
University of Central Florida, Orlando
University of Florida, Gainesville
University of North Florida, Jacksonville
University of South Florida, Tampa
University of West Florida, Pensacola

UNIVERSITY PRESS OF FLORIDA

*Gainesville · Tallahassee · Tampa · Boca Raton
Pensacola · Orlando · Miami · Jacksonville
Ft. Myers · Sarasota*

The Peace of Blue

WATER JOURNEYS

Bill Belleville

A Florida Quincentennial Book

Printed in the United States of America. This book is printed on Glatfelter Natures Book, a paper certified under the standards of the Forestry Stewardship Council (FSC). It is a recycled stock that contains 30 percent post-consumer waste and is acid free.

This book may be available in an electronic edition.

19   18   17   16   15   14   6   5   4   3   2   1

ISBN 978-0-8130-6009-5

Library of Congress Control Number: 2014937648

The University Press of Florida is the scholarly publishing agency for the State University System of Florida, comprising Florida A&M University, Florida Atlantic University, Florida Gulf Coast University, Florida International University, Florida State University, New College of Florida, University of Central Florida, University of Florida, University of North Florida, University of South Florida, and University of West Florida.

University Press of Florida
15 Northwest 15th Street
Gainesville, FL 32611-2079
http://www.upf.com

To Beth, Chuck, Ray, and Will Crawley

Contents

THE PEACE OF BLUE

Introduction

> If there is magic on this planet,
> it is contained in water.
>
> Anthropologist Loren Eiseley

I went down to Rock Cub spring the other day to see if it was still flowing. We've been in a prolonged drought here in Florida, an event that aids in the progressive destruction of natural landscapes around us. The effects of that drought are magnified by the great thirst of resident Floridians and by the millions who come to visit as tourists every year.

The springs are inside a state forest not far from my home. Although land around it is in public ownership, the delicate balance of its ecology is in jeopardy because the private land far beyond its boundaries affects its health. Our Florida springs are "recharged" by rainfall seeping through the porous uplands. There's already a massive storehouse of this water down in the aquifer below. But most of it was accrued long before modern growth and its caffeinated promotion set in. It's easy to have a functioning aquifer in a state with 2 million people—which is about how many lived here in the 1950s. But when that population is multiplied nine or ten times, the native stasis that nourishes these springs is thrown all out of whack.

Limestone boulder in the shape of a bear cub that sits in the middle of Rock Cub spring.

Indeed, the vitality of both our surface and groundwater in this sea-level state often depends on the kindness of strangers upstream—and the strangers have not always been kind. We have worked diligently over the last century to uproot our rare and naturally bountiful places—dredging, draining, and burning to make way for fantasy worlds and walled, upscale developments and glitzy resorts. Now, periodic droughts and the fires that follow in their wake continue that human-driven work. It was only logical that I should worry about the health of a tiny spring.

Rock Cub is actually a series of four or five separate seeps that splay out of the bottom of a high bluff. The topographical map that first led me to it a few years ago showed the landscape dropping dramatically forty to fifty feet down a sloping terrain. At the bottom, the slope leveled out onto a blackwater swamp. The first time I walked down to the little springs, I had to hang onto the limbs of small water oaks and bay magnolias, grabbing the occasional frond of a sabal palm to keep from falling on my butt. There was no path here, not even one made by animals, and my only trail marker was the hope that the bluff would, sooner or later, flatten out into the swamp below.

My most recent visit was more of the same—an ungraceful slow-mo freefall down the seepage slope, dodging the prickly catbrier vines and the finely woven webs of the golden orb spiders. At the bottom, the springs still streamed from the base of the limestone bluff. The outflow was only a few inches deep, but it was enough to polish the fine grains of silica and shell and lime rock in the spring run so they glowed luminously when shafts of sunlight hit them. A limestone boulder in the shape of a bear cub sat in the middle, and the ether of the clear water flowed up and around it.

I have visited this boulder and its springs during different seasons—by winter, with no foliage canopy to provide shade, it is stark and bright, the rock itself bare and gray. By summer, with the thick crown of sweetgum and tupelo and oak above, and ferns, lichens, and mosses below, the scene changes: bromeliads spike the branches of the water oaks, and the bear cub grows a rich coat of jade-colored mosses. The springs, insulated by the thick, surrounding jungle, seem to actually resonate, each refolding itself into a gentle gurgle, as if the lime-rock bear itself has taken life and is sipping from them.

I wonder at the sheer timelessness of such places, of how swamps and seepage slopes that sometimes feed them are among the least changed features of the landscape. If they have not been mechanically dredged and excavated and destroyed, these relic shards of nature can be portals to an ancient world. What I see today is not dissimilar to what other humans must have experienced when these springs first began to flow here eight to ten thousand years ago.

In this way, swamps and marshes function as time machines, places that that can transport us back to a very real, water-driven wilderness. If they afforded no other benefit, that alone would be worth the price of admission. But they allow a multitude of riches—storing and filtering water, keeping our climate and landscape moist, and housing a vast biological storehouse of animals and plants.

Our flowing rivers—whether they arise from a waterlogged swamp or marsh or as the collective outflow from scads of springs—function in a similar fashion. The larger rivers also served as aquatic roadways, allowing early Native Americans to navigate what amounted to a subtropical rainforest sitting atop a saturated sponge of water in Florida's dense interior.

But the pervasiveness of water doesn't end there. The Gulf of Mexico and the southern Atlantic swash the shores of most of peninsular Florida, creating what amounts to a flat, linear island tethered to the mainland by a slab of undulating sandy terrain.

Water is the singular feature that has made Florida what it is today. Add a warm, temperate, and subtropical climate to that, and you find a place where the diversity of animals and plants soars, both under the water as well as atop the landscape nearby. And, as the scientist Edward O. Wilson has astutely observed, "the greater the biological diversity of any place, the greater the cultural diversity." Perhaps that's because humans who occupy a more complex landscape acknowledge the capacity for multiplicity on some deeper level. If that is so, then maybe the variety of habitats expands the cultural vision to include all those provincial behaviors that have radiated out to fill the many niches in the landscape.

Geographically, the islands of the sprawling Caribbean are considered a subregion of North America. But if you reverse the ethno-territoriality of that perspective, you will also see that Florida is regarded as part of the Caribbean Basin. Currents that sweep through the Caribbean often brush up against our shores. Indeed, plants and other living organisms of the Caribbean—including Florida's official "state butterfly," the zebra longwing—have also alighted here over time. Many have ridden prevailing currents of air and water for hundreds and thousands of years in this way. Politically, Florida may be a world apart from the thousands of islands of the Bahamas and the Antilles, but biologically, these places are deeply intertwined.

Like any highly diverse bioregion, our Florida watersheds should be managed in a way that keeps them healthy and sustainable—by using the higher truth of ecological realities rather than political ones. Although the mouth of a deep, wide river may seem vastly different from its distant soggy genesis, a mature understanding of the entire natural gestalt of that waterway is needed if it is to be fully understood.

Many of my excursions in this book take place in this Florida because that's where I've spent most of my adult life. But some stray into the Caribbean because that's where I've sometimes gone to report on expeditions, or other scientific projects that have to do in some way with water.

For someone trying to get a feel for water, the larger bioregion of Florida and the Caribbean is surely a great place to begin. The ocean, springs, rivers, and lagoons are generally blue—when not busy being turquoise or tannin, cobalt or gray. But a deeper, more personal look reveals another side, one that goes far beyond color and form, sometimes even skirting the edges of the great ecological unconscious itself. And once that "blue" is breeched— both physically and metaphorically—there's no telling how far the perspective may roam. If we're lucky, during the very best moments of a water experience, we might even come to know a very real peace.

While I've done my share of expository reporting early on, my natural inclination is to personally chronicle the observations and feelings and actions that imprint themselves onto a life. After all, as a little boy, the larger world first opened itself to me when I sat on my grandmother's lap as she read stories to me from books. And as an adolescent, I grew up in a relatively isolated countryside where so much of the culture still relied on storytelling for information.

By the time I was well into adulthood, I realized that the comforting childhood fondness for allowing a narrative to explain life had traveled along with me. And I found that some very astute authors were explaining the dynamics of this. "Everything is held together with stories," the nature writer Barry Lopez has said. "That is all that is holding us together, stories and compassion."

In this same way, my childhood life in the then-remote peninsula of the

Eastern Shore of Maryland where we lived was also defined by nature—which was acknowledged by playing outside, sometimes roaming for miles across a rural countryside veined with creeks and rivers and dotted with lakes. If I appreciated the notion of "story" on a fundamental level, I felt every bit as strong about nature because it had left such an enduring mark on my life. When I began to tease apart the many ways this "environment" has been meaningful to me as an adult, I found one very potent universal thread—and it was water.

And so, in this collection, I have tried to illustrate this connection in as many ways as possible. As a result, it may be realized by paddling a kayak in the full darkness of night, scuba diving or snorkeling, hiking in the bottom-lands of a remote swamp—or simply walking with my little sheltie along the shore of a "domestic" lake. It may also be evoked when I immerse myself in the ancient, desert-like scrub and sandhill communities that exist because they were once shoals and islands and sandbars when the peninsula that is Florida first emerged from the sea.

While you may find pragmatic data about water woven into many of these narratives, I hope that information won't overwhelm the story itself. Although I do explain scientific aspects of the water equation now and then, I leave the more detailed abstract writing to others who excel in the expository approach to earth science.

The essays of *The Peace of Blue* are not intended to be polemics that attempt to herd readers into water advocacy. Rather, they are one man's experiences in trying to fully inhabit a "place." In doing so, they rely as much on our sensibilities as they do on anything else. As the Pulitzer-winning author Richard Rhodes has advised, "The great benefit of experience is that your senses gather information directly and you feel it. No collection of documents is as ever as rich in detail as experience itself."

It is direct experience that helps each of us understand our landscapes more fully. In doing so, we acknowledge the emotional boundaries of a place—realizing not just the lineage of its culture and its science, but expressing how it makes us feel. In this way, the full knowledge of a certain place can also sculpt our identity in profound ways. Even if water seems to play only a minor role in creating the milieu for a story that may not dwell on its presence, it's still there—and it still embodies a universal and elemental dynamic.

I do hope these chronicles will illustrate how "blue" in all of its many incarnations might play a role in the dreams and memories of our own human lives. If we're fortunate, it might function as a portal to lead us to a vernacular experience in nature, one that's inextricably intimate and real. After all, the energy of water will be there, and we will know its power on some deeper instinctual level. Why not alert the conscious to what the great yawning unconscious already knows? I'm figuring that Carl Jung might raise his paddle high to that possibility.

When I finished assembling the essays that reveal my own personal toehold on the sway of blue, I actually wondered if I even needed to write an introduction explaining the primal and everlasting power of water in our lives. Certainly, water is the solution of our freshwater springs and rivers, bays and oceans—indeed, it is the element that covers three-fifths of our planet, the driving force of a true global reckoning. It is where our distant ancestors were first nurtured into life, where our fetal development mimics the progression of the water-bound life form that has gradually and painstakingly become terrestrial and human. After all, with over 70 percent of our bodies occupied by water, we are not just surrounded by it—and bred to it—but we are virtual walking vessels of it.

Nonetheless, in our era of überspecialization, we linear-minded moderns tend to see the water-driven "environment" as a place apart from ourselves—a place maybe in need of tinkering, exploiting, or even restoring. Yet, a more whole approach—such as that still found in many native cultures—helps us realize that it also lives inside of us, literally and otherwise.

My intent is not to create an intellectual précis about water, but rather to describe some of the excursions that have informed my own life. In doing so, I've tried to be honest about the true intimacy of place. As the writer David James Duncan has frankly noted, "The rivers that have moved me are those I've fished and fallen into and canoed and swam and slept beside; those I've lived on, nearly drowned in, dreamt about, sipped tea and wine by, taught kids to swim in, pulled a thousand fish from, and fought to defend."

A corollary of this truth also explains why otherwise well-meaning eco-advocates sometimes miss the boat by immersing themselves not in the heartfelt experiences of nature, but in the strident rhetoric of intellectual righteousness.

As for me, I've carefully banked my own water memories since I was a little boy. They date to when I first heard the crash of the ocean on the sandy beaches of the Atlantic, when I learned to fish and crab with my family—and where, as an adult, I have had some of the greatest adventures anyone could dream of. As a kid, I simply loved being around water. As an adult, I have found inspiration, discovery, and a generous dose of Loren Eiseley's magic there.

All great love stories have a beginning, and my own relationship with water was launched when I looked through a mask for the first time as a seven-year-old in a swimming pool and found that another world existed just under the surface. It wasn't a natural world, and the lower bodies of the others standing there in the shallow chlorinated pool water didn't make it any more so. But it did leave me with the ingenious notion that I could take that mask—and others like it—to just about any place where there was water. Once there, I might actually see through to another dimension, to the other side of blue.

A few years after my first underwater satori, I found myself using another mask to join Danny, a childhood friend, in a hunt for an old millstone in a lake near our country homes. The small lake was fed by an upland creek, and when the pond water flowed over a little waterfall, it tumbled down into another, slightly lower stream. The subtle gradient of the landscape would transport that swamp-bred water away to a deeper and wider river, until finally, it reached a massive bay and then the sea itself.

I was in my early teens then, and it struck me that the terrain itself played a large role in how water moved—or how it stayed relatively still. It was the gradient, after all, that made this lake particularly useful since the local business of grain farming could be more fully realized by a water-powered grinding mill.

The mill was emblematic of a time when mechanization was first harnessed to do the work that historically had been accomplished by brute strength. But the availability of electricity and an improved transportation system would eventually spell an end to the old mills. Most were simply abandoned, with the picturesque wooden mill houses left to slowly rot away, and the massive round-flat granite stones left to fall into the waters of the lake or stream where they had once held such vital sway.

Danny had done his own exploring on and under the waters of that little lake, and one day he had been rewarded with the discovery of the millstone itself. By the time I was invited to visit and fin out to the submerged stone, Danny was certain of its location. It was only a hundred yards or so from shore, near the place where the lake still spilled out into a lower creek. The water was as murky and cold as any I would later experience as an adult, and my visibility from inside the little mask was only a few inches. Still, the thrill I first experienced when I found the stone and ran my hands across its rough granite surface far exceeded any discomfort or cold or murky water.

These early discoveries were springboards to the adventures I would later have as I traveled as an adult to other water-infused landscapes. I soon learned that if I were curious and stubborn enough, I could prevail over just about any unpleasant challenge that might be looming there in my cherished world of blue—whether I experienced it underwater or on land.

Water—often just the memory of it—helps jar me out of that technological trance that our prosperous American society keeps trying to lull me into. And that has been reason enough to do what I can to connect with a landscape in which fresh or salt water has played an essential role in the human experience. Geographers sometimes use a term to describe our particular affection and caring for a certain place. It's "topophilia," and if you've spent any time at all chasing after landscape-driven experiences, you'll know what this means—and, if you're really lucky, you'll know how it feels.

If I'm going to stray down this philosophical slough, I'll also need to consider a broader perspective about the peace of blue. Water may be "managed" in a great many ways by us humans. But the ultimate truth is that water is a timeless and essential force all by itself. As such, it exerts its own very real "management" on the human race, whether we acknowledge it or not.

Some of this energy surely has to do with enchantment—and with our never-ending human infatuation for it. But there's something very primal going on here as well. We are air-breathing mammals. And regardless of the clever methods we've invented to take us across and under the water, the aquatic world will never be as directly accessible to our senses as a terrestrial habitat. It is no wonder that astronauts in training for space learn fundamental behaviors by being submerged in a tank of water. Since we cannot breathe underwater without an artificial aid of some kind, any liquid habitat will always be less known, less explored, and less understood. It is and always will remain truly wild because of this.

But there is more. According to the World Health Organization (WHO), "Water is probably the only natural resource to touch all aspects of human civilization—from agricultural and industrial development to the cultural and religious values embedded in society." Although it doesn't use the term "sense of place," the WHO does note, "The way water is used and valued constitutes an integral part of a society's cultural identity."

So while you're unlikely to find any essays here that deconstruct the notion of a "cultural identity," I hope that the shards of emotional information in these stories will help reveal that connect-the-dot rationale we humans often seek when we roam about in nature.

I may rant a bit every now and again at how wealthy scoundrels and their political toadies are sucking the liquid blue out of our landscapes, and how—if allowed to continue—they will destroy the very nature that first drew humans to any given place to begin with. While I surely advocate a sustainable approach to water use, I take great satisfaction in knowing you will find a very informed and eloquent library of both journalism and literature elsewhere to help you understand what is happening with our shared water "commons"—and why you should not allow it to continue. You'll find excellent advocacy-based case studies in books ranging from Cynthia Barnett's contemporary *Blue Revolution* to earlier works by Rachel Carson and Henry David Thoreau, all of which reflect commonsense discourses dating to the ancient Greek philosophers.

Similarly, I won't be expounding on any higher economic value of fresh- or salt water. Certainly, I do understand that folks sometimes must resort to that argument when making a case to save a stream in a wooded park, a freshwater spring, or a river. Our Western world is very good about assigning arbitrary values to material things and natural places—because that's the only worth some folks will understand. Still, I feel that by playing that game, we validate it in some way and that validation makes it more difficult for others to bond with the full emotional and spiritual energy of that place.

Consider this: the Zen master Thich Nhat Hanh has been practicing meditation and mindfulness for more than seventy years. By most accounts, he radiates an extraordinary sense of calm and peace. Thay, as he is known to his followers, says the current trend that puts an economic value on nature is similar to layering plaster on a gaping wound. "I don't think it will work," Thay told the *Guardian* in 2012. "We need a real awakening, enlightenment, to change our way of thinking and seeing things."

Thay says change will happen on a fundamental level only if, instead of assigning an economic value to our springs and coral reefs, we fall back in love with the planet that birthed and nurtured us. "You carry Mother Earth within you," says Thay. "She is not outside of you. Mother Earth is not just your environment."

And, really, the notion of "topophilia" arises out of an earnest caring for a specific place—just as a topographical map is created to chart the contours of a particular landscape. Technology and its diagrams may help lead us to a place—indeed, its many moving parts may power a plane or boat or scuba tank. But these are simply tools to understanding the water-crafted landscape and not ways to dominate or exploit it in a more efficient manner.

To fully appreciate the value of "sense of place," identify the most predominant and enchanting natural feature where you live, or where you most love to travel. Then imagine what that place on earth would be like if that feature were to vanish. There's no dollar figure in the world you can put on such a loss. It goes far beyond the economics of waterfront real estate and retail sales and seafood landings, and strays into the desolation of loss-driven despair.

Certainly, introducing readers to any commodity of blue is not intended to arm them with covetous and arcane information. Instead, it encourages bonding with a place on earth, one invaluable emotional contour at a time. From that bond, a real-world ethic may sprout, even flourish. After all, as the ecologist Aldo Leopold once advised, "We can be ethical only in relation to something we can see, feel, understand, love, or otherwise have faith in."

Properly informed with our own personal discoveries, we might then resist the narrow perceptions that our so-called modern Western culture often places upon a liquid, organic world that is still wonderfully alive with wisdom and discovery and light.

1   A Florida River at Night

The Incredible Lightness of Being

We drive down a dirt road atop a massive pre-Columbian Indian midden, bleached and knobby snail shells packed tightly just under the patina of grasses and fresh, white, modern gravel. The river is flowing ever so gently just as it has for thousands of years, and the midden slopes down as if to greet it.

Paddling under large bow in a tree limb. Photo by Michelle Thatcher.

I park as close to the shore as I can and undo the straps holding our kayaks on the car roof. My friend Michelle is with me, and she works the straps on one side of the cab while I do the same on the other. The sun will disappear below the horizon in an hour or so—but it will hide behind the tree line of cypress and sweetgum and bay before that. The residual light of day is a luxury now, and it allows us the clarity to get our small boats down and into the water without stumbling or otherwise losing context. When we return to this shore later in the night, it will take much longer to reload in the dark.

We're here for the rising of the full moon over this subtropical Florida river, an event that will take place in a few more hours. The sight of a full moon over water has always fascinated me; there's something comforting in the way the pale light glows as it's reflected in the dark liquid. Almost as if it marks a place, for just now, where the heavens and the earth join. Years ago, when I started paddling, I realized a small boat allowed me to go beyond the role of a mere spectator on the shore and to actually become a participant in this theater of nocturnal light.

Certainly it's an aesthetic that goes far beyond the visual image—particularly one seen from a remote or safe distance. It's a whole experience of the senses, one you can at once smell, feel, hear, taste, maybe even intuit on a more sublime level. And you can also move atop the actual liquid itself, allowing the reflection of the pale light to close around you. Early lyricists, like the Chinese poet Lu Yu, were taken with this notion, even when it happened on land. To walk in the moonlight, the twelfth-century poet wrote, is to "ride the moon." To float atop it evokes the same notion. But out here at night, it seems even more encompassing, as if the water in your body is also responding in some deep, visceral way to the touch of the sky.

I often go it alone on such paddles just as I do on some of my long wilderness hikes. In those cases, the solitude is a way to fully *feel* the landscape around me, as well as to listen to those enduring voices in the heart and in the mind. But I also enjoy companionship with thoughtful and curious partners who appreciate the immediacy of the moment and are not afraid to give themselves over to it. Michelle is one of those partners who is able to unshackle the ballast of socialization and fully inhabit a moment, and I am grateful for that.

We push away from shore, catching the slightest flex of the current that pulls us downstream. Instead of staying in the main channel—which I seldom do, under any circumstances—I firmly plant my paddle to turn my kayak, and then head for an opening in the shoal of vegetation at midriver. There's enough room for narrow kayaks to make it through here, although barely. As we go, large mullet spook in the shallow water around us, some of them creating loud sploshing sounds with their bodies, fins, and tails, the fleeting silver of their bodies catching the remaining shards of twilight.

Along the shoreline, the water plant known as pennywort is thick here, and I notice its roundish leaves are larger than usual, each the size of a small, green saucer. Although gentle, the current is ceaseless. Its days and nights of flow have neatly trimmed the edges of the fields of pennywort so rigorously that it seems almost coiffed, as if some human has been out here manicuring a very linear garden of green saucers. It is thick enough so that it seems like a natural understory to the trees that rise up behind it, a green pasture almost substantial enough to walk on.

The sun has fallen below the top of the tallest cypress now, and the refracted late-day light is working its particular magic on the river world, tracing a delicate balance between fading sunlight and gathering dusk. Twilight does this most everywhere, of course. But it seems particularly pronounced here in Florida, where the ever-moist subtropical air imbues the sky and water with a thousand versions of crimson, saffron, ocher.

Just ahead, a dead branch of a tree pokes from the water, and a black-crowned night heron—a rare wading bird that hunts after dark—crouches, looking more like a skinny owl than a heron. Elsewhere, great tangles of vines and leaves trail through the forest like topiary, mimicking the shadows of the mastodons and giant sloths that once hunted these same waters, an ice age or so ago.

It's still February, but the bare trees are already sprouting new green, and the animals are beginning to wake from the mild dormancy of our Florida winter. The specks are bedding, and some of the birds beginning to nest. A flock of large red-breasted birds flitter in the treetops, and I see it's a band of robins headed north to announce the arrival of spring.

There's something ineffably lovely about the light and the way it settles upon this place. It helps me understand better why the landscape painters from the Northeast traveled here in droves in the nineteenth and early twentieth centuries—Heade, Hunt, Herzog, McCord, Moran, and others. The images of water and light they captured spoke to an intimacy with a landscape—as well as to a skilled and precise art that could capture a fleeting moment in one special place on earth.

If twilight is ephemeral by its nature, it most certainly is here on this Florida canvas where one color effortlessly morphs into another before melting forever into the night. Art historians describe the style of those early Florida landscape painters as "evanescent"—each precious and heartbreakingly lovely image they captured looking as if it were ready to dissolve into the ether. And, of course, that is exactly what that real-life moment was also preparing to do.

All of life is that way, of course, far more fleeting than our ego-driven mammalian brains would ever allow us to admit. But here, on the cusp of light and darkness of a Florida river, it is not a matter of intellectually accepting or denying truth. The half light of this river will quickly be gone. And like a stunningly brilliant and beautiful woman you once knew—one who would have to leave because she was destined to do so—the aesthetic of it will be made even more intense and vivid by the knowledge of its impending departure. It is not a choice; it simply is.

A few yards away, a large gator—startled by our noise—propels itself almost entirely out of the water, vertically. Its loud splash interrupts the silent grandeur of the moment. But, within seconds, all is calm again, almost as if the river has transported the memory of the experience downstream with its flow.

The full moonrise is imminent, and in time will announce itself from inside another tree line, ascending into the eastern sky, nearly opposite from where the sun has now disappeared. For now, vines in the forest seem to become animated by the light, quivering like large-bodied snakes. A visual memory from an experience I once had in the Amazon flashes in my head now, and I get a very real gut rush from it. I'm comforted by being in a place that has the power to evoke such a memory, and for right now, that's all that counts.

If transience fuels this moment in nature, so too does the rich diversity of color and life—it is so much more than what a temperate landscape would support. I figure if the exotic lushness of this place wasn't enough to overwhelm the senses of early visitors, artists, and writers, then the surreal opportunity of being attacked by giant lizards, cougars, and assorted vipers likely was. If La Florida wasn't too pretty and too luxuriant and too ripe, then it was too dangerous.

Michelle and I paddle instinctively now, no intellect to bogart the moment. In a very real way, it occurs to me that the energy of the senses has been freed to create its own momentum, a reality as sure as the V-line of the wake my hull leaves behind in the dark liquid of the night. Although she's only a few yards away, I can barely see her. But when she paddles into a stretch of water illuminated by the moonlight, I see she is smiling a great smile of happiness.

And yep, we're essentially in an unknown place for right now. Nonetheless, the particular scent of the water can be acknowledged; the fresh coolness of the air can be absorbed by the pores of the skin; the calls of the birds and the animals can be heard, somewhere beyond the final echo of the sound. What emerges is a profoundness of being, one that trumps any intellectual pretense that may have tried to smuggle its way along. Despite all we have done to sweep it clean from the imagination, the true natural Florida remains, inextricable and sure, and I am thankful for the everlasting possibilities of its soul.

More fish jump and splash, a gator groans, and a radiant, pale glow rises from behind a crown of cypress to the east. Paddle in hand, I push forward onto where it's reflected on the surface, thinking one last time of the twelfth-century Chinese poet and his seminal metaphor of celestial light.

Michelle and I are riding the moon as fully as we can into the blackness of this Florida river night. As we do, we listen silently for the ephemeral lyric of its wildness. It's not a swaggering, fearsome lyric, but one that speaks in quiet whispers to the human soul.

2 Wading through the Walt Whitman of Habitats

Scrub and Sandhill

Shouldering my backpack, I walk atop a dirt road that skirts the cusp between a high ridge of porous white sand and a low, darkly wooded hammock.

Walking on a sandy trail in the ancient shoals known as the Florida scrub. Photo by Jane Goddard.

Although the sun is not far above the horizon, the uplands mapped as "Sulphur Island" are already radiating a heat that will intensify as the day goes on. The stunted forest of twisted trees, saw palmettos, and gristly plants offers almost no shade, creating what amounts to a patina of green atop a rolling desert. I take the first trail that opens into it, a narrow aisle that ascends to a distant past.

I have just come from exploring a small, remote spring at the base of this sandy dome, a wild oasis tucked in by a thick, amber-tinted grid of tupelo and hickory, cypress and sweetgum. Now I will see where the aquatic energy that powers this tiny magic enters the earth, to more fully know where it begins its patient and timeless seep down into the soil and soft rock that brings it to life. It looks like, if I pay attention, I may also see some other neat stuff along the way.

Geologists describe the uplands here as "sandhill karst," a word-squeeze of two very different realties. The well-lit, dry "scrub" and sandhills I am walking through rest atop a dark underworld of consolidated coral and bone and shell. "Karst" is the name given to this porous limestone, the soft rock of the aquifer. Water flows through its fissures and bedding planes, hidden rivers and streams.

Despite all our losses, a relic wilderness remains in the interior of Florida, much of it inside large public swaths of conservation land, from ten to more than forty square miles in size. If the preserve is large enough, as it is here in the Seminole State Forest, I can see most of the plant and animal communities of this richly varied peninsular state within just a couple miles of each other. The swamps and rivers, of course, are at the bottom, while the sweeping, dry uplands of scrub and sandhill are at the top.

The gradients in between are jammed with the diverse ecotones that define the margins of the dozen or so habitats that stair-step their way up and down the slopes. Each distinguishes itself with specialized mixes of moisture and soil, customizing its biota with the particulars of geography and climate and the inextricable passage of time.

I walk toward the crest of this sandy Florida mountain, up to where my topographical map shows rises of sixty and seventy feet above the swamp. This arid mesa is barely two square miles in size, an ancient island that first arose from a retreating sea over a million years ago. Between several more glacial ebbs and flows, critters and plants gradually colonized this island, ranging out across a vast desert that stretched from the continental Southwest and Mexico to Florida.

The rising sea stranded new residents like scrub jays and lizards and tortoises here, and they learned to do a lot with a little. Now that the ocean has retreated once more, the millennia of island survival have left their imprint on plants and animals alike. With no sea to isolate them, they could fly, crawl, or drift to lower ground. But speciation is a powerful force, and this timeless scrub will forever be their home.

When the naturalist William Bartram first explored Florida in the 1760s, he ranged to the west beyond Salt Springs and then Lake Kerr, out to where the darker soils of the hammock gave way to the white sand of the Florida scrub. It was an "endless wild desert," Bartram reported, unlike the water-driven landscapes he had been experiencing. Bartram didn't have the luxury of sticking around to figure out this endless wild desert. If he had, his core understanding of what we know as "ecology" would have told him much.

This gnarly, chest-high forest seems ruggedly arid, distinctly apart from the younger and more diverse Florida landscapes of the lower altitudes. Most of the plants that have learned to live here have defensively armed themselves with potent forces: thorns and spines, leather-tough leaves, and volatile oils with aromas that discourage chomping by hungry, vegan predators. The warm sun releases these natural fragrances today, allowing plants like wild vanilla to inform my own human sense of smell. It is wild and pleasantly fragrant, and it broadens my sensibilities beyond mere sight and sound.

I spot a native scrub jay, the crest on his head rounded and his blue plumage far more vivid than that of other jays. Thoreau one wrote that the "bluebird carries the sky on his back." If that is so, then the scrub jay carries the very best colors of our deepest Florida springs. A second one joins him, and instead of fleeing, they scuttle about in the low boughs of myrtle oak and sand pine. They always seem gregarious and friendly, but I realize that's my own human-mammal precept. The low altitude of the stunted forest here keeps them from flying to higher branches—but, more to the point, they evolved without the sort of predators that might make them want to do so. Ancestors of this sweet bird still live in the distant Southwest, their premigratory anatomy largely intact.

I am still ascending this old island, and if its rise is subtle, the muscles in the backs of my calves recognize the difference between walking on flat land and climbing an ancient Florida dune. I pass wild blueberry bushes, tiny canopies of shiny leaves and unripe red berries, all clustered together like a bonsai forest. I figure every black bear who lives nearby has stored away the seasonal calendar of each plant, the ripe geography of sweet, dark-purple berries chiseled into its memory.

A gopher tortoise, her scutes as worn as a handmade monastery brick, moves slowly along the trail toward me, never a need to rush, 200 million years of genetic memory on her side. As she gets closer, I bend down so I can better see her ancient chiseled face, and she stops. Her enormous dozer-like front flippers, scales fitted atop them like miniature shingles, retract ever so carefully.

I look more closely at her dark, moist eyes, and it feels as if I am staring through tiny telescoping portals of time, little windows that reveal a glimpse of the distant history she has known. For just a moment there, I see a land-scape of smoldering volcanoes, ferns as large as the highest trees, reptiles with horny beaks gliding overhead like giant swallow-tailed kites. With surprising grace and speed, the tortoise then rises up on her legs, gallops a few yards away, and slips through the sandy portal of her burrow, disappearing into the cool darkness under the earth. I notice the mouth of the burrow is shaped to accommodate her shell, rounded at the top and flat as her plastron at the bottom.

The theologian Thomas Moore has said that the soul needs a vernacular life, a place full of intimate details with authentic meaning, a world of particulars. All of nature is vernacular, of course, special to the place it populates. But the Florida scrub may be the most vernacular of all, a rare microregion of ecology detailed with the crosshatch of nuances: the plants and their aromas, the specialized tortoise and blue jay, the truncated trees and plants that have transformed to survive here. Diversity is notoriously low, but endemism—the number of species unique to this place—is almost off the charts.

Certainly, a shopping mall with corporate chain stores is also loaded with details. But shopping malls don't arise from a particular landscape that helps define where you and they are in the world, at any given time. Nature is art, pure and simple, and for me, it seems newly created each hour, each day, each season. To connect with it is to come to understand just a little bit more about my own identity, about my own singular place here on earth. The nature writer Barry Lopez explains this notion well: "The key, I think, is to become vulnerable to a place. If you open yourself up, you can build intimacy. Out of such intimacy may come a sense of belonging, a sense of not being isolated in the universe."

Although the springs first captured my imagination as a boy, it is this Florida scrub that holds intrigue for me as an adult. My earliest relationship with scrub was forged by simply walking through it, feeling the soft white sand slipping under my shoes, carefully watching the diminutive forests around me for their finely localized vignettes to unfold. On those walks, I'm in Florida, but I'm also somewhere else—maybe the Sonoran desert, its giant treelike saguaro cactus mimicked by the tiny prickly pears, pad-like limbs spiked with lush yellow flowers.

Most of the xeric terrain here is made of "entisols," little more than ground quartz. It's nearly devoid of silt and clay and organic matter. The slightly higher sandhills of longleaf pine—the broad pinnacles atop the undulating hills of scrub—are a bit more enriched with nutrients, more likely to have been cultivated by the hardscrabble Crackers who once homesteaded in the frontier of the wild Florida interior.

To visit this scrub is to time-travel backward. Most of my excursions in Florida and around the world have to do with water, whether in oceans and lagoons or rivers and springs. Water certainly has shaped this place too. But the prehistoric memory of it is all that remains. Now, when water arrives as rainfall, it passes quickly through the porous shoals and dunes. Plants have designed themselves to adapt to this, growing waxy, curled, or needle-like leaves to resist evaporation. Some, like the scrub holly, aim their leaves toward the ground so rainwater drips right above their shallow roots.

In my walkabouts, I've learned this ancient scrub of Florida is our most distinctive ecosystem, and that alone has made it worth getting to know. Arising from a primordial sea, the sandy islands that first spined the middle of the peninsula of Florida have remained with us as north–south ridges, and the visual clues of that history are somehow reassuring.

But that knowing is tempered with a certain awe. I have come to realize that the scrub—if it is to endure at all—can never be domesticated or tamed. The lichen-covered trees of the hammock can sometimes be transported, even imitated. Gated subdivisions can sometimes commandeer freshwater springs inside their walls. But the scrub is its own fiefdom. It is driven not just by the sun and the soil, but by the nobility of its venerable and historic genesis. When scrub plants and animals are removed or corralled into a more entertaining landscape, the result can be jarring, not unlike the image of a gopher tortoise, festooned with glitter and marching in a Disney parade.

Rich soil heavy with moisture may enliven most plants and trees, but it will usually overwhelm the minimalistic needs of xeric plant roots, causing fungus and rot. Conversely, non-native, exotic plants that plague so many of our natural landscapes are least likely to take hold here.

Florida may have its share of jungle safari rides and water-themed parks for tourists, but it is unlikely to ever promote its most cryptic and endangered ecosystem as "Scrub World." It is this eco-tenaciousness that helps express my own affinity for Florida's scrub. Walt Whitman, the true democratic American poet of nature and spirit—a man with enough confidence to embrace both transcendentalism and realism—once lyricized in *Song of Myself*: "I too am not a bit tamed, I too am untranslatable / I sound my barbaric yawp over the roofs of the world."

Of all of our habitats here in this Land of Flowers, it is the Florida scrub that most resists taming. And even within the context of science, this scrub is not easily translatable. The high and dry landscape can be plowed under and destroyed to make way for rows of citrus or extruded real estate developments—indeed, that is how we have lost almost 90 percent of our historic Florida scrub. But it can't be transplanted, or coiffed up, or otherwise ripped out of its primal context with much success. Its timeless, complex, and cryptic charms resist commercialization.

It occurs to me that scrub may be our Walt Whitman of landscapes. Like the poet, it surely has its very own "barbaric yawp." And while it may not sound out its wildness over the rooftops of the world, it may quietly hum it, late at night, over the tops of the rusty lyonia and Chapman's oak, saw palmetto and wild rosemary. Snug deep in its burrow, the gopher tortoise may hear it and feel there is hope, after all.

If this scrub is to be most fully understood, it may be through doors unlocked by art and literature, mediums that seek an instinctual connection with the human spirit. Certainly, its natural gestalt is subtle, almost secretive. It is so much more than just the sum of its individual parts.

Nonetheless, when it comes to natural Florida places that humans find endearing, "scrub" has a bit of an identity problem. Dictionaries tells us that word may mean stunted, insignificant, inferior, even in need of cleaning. In one curriculum plan devoted to the Florida scrub from the Archbold Biological Station on the Lake Wales Ridge, the writers apologize to students for the feeling the name evokes: "Sorry the habitat name is not more inspiring. If Florida habitats could be named all over again, maybe scrub could be the Florida Dwarf Forest, or the Florida Elfin Woods, or the Florida Pygmy Woodlands. Alas, it is too late to choose a pretty name."

But then they get real, figuring that the name has its own kind of gutsy symmetry: "Florida scrub is the original name, the tough name, the name that makes no promises. Maybe it's an appropriate and meaningful name after all."

On a bright and early Sunday morning, my friend Jane and I drive deep into the Ocala National Forest, a massive landscape that sprawls between the St. Johns and Ocklawaha Rivers. The national forest protects the largest contiguous sand pine scrub forest in the world. S.R. 19 carves a narrow line of asphalt through the middle of the forest, transporting us past its dry ridges of scrub, its vast prairies, and its dense hammocks of springs, many fed by the porous uplands inside this preserve.

The Lake Wales Ridge, which spines the center of the state from Clermont to Venus, is the oldest of our scrub islands, and the one with the most endemic plants and animals. But it is this Ocala tract that holds the most appeal for me because of the way it has embodied a true "sense of place."

The Pulitzer-winning novelist Marjorie Kinnan Rawlings, ranging out from her nearby home in Cross Creek, got to know this landscape and the Crackers who lived here as well as anyone ever has. Inspired by the depth and complexity of this information, she deftly wove it into some of her novels.

Unlike landscapes used by writers as a backdrop for their narratives, the scrub and sandhill became a character in Rawlings's stories. It was a primeval, mysterious force that evoked solitude and ruggedness and singularity, providing insight into the way her human characters were shaped by the landscape. The real people who once lived here may have vanished. But their spirits live on, both in literature and in the clues they left behind. In *South Moon Under*, Rawlings wrote: "The scrub rolled towards its boundaries like a dark sea. It cast itself against the narrow beach of swamp and hammock that fringed the rivers. The two types of growth did not mingle, as though an ascetic race withdrew itself from a tropical one and refused to inter-breed."

Today, we are headed to the Yearling Trail, a sliver of snow-white sand meandering through the chest-high vegetation of the scrub, following the topography an ancient sea created so many million years ago. At the top of this ridge is the sandhill mesa where the fictional Baxter family once lived. Trails in parks and forests nowadays are designed for a variety of reasons— but few are marked to honor literary tales and the people whose lives once played out inside of that art.

And so the compelling stories of Rawlings have led us here today, two grown-up kids who relish the ways in which a well-told story can still flavor our world. *The Yearling*—and its coming-of-age tale of young Jody Baxter and his orphaned fawn—may have been fiction, but the sway of the land and the heartfelt grit of its people were very real.

Nature writer Lopez, in considering the true value of a compelling narrative like this one, says we need such stories to more fully give meaning to our lives. But storytelling involves great responsibility. "The intent of the storyteller," says Lopez, "must be to evoke, honestly, some single aspect of all the land contains." This higher understanding—a feat Rawlings painstakingly achieved—can be revealed as long as stories are crafted to show how the human heart and the land are so closely intertwined.

When we pull into the dirt parking lot for the Yearling Trail, it is clear that not everyone is as transfixed with narrative and cryptic landscapes. Already, the parking lots for the springs this scrub nurtures downhill from here—Silver Glen and Salt and more—are packed with cars. But we will have the Yearling Trail and its acres of prehistoric dunes and their intertwined stories to ourselves today. If given the choice between a congested queue at Space Mountain and the lonely, mysterious desert of the Florida scrub, the choice is a simple one for us. There are never any crowded parking lots at Scrub World.

In *The Yearling*, Penny "Pa" Baxter—emotionally hurt and scarred by the world—felt safe within the solitude of this scrub, a place where he could experience a certain calmness. This very special geography, this "vast wall" of palmettos and myrtle and oak, functioned as a sanctuary.

"Penny," Rawlings wrote, "had perhaps been bruised too often. The peace of the vast aloof scrub had drawn him with the beneficence of its silence. Something in him was raw and tender. The touch of men was hurtful upon it, but the touch of the pines was healing." In a way, the same primal force that Penny Baxter sought still endures around us today, an enigmatic, wild landscape ready to extend comfort to every sensitive human willing to fully inhabit the moment in this most ancient of Florida places.

Just beyond the trailhead, we pass a metal U.S. Forestry Service warning sign advising we are entering a restricted "Wilderness Area" where "hikers must assume risks such as fallen trees, limbs, lack of vehicle access, animal encounters, bad weather," and the like. I guess I've been poking about in remote places so long that the warning seems obvious, almost redundant. If wilderness were safe and domestic, what would be the point?

We walk slowly, savoring the scents of the landscape, looking for tiny clues. After only an hour of this, we are far beyond the reach of any mechanized sound, fully enfolded inside the experience of an authentic and wild place. Clearly, there is a sacred natural antiquity that informs the sensibilities of the moment. It is beyond the imperfect authority of the intellect, burrowing somewhere deeper into the knowledge of the unconscious. Jane remarks that this rugged landscape is both complex and desolate at the same time, and I smile at the wisdom of that notion.

Philosophers of nature sometimes describe a wilderness as uncultivated, undeveloped. Roderick Nash once wrote that "wilderness is any place where a person feels stripped of guidance and is lost and perplexed." Other than our little trail map, we have no organized "guidance," and other than a compass, no tools to navigate for us. We expect to get lost, and several times, we do. Still, we move across this arid, wild place with something akin to comfort, connecting on some vital level with the spirit it seems to exude.

Surely, Rawlings knew of this connection. As she once explained, there is an "invisible Florida," one that visitors and residents may vaguely acknowledge, but don't really process or try to understand. "It is invisible because its beauty must be seen with the spiritual eye as well as the physical," she once said. "I've longed to re-create, to make visible, this invisible beauty."

Upward we go through this rolling, increasingly visible sea of scrub, sometimes stopping when curiosity alights. Despite the arid nature of the place, we find lovely, tender little flowers practically glowing under the low boughs of sand pine and the stiff fronds of saw palmettos. The butterfly pea, pale with a deeper purple splaying from its throat, is the size of an old silver dollar. The passion vine, with a lavender blossom as wonderfully baroque as any I've ever seen, is a riotous parade of stamens that can't seem to figure out if they want to imitate the exhaust of a space rocket, or be inside the corona of a flower.

Like all natural systems here in Florida, scrub is fire-dependent, learning to live with the high frequency of natural lightning strikes. The little sand pines, the perfect "Charlie Brown Christmas tree," are loaded with small, compact cones full of seeds that are only released when fire dissolves the resin. That same fire keeps the sand pines from growing taller, losing their utility for the low-flying scrub jays. Other adaptations come in handy too: during those fires, the tortoise retreats into its burrows; so too do the dozens of other species that use these little caves for shelter.

Jane spots the swift movement of something small at the top of an old weathered post. It's an endemic scrub lizard, two bright streaks of blue glowing from each side of its belly like tiny reptilian racing stripes. It flees at my movement, but finally shrugs into camera range for her.

One animal we don't expect to see today is the sand skink. It lives somewhere under us, literally swimming its way through the porous paleo-dune. Smooth and shiny, the endemic skink has small eyes with a transparent window in its lower eyelids, allowing it to see prey while navigating through the darkness. The skink lives nowhere else in the world except these few counties in the scrub. Between 40 to 60 percent of all the plants and animals here are special to this place. So, too, were the rugged pioneers who migrated to Florida in the 1800s, iconoclasts who chose to live up here on the ridge rather than near the rivers, where the luxuries of water, food, and transportation were readily available.

There are no real trail markers here, so the only way we know for sure that we are headed for the top of the ridge is by feeling the very gradual ascent. Finally, the low elfin forest begins to fall away around us with the appearance of a single, venerable hardwood tree. With its bare, arching limbs, it seems to be welcoming us to the higher plateau of the pine sandhills.

Another hundred yards and we are inside the canopy of this ancient shoal, surrounded by much taller longleaf and slash pines, the more dense understory replaced by wild coonties and rosemary and wiregrass. This is still a long way from the cooler hammocks of the springs, but it's far more comfortable than the open scrub. I notice the ground, while still sandy, is darker, better able to hold the nutrients, and certainly more suitable to growing crops and nurturing livestock.

We are on a wide pinnacle atop this sea of scrub, near the crest of what is mapped as "Pat's Island." The Reuben Long family migrated here after the Civil War in 1872, poor but hardworking Appalachian natives who cherished the free land that a homesteading grant offered. A dozen other families lived here on this 1,400-acre island by the turn of the century. But by the time the Ocala National Forest was created in 1908, the population had already begun to decline.

In the 1930s, Rawlings spent several months living here with the Calvin Long family, learning about the landscape and hearing stories about their lives—including that of a fawn Calvin raised when he was a boy. The people who lived here were clannish, insular, and apart from the rest of the world, the living embodiment of the rugged landscape itself. To an outsider, they might seem simple and one-dimensional, but to Rawlings, they symbolized the complex and subtle mysteries of their chosen landscape.

On the ground around us, large shards of worn blocks and limestone from aged building foundations are scattered randomly, like amber-entombed capsules from a distant time. From where we now stand, the edges of this "island" literally drop away, as if we're atop a high building. In reality, the drop is slight, no more than a few yards. But our gradual immersion into this world has magnified the nuances, making the unseen much less so.

We walk a bit more to the old cemetery of the Long family, enclosed inside a wooden picket fence with a small gate. The feeling of being here, where the living prototypes of the Baxters are buried, is akin to being inside of an author's imagination, or perhaps somewhere inside the residual spirit of the Baxters themselves. It is a place at once mythic and very real, a landscape and culture that have become more "visible" because of the generosity, skill, and grace of a single tenacious author.

One of the gravestones is marked: Reuben Long, Confederate States Army, Jan. 1832–Sept. 1915. Jane reads more inscriptions, all of which hint at how difficult life in this Florida frontier really was: a sixteen-year-old was killed in a hunting accident; a four-year-old died after playing too close to a cooking fire. Clearly, Rawlings had a great appreciation for the moral sinew that both motivated and set these people apart. They represented the clear dialect of the hard Florida scrub, walking metaphors of the vernacular and of every truth-driven detail that ever informed it. Certainly, this scrub was undomesticated ground for her, a place where survival depended on an intimate relationship with nature. When the last of the Long clan left, the island was abandoned to nature and time, a place that had never been conquered and was, for one brief century, only slightly compromised.

This is still the natural face of Florida that has changed the least. Rawlings respected that, memorializing both the distinct landscape and the "primal quality" of its people, seemingly comforted by the very real particulars of it all.

There is one last place we want to see before we leave today. We walk across the top of the sand hill to where some hardwoods are clumped together in a hammock. Here, in the midst of tall oaks and hickories, is a deep sinkhole. It is the sort of feature that fits with the rolling karst terrain. Created, like all sinks, when the limestone caves below lose their water and the earth falls into the empty cavern, this one is particularly special. Formed long ago, the funnel-like sides of the 100-foot-deep sink are now colonized by all manner of plants and trees, nurtured by the water that once flowed here.

Jane and I sit at the edge, atop a log, and remember. On the cover of one edition of *The Yearling*, artist N. C. Wyeth faithfully conveyed one moment from the novel, an instant that revealed a much higher truth. In it, a barefoot Jody caresses the neck of his orphaned fawn, Flag. Next to him, Pa Baxter stands with a wooden oxbow across his back. The rig held two buckets that hung from both ends of it. Without money to dig a well, the Baxters gathered all their water from this sinkhole with buckets, just as the real-life Long family had done.

It was difficult work, but—like all other shards of the very real landscape—the sink also embodied its own special art. It was, wrote Rawlings, "a great cupped garden, feathered with green leaves, cool and moist and, always, mysterious . . . a lush green heart."

Our groundwater in Florida has been dropping for the last few decades.

So the lateral veins of the aquifer that once leaked sweet freshwater from lime-rock vents into the sink have now run dry. But the deep earth and rock have kept it cool and moist, feathered with leaves. It remains a great lush oasis in the midst of the desert-like terrain.

The sink beneath us is cryptic, mysterious, enchanting. Like all the other shards of this rare landscape we have seen, it plays an essential role in reassembling the world around us into a functioning whole.

Some may describe our walk through the distinctive scrub and sandhill today as a study in enviro-cultural ecology. But I guess I see it as a way of conjuring the deepest and most evocative memories and dreams available to us, a way of redeeming the spirit by returning it squarely into the sacred moment where nature and people again coalesce.

As Jane and I prepare to leave, I silently thank Marjorie Rawlings and Jody Baxter and Calvin Long, grateful for the way art can create mirrors and stories that reflect far more than we can physically see—for the way it can reveal the glorious and transcendent magic of the human heart.

3 Me and Buddy and the Speed of Light on a Florida Lake

It's Tuesday, early evening, and the crescent moon is a sliver in the southern sky. It's waxing inside a radiant canvas of astral colors, a blissful work of natural art that captures my attention more than usual. I do some quick research and learn it's about 17 percent of full. By the time I'm done writing this, it will likely be just a little bit more so.

I stand with Buddy atop the edge of the peninsula on the southern shore of Lake Monroe as the sun sets lower in the sky and the constellations begin to gradually reveal themselves. Photo by G. K. Sharman.

I snap a leash on my sheltie, Buddy, and we take the sidewalk down Park Ave. to where it dead-ends into the southerly edge of Lake Monroe, where we can see the crescent high atop the surface of the slowly flowing water. It's 5:15 p.m. in the early Florida winter so the moon is still a lighter shade of pale, no dark sky yet to backdrop it.

Buddy came from a rescue shelter, and is still half-wild, not quite used to walking with a human, even one who cares for him as I do. Even after a year, he tugs and pulls, for no reason other than the one only he can sense, his olfactory world so much richer than mine. I smell the slightest hint of a southern blackwater river, a burst of a nearby auto exhaust, and that's about it.

Buddy, on the other hand, acknowledges the golden retriever who lifted a leg here in the strip of St. Augustine grass between the sidewalk and the road two days ago; the young standard poodle who pranced through the same grass a day later; the lab/shar-pei who trotted nearby, exhaling one very deep bark, the vibration of the sound settling into the tissue of the scrubby little wildflowers nearby, oxalis, Cupid's paintbrush, something that looks like innocence. All this happens in maybe ten seconds, and by then, caught up in my higher mammal quest for movement, I urge him onward.

We walk across the street next to the river, stopping briefly to watch the local drivers here in Sanford confuse themselves with the traffic circle—rotary, roundabout—that the city installed a couple years ago. I stood here one evening and watched a guy in a beat-up American pickup drive around the circle three times before figuring how to get out of it. Cheap entertainment, I guess. Across the river street is the river, natch, and at its edge is a small, bulkheaded peninsula that juts out a few hundred yards into it.

Many years ago, when Sanford was a functioning small farm town and most of the people who lived here had grown up locally or somewhere nearby, there was a band shell at the end of the peninsula. I'm guessing small bands would come and play here, maybe on a Sunday, just like they did in the big gazebo of a band shell in the city park of the small town where I had grown up. And unpretentious folks would come with blankets and chairs and wicker baskets of fried chicken and iced tea, families and friends letting the glorious richness of the moment fully settle in. It was not unlike the way Buddy allows all his senses to settle in today, informing him of things he would not otherwise know while his human makes do with what he can.

The band shell is gone now, and the peninsula has been renamed Memorial Plaza because it memorializes various wars our country has fought, from the very un-Civil one, to World Wars I and II, Korea and Vietnam, and some more recent. Interpretative signs with historic photos explain the various conflicts, and granite place-markers engraved with the names of soldiers rim the inside of the walk. A large American flag flies overhead, one that, when unfurled, looks as if it could shelter an entire platoon of soldiers. There's more "hardscape"—as the landscape architects call it—deeper in atop the peninsula, and it seems to create a stylistic stage, one made of some sort of igneous rock, polished smooth, like the granite.

Buddy and I walk the U-shaped sidewalk that follows the perimeter of the peninsula, Buddy stopping to lift his leg every so often to communicate with a departed scent, and me, with my eyes on the flat blue-gray of the lake-river surface, a massive body of water that is now as gentle as the bath drawn by loving parents for their small child.

A very pretty woman jogging by looks at Buddy and then at me and smiles engagingly. My own senses quiver in a pleasant way, somehow proud of ushering that information to my gut. Then, a young boy with his dad sees Buddy, and since Buddy looks like a miniature collie, he calls out excitedly, "Lass-ie!" and his dad grins. I walk to the end of the peninsula, as close to the water as I can get without falling in, and stand on the flat concrete ridge that overlays the bulkhead. Buddy sits so he's prone, and puts both of his front paws up on the bulkhead too, maybe to get a better look, maybe to comfort his human with his imitative behavior. The sun is at the horizon now, and the water around us is a light crimson with its reflection. I notice that the heavy, robust fronds of the palms rimming the peninsula now glow with a hint of the reflected color.

Nearby two homeless people with a small chicken are sitting in the grass at the edge of the bulkhead. I have seen them here before and have talked a bit with them. They seem worn, beat, but they remember me, and the woman gets up to come over and say hi. I ask them about the chicken, and they say they have had it since it was a little yellow biddy. The chicken looks up from its serious chicken business of pecking at a piece of discarded po-tato chip and *cawwks* on over until it is just a foot from Buddy. The chicken then stops and looks at him, and they are eye to eye, snout to beak, neither moving nor making a sound for a good minute.

"Mexican standoff," I say to the homeless woman, and she thinks this is hilarious and laughs a long, hearty laugh, one that she may have first known when she was a young woman, maybe with a family and a dog and a real home with a roof and a bed. My heart goes out to her, and as usual, the notion of "six degrees of separation" is squeezed down to barely less than one.

A third homeless man is nearby, also near the water, and he walks over, bends down and pets and rubs Buddy. Then after a minute or so of this, he looks up and says, "When was the last time this dog was bathed?" I wonder somehow if he isn't trying to sell me a sort of doggy bath deal. Then I realize that it's been a few weeks. Buddy's mostly an outdoor dog, roaming the dense jungle that is my fenced backyard, having serious dialogues with the gray squirrels that forever challenge his territory. A lot of running and wallowing and stealthful hunting from the thick weeds and wildflowers come into play. Nonetheless, the fact that a homeless man has been commenting on my dog's hygiene is one of those deeply satirical moments that the novelist Franz Kafka would have appreciated.

We walk on a bit and then sit on one of the wooden benches at the water's edge, me on one corner next to the armrest, and Buddy jumping up right next to me. Often he stands and puts his face into the wind—even if it's the slightest hint of a breeze—that usually rises up by early evening from the river/lake. I look up to the south at the crescent moon, and see that the quickly darkening sky is contrasting nicely with the new white of the crescent so that the moon seems to pop out, as if rendered in 3-D. There is a bright starlike glow, also in the south, and I know that to be the planet Jupiter, since that's where it should be right about now.

I look for Orion because that is what I sometimes do when contemplating the night sky. Just south of the Orion's Belt constellation, I also see the faintest traces of the Orion Nebula, a massive cluster of distant stars, emitting a light I couldn't have seen at all when I first walked out here. I traveled to the Yucatán once and saw some of the Mayan ruins, including a cenote. I would dive into a sacred cenote years later in another part of Latin America to watch scientists retrieve the relics of a vanished civilization from its forever-dark and deep bottom, and my life would change in subtle ways because of it, opening a spiritual portal to the ways in which nature and gods exist as one.

Earlier, in the Yucatán of Mexico, I learned some essential information about the Maya; some of it had to do with the stars, because the night sky—indeed, all of nature—was embedded into a complex mythology of honor and fear. Orion, the Mayan believed, represented Xibalba, the Underworld.

I have seen enough for now, so Buddy and I walk toward home atop the brick streets and their delightfully uneven bricks, under the boughs of live oak thick with moss. I walk into my driveway, next to the front walk lined with small coonties I planted last year, the palmlike cycad finally seeming to come into its own on this fine Florida fall evening.

Inside, I feed Buddy and then turn on the water in the tub in the bathroom down the hallway. Righteous observations can be found almost anywhere these days, and just because the guy making the doggy hygiene comment was homeless doesn't make his opinion any less true. Maybe a bit ironic, but not untrue.

As I wait for the tub to fill for Buddy's bath, I go to my computer and check the status of the crescent moon. It is 18 percent full now, bringing just a bit more cosmic darkness into the light. I review some figures on time-light travel, and find that it takes hardly two seconds for the light of the moon to travel to the earth; for Jupiter, it takes forty-three minutes. For the Orion Nebula, it takes 1,500 years.

I wonder absently how long it will take the exhalation of a large black dog to reach Jupiter, the smile of a pretty woman to finally reach Orion, the sweet and nostalgic music from a town's band shell to reach the outer edges of the universe. And I figure, finally, that the math of it all doesn't much matter. What matters, really, is that those behaviors have happened, if only briefly, and that once exuded, they may take on a life beyond the curvature of the human heart—perhaps even beyond the surface of the earth.

There's no telling, really, how far the energy and light of any heartfelt action—any meaningful journey—will travel, and where, if ever, it will really end.

4 Los Roques

Realizing the Timeless Promise of the Unknown

Time has vanished here in the Venezuelan island chain of Los Roques. But then again, so has Jose, our native boat captain who bid us adios as we splashed backward from the gunnels of his open fishing boat.

Now, as the needle on my depth gauge edges past the 100-foot mark, Jose—with the Amor de Madre tattoo on his forearm

One of the islands of Los Roques from the air shows the swath of clear Caribbean water and reef around it.

and cerveza Polar in his hand, has disappeared. But the wooden hull of his *penero* is as clear as if I were back on the beach and it were floating in the air above. And, really, I know Jose is in there, just this side of the clouds, waiting.

As for us—Venezuelan outdoorsman Frank Ibarra and American photographer Tim O'Keefe—we drift along in the strong five-knot current next to the mini-wall with its seven-foot-tall gorgonians and bright orange sponges, twitching our fins as if they were overgrown pectorals to drip or turn, rise or fall in the water column. I am in a place that two weeks ago I didn't even know existed, in an isolated archipelago of bucolic limestone islands, red mangroves, white beaches, and plunging coral walls washed with the clean, oceanic waters of the southernmost Caribbean Sea.

Back home, my Rand McNally had charted Los Roques as a couple of mere dots some 106 miles north of Caracas, and a guidebook warned: "No opportunities for scuba diving exist here." Yet I am here anyway, having long ago traded in my knowledge of familiar and worn geography for the chance of poking about between the known dots on the map, looking for a place where promises can still be made and kept.

Actually, if we're counting dots, Los Roques should be worth at least three hundred or so, all scattered about a kidney-shaped lagoon of a half million acres on a latitude somewhere between Bonaire and Grenada. Taken wholly, it's one of the Caribbean's largest and oldest marine parks, protected—on paper, at least—as Parque Nacional Archipiélago de Los Roques since 1972.

Here, simmering in a rich food chain under Windex-colored waters, are sea turtles and giant spiny lobster, pods of bottlenose dolphin and sleeping sharks, massive schools of yellowtail snapper, and, in the grassy shallows, ten-pound silver bonefish tailing for benthic shrimp and crabs.

On the main island of Gran Roque beneath the crumbling lighthouse are village casas with shell-crushed stucco walls and corrugated roofs, wooden shudders and shed-like doors—all tinted in shades of turquoise and pink— thrown open to the generous trade winds. On the playa of the protective lee coast, deeply tanned fishermen are weaving new seines. Their hand-built wooden *peneros*, trimmed in a spectrum of primary colors, lie beached just above the high-tide mark nearby. At the village square, where a wall mural of a blue-eyed mermaid watches protectively, bright-eyed, barefoot children are playing marbles and hopscotch in the dirt streets.

It is a place far outside the dots—a place that might not exist, except for just now. But Los Roques and its authentic charm and clear waters do exist, of course. I know this not just because the off-the-map promises of this place make my romantic sensibilities so taut they vibrate like a snare drum. Nope, I know they exist because, at 120 feet, I can still see Jose's propeller spinning, promising to Cuisinart anything that comes near. It's a sight that cuts through every last ounce of nitrogen-induced stupor of the depths to remind me of how tenuous a path we create for ourselves when we bring technology like scuba-diving gear to such a place.

↓ ↓ ↓

Caraqueno Frank Ibarra is a mechanical engineer who loves the water and fishing so much he quit his job to try to make a living at it. To do so, he takes sport anglers into the Venezuelan Amazon to fish for peacock bass, over deep oceanic waters to hunt billfish, and to the offshore islands for bonefish and permit. When I learned of this, I called Ibarra to ask, if I came to visit, would he help me explore the underwater world of his backyard?

Ibarra, a good-natured fellow who likes to laugh a lot, answered by telling me about the jungle rivers of the Amazon where the pink freshwater dolphin frolic in the wake of fishing boats. And he told me about Los Roques—the rocks—that sprawl in virtual obscurity off the coast of his country, little Cozumel-like islets of limestone surrounded by strong, clear pelagic currents. Ibarra had visited both of these places—but only as a fisherman. In both cases, what we find underwater will be, as Ibarra put it, "a big surprise."

I asked him to narrow that down just a little bit. "Okay," says Ibarra, "now is the dry season. And in the Amazon, the piranha will share the same deep holes with the dolphin. It will be good for the piranha, but maybe not so good for us." A headline flashed before my eyes: Crazy Gringos with No Sense Eaten Alive by Little Fish. Thinking the river dolphins may not be such a hot idea right now, I decide on Los Roques. "It is a good choice," says Ibarra. "The ocean may send us many things." And with that, I am off to Caracas, ready for what the ocean may bring.

On arrival, Elias Dib, an earnest young fishing guide who works with Ibarra, greets me at the airport, ushering me past customs with a wave of his hand and through the crowded airport as if he is strolling down a street where he has been many times before. I am brimming with confidence about this trip and how well it is going when Dib stops at the curb next to a battered Ford LTD that looks like it has been stripped by burglars. Dib walks to the rear and hits the trunk hard with his fist. It opens and he motions for me to put my bag of gear inside. "It is okay," says Dib. "There is no trouble with the car. It only looks not so good."

I settle into the passenger seat, where the upholstery from the roof sags down onto my head and the hole where the radio used to be glows with some tiny light from deep within. Not one but three miniature statues of Catholic saints stand guard on the pockmarked dash, which is fine because I figure we can use all the help we can get—spiritual, secular, and otherwise.

As we hurry through the raucous night streets of coastal Venezuela, the shacks of the barrios cluster above us like giant mud wasp nests against the clay foothills of the Andes. The dimly lit sidewalks and *mercados* glow in the darkest of ambers, almost the same color as the radio hole. We seem to be passing through an Oliver Stone movie set designed to evoke the foreign shadow dance of South American coastal mystique.

Morning arrives as a warm tropical sun, and with it, a prop flight north, beyond the massive, cloud-topped Andes that abruptly cascade into the Caribbean Sea. With a few exceptions—like the Morrocoy National Park west of Caracas—coastal waters here carry too much suspended silt from mainland runoff to nurture vivid corals or clarity. But the deep-blue oceanic sea off the continental shelf tells a different story.

Before long, the tallest island of Los Roques appears, a single ancient chunk of weathered igneous rock that melts into a plateau of sand-covered limestone, spreading out to green tropical flats, ocher-inflamed corals, and beds of sea grass. Back in Caracas, local dive pioneer Mike Osborn, who first set up a shop in Venezuela in 1970, had told me that underwater, Los Roques is as healthy as the Netherland Antilles island of Bonaire, and I am excited by the possibilities.

On Gran Roque, we settle into a small inn with the grandiose name El Pelicano Club, spartan but clean rooms inside a walled courtyard, whitewashed like a Spanish mission. Later, in the rustic little café across the dirt street, I watch a grand sunset through massive glassless windows, while scores of waterbirds—pelicans, boobies, terns—madly dive into the food-rich waters, an entire flock at a time.

It is here I meet Saul Wainschtein, our dive guide-to-be, who steps from the beach—¡Buenos tardes!—into the dining room through one of the low, open windows. Despite the earlier disclaimer I read about no available scuba opportunities, Saul has recently opened a tiny dive shop here. Saul tells us he has hired a local fisherman to take us diving in the morning, and we are beaming with the promise of it all.

That night, lying in my single bed in a room cooled by a lone ceiling fan, I sleep and dream of seabirds swimming through windows of coral, sometimes with piranha at their sides, tiny teeth snapping like castanets.

↓ ↓ ↓

Our twenty-eight-foot *penero*, peaked at the bow like a dory and fitted with a center row of scuba tanks, carries us south from the beach at Gran Roque across the vast lagoon. We bounce about on little benches, drenched from plumes of seawater as Jose—all steely glare under a *biesbol* cap—keeps his twin Yamahas cranked at full speed. The inside of the boat is a bright, moist orange, as if someone has halved a giant mango and fiberglassed it. O'Keefe stows his topside "dry" cameras in what he thinks is a safe spot, inside a hold in the bow. Later, when he retrieves the bag, he discovers it has spent most of the day atop a pile of breathtakingly pungent dead fish, split and butterflied to dry.

Of the three hundred islands of Los Roques, only seventy-nine are named. Many are little more than clumps of mangroves, or dead coral rimmed with sand. Soon we pass the islet of Rabusqui, near where the sleeping bull sharks are said to be, and beyond that, several shallow ridges of sand and turtle grass that Ibarra identifies as prime bonefish territory. In these clear, undisturbed waters, the color green flashes vividly in all its known incarnations.

It is hard to imagine all this remote, barely charted water and land as a national park, but that is what it is. As such, it has rules by which all islands in its boundaries are "managed." But the territory is huge, funding for rangers is meager, and enforcement is difficult. I see at least five illegal fishermen's camps where fish and conch are drying on lines between sheds of driftwood and corrugated tin.

Later in the week, we will stop between dives for lunch on Cayo dos

Mosquises Sur, where the non-profit Los Roques Scientific Foundation has a field research station. Here, among tanks of young sea turtles raised from eggs, I will learn that poaching of sea turtle eggs and overfishing of conch and lobster are major conservation problems, even in these insular cays. Each season it is a race to the sea turtle nests to see who gets the eggs—the fishermen or the mariculture-minded biologists.

As we approach the site where Saul has decided we will dive, Jose cuts back on the throttle and we quickly hoist on our tanks. Within minutes, we are overboard in an aquatic freefall through stunningly clear waters. We all have our individual styles—O'Keefe in a gentle wallow with his underwater cameras, Ibarra attentive to his gauges and straps, and me, knees bent, head back, pretending I am plunging in slow motion from the distant clouds.

At depth, the current is strong and coral covers the steep wall that rises before us in a wealth of hard and soft varieties. We are diving on the southern rim of the island chain, just off a high sandy island called Boca de Cote, at the edge of the channel where five- and six-knot ocean currents wash into the lagoon. Like most of the windward sites here, the wall flattens out into a plateau at somewhere just under two hundred feet and then stretches flat for another five hundred before plunging down to a five-thousand-foot bottom.

Since the best and brightest of marine life is in the upper regions, where it can be kissed by the sunlight, we remain between sixty and eighty feet most of the time, drifting along in the swift current. Occasionally I stray to 120 feet, just to make sure I'm not missing anything.

Midway down the wall, gigantic beige-colored sea whips taller than I am reach up to the surface light, their tiny polyps extended to feed by day, silently rustling in the current. On a small sandy ledge, a foot-long lizard fish, almost perfectly camouflaged, rests on his fins.

Tropicals dart everywhere—damsels, gobies, a juvenile French angel—and anemones hide in the crevices, blunt tentacles waving their tips of blue. A five-pound Nassau grouper skitters a few feet below; I drop down for a better look and through an opening in the coral see part of the massive body of a green moray, almost a foot wide. I look over my shoulder, away from the wall, and see we are being escorted by three yard-long barracuda. Later, Ibarra will tell me that a six-foot-long 'cuda spent the entire dive shadowing me just a few feet above my head.

The clarity here seems to defy basic laws of physics: primary colors usually lost at half the depth are still present, glowing in the unworldly blue light. Jose, who has been following our bubbles from a distance, zooms in when our air wanes and we begin surfacing, one by one. His technique is skilled for a fisherman, but the sight from below of a constant propeller churning above is less than comforting. Although a portable dive ladder magically appears on this first dive, it just as magically disappears on the ones to follow. Subsequently, we unfasten our tanks, flop over the worn gunnels like netted tuna, and then hoist our respective tanks and gear into the boat.

At Boca de Cote, the archetypical desert isle, we put ashore for lunch: Spanish mackerel steaks from last night's dinner, mangoes, and Cokes in the shade of a rusting tin fisherman's shed. Nearby, piles of empty queen conch shells are bleaching in the tropical sun at the edge of the gin-clear shallows. The supremely clear water and healthy marine life that have drawn us here also attracted early indigenous peoples from the mainland.

Archaeologists have found pre-Columbian Indian sites on fifty-six islands in Los Roques, representing seven different Indian groups. Before vanishing back into a black hole of history, the Indians left behind middens of conch, fish bones, and turtle shells, as well as red clay bowls and vases, sometimes elegantly carved into likenesses of their gods.

As I reflect on those who have been here before me, I feel something move across my foot. I look down and discover one of the ten-inch-long black lizards that are the main inhabitants of the cay. Saul tosses a mango rind to the ground and lizard pandemonium ensues. "They eat anything," he smiles, grinning. I learn that Saul has explored these waters over the last two years, hiring local boats whenever enough Latino divers find their way here to make it worth his time.

On the inside of the shallow lagoon surrounded by the islands, coral grows in waters less than a meter deep. On the outside, the plunging high-profile walls tell a different story. Unlike islands that accrue on ancient coral reefs, these islets actually sit atop the rim of a plateau, one that was created when a prehistoric volcanic erupted from the depths.

On the afternoon dive, we continue our drift odyssey at a nearby site, past massive colonies of reef-building star corals, hulks of brain coral squeezed onto narrow ledges, and miniature barrel-like sponges upholstered in a sky blue. A two-foot-long stoplight parrotfish noses about, crunching live coral in his beak-like mouth, while a small sharpnose puffer fish half the size of my hand browses nearby. Around the next corner, I am surprised by five large and fearless southern puffers—more puffers than I have ever seen together in one place.

Back at Gran Roque, after the sun goes down and as the balmy trade winds waft across the island, we sit in the dark on the little brick wall next to the bust of Simón Bolívar in the village square and reflect on the puffer situation. I tell O'Keefe this area must be truly unexploited, else the puffers would fear divers—who sometimes thoughtlessly squeeze the sluggish little fish to get them to puff up, a defensive reaction. O'Keefe figures some puffers actually like divers to inflate them, and hang around for that very reason. I ask O'Keefe if he would enjoy being puffed up by a two-hundred-pound sharpnose puffer.

The next morning, we are back on the water by 9:00 a.m. for two more dives, this time across the lagoon on its southern edge. With us today are Toni and Inaki, owners of a dive shop on Isla Margarita, a large resort-style island with nearly a half million residents closer to the Venezuelan mainland. But, with its murkier, nearshore waters, neither corals nor visibility fare well there.

Toni tells me that most visitors to Isla Margarita come for the beach, to party at island bars, and sometimes to sport dive for little pearls found in a local mollusk. If Los Roques turns out to be as good as they think, they may shuttle more advanced divers here, flying them over in the tiny jet-prop commuter planes that earlier transported us, the ones with the thick carbon residue covering the metal skin outside each engine.

Our morning dive is not good: the water is thick with plankton and the visibility is less than thirty feet. Saul says the ocean currents sometimes inexplicably change, bringing the sediment-rich lagoon waters outside. The natural process that flushes the lagoon in this way is an intricate part of keeping this system as healthy as it is. Sometimes as visitors, we fall into the condition of expecting even environmental realities to conform to our preconceptions; but the real world is not made of picture postcards. The most successful adventure travelers seem to be the flexible ones who roll with the punches, using each day as a true learning experience.

By afternoon, the currents have shifted again, and the outside of the cays where we dive are as blue and clear as they've ever been. Here, at ninety feet, I fight my way against the strong current inside a bedroom-sized cave carved back into the rock. It's dark in here, so I pull a small, bright dive light out of the pocket of my buoyancy compensator vest. When I turn it on, a coney grouper blasts through a thick school of blue chromis in the mouth of the cave. Under my light, massive gray angels flip their bodies at me sideways, showing their girth. In the recesses of the cave, a Peterson's cleaner shrimp—striped like a peppermint stick—rubs his tiny antenna together.

Back outside, I move along the wall, past mounds of pillar coral stacked atop each other like huge, triangular party hats. I drift through a school of small fish I can't identify—light blue, tipped with yellow noses, and striped with indigo—and they move away from me and then toward me in perfect unison like blades of meadow grass in the breeze. A sleek, silvery Spanish mackerel, just like those we've been eating, pokes about near the ocean triggerfish. I look down to see three tiny blennies, almost transparent, balanced on their pectorals on a slab of sand between the coral. Away from the wall, a school of large bar jacks, predatory and wary with bulldog like faces, move quickly by us. They are on the prowl.

Finished with our diving for the day, I am back on Gran Roque, in shorts and tennis shoes now, hiking by myself to the top of the worn volcanic mountain where the sad old lighthouse, El Faro, still watches, bereft of its light. Carefully, I look down from the windward side of the plunging cliff where the whitecaps pound on the rocks, and imagine this to be covered with water someday, just like the walls I have been diving next to—all of it a function of time sweeping across the sea, and me here, seeing it just for these brief moments.

Below me on the other side of the light, the rock and rubble slope gradually give way to the entire square-mile worth of island, its little cemetery of stone crosses and tiny houses for the spirits of fishermen lost at sea, its sandy streets full of barefoot children moving in schools like yellowtail snapper.

In this second, a sliver of a new moon glimmers low in the early night sky, crescent tips turned upward, smiling benevolently like the blue-eyed mermaid in the village square, promising, always promising.

5 Spring Hunting in the Native Terrain

A Topography of Wholeness

It's a crisp and cool autumn day, and my hiking buddy Bruce and I are hunched down atop a rare patch of open shore on a small, isolated pond deep inside a particularly wild Florida landscape. We're under a bright sun, and the splotches of blood on my forearms glow in a vibrant shade of red from the scratches and punctures of the thorny catbrier and serrated palmetto fronds we pushed through to get here.

A large gator blends in at surface with the reflection of a tree from above.

The desolate pool of water next to us seems nearly symmetrical, rimmed by native sawgrass and shagged every so often with a clutch of cattails. Sweetgum and maples rise just a few feet beyond, their leaves quietly smoldering in muted shades of yellow and red to oblige the nuances of our changing Florida seasons.

With its light-infused backdrop of hardwoods, the pond and its surrounding wilderness seem lifted out of a luminous nineteenth-century Florida landscape painting rendered by William Morris Hunt or Martin Johnson Heade. Above, the sky is so clear and brilliant that the outline of the swollen gibbous moon is faint, just the scantest reminder that it is there at all. By night, I imagine it will be bright enough out here to commandeer much of the sky, glowing like a giant beacon with no artificial light to dilute it.

We are really only eight or nine miles from an asphalt road. But the lush subtropical tangle native to certain unmanicured landscapes of Florida is pervasive, evoking a wild and majestic place from another century. What appears to be a set of gigantic eyes has been patiently glaring at us for the last twenty minutes or so from the other side of the pond, about a hundred yards away. Gnarly, primal, and black, they protrude just above the surface, doing a great imitation of the eye console of a very large gator. But both of us have already rationalized that a gator of that size would be way out of scale for this little pond. Must be small muscular-looking stumps, a peculiar set of wooden snags, something like that. Besides, most wild gators tend to submerge or otherwise hide when upright walking mammals bumble into their territory.

It is only when the rest of the reptile attached to the eyes suddenly emerges at the surface, turns sideways in a particularly commanding manner, and cruises aggressively toward a cleft in a stand of sawgrass that we realize this is indeed a massive animal, somewhere between twelve and fourteen feet in length. And for a reptile of its size, it's traveling with remarkable speed.

"Wow," says Bruce. "It's moving through the water like the *Queen Mary*." I chuckle, since that seems healthier than expressing fear and exuding adrenaline. And then, say, "Yeah, like it's driven by a really powerful engine, turning a sort of reptilian propeller."

Then it occurs to me that the open, compacted mound of dark earth and sweetgum roots we are hunched down on is likely the home turf of our new animal acquaintance, a great vantage point from which to survey the rest of his world. It could even be the classic gator "mud slide" as reported by earlier observers of Florida waters, from Bartram to Sidney Lanier. If an animal weighing seven hundred or eight hundred pounds routinely lounges here, that sure would explain why the otherwise muddy pond shore under us is packed down as it is. I wonder absently if he's simply been waiting for us to vacate his patch of prime waterfront real estate—or if he's trying to figure out if it's worth it to gum up his teeth with all that leather and fleece and fabric to get to the morsels of fresh mammal meat inside.

It's taken us almost four hours to get here on our annual "Black Friday" hike, but it has been worth every step, every golden orb spider web full in the face, every forearm puncture and scrape. Bruce is a professor of environmental studies at a college down in Winter Park, while I am a nature writer living not too far away in the old farm town of Sanford. Our jobs really do reflect far more than how we make a living: they define us, since what we do has organically grown out of how fully we care about natural places and what they offer to the human soul.

The idea of a Black Friday hike was hatched a few years ago after we joked about how contradictory our culture can be when it comes to aggressively spending money for a holiday that, historically, was devoted to charity, sacredness, and goodwill. Although the term "black" was coined to imply that merchants would go into the fiscal "black" because of the stepped-up profit on the Friday after Thanksgiving, it was clear the anxiety of it all created a true emotional darkness, a condition where the human soul gets sucked out and Cuisinarted in favor of getting a deal on the trendy techno-gadget of the hour.

Oddly, whenever I start to feel I should be more generous about this particular shopping extravaganza, some metaphor comes to life and actively rekindles my aversion to it. Last year, Christmas shoppers started macing each other to improve their position in the queue. Other times, fistfights have broken out, inspired by disagreements about who deserves a better shot at the coveted merchandise. Since this happened a day after our national feast of gratitude and before our national celebration of spiritual birth, it was as if one of the great American writers of surreality—Tom Robbins or Kurt Vonnegut—had conjured up these ironies, maybe as a way to better create a more distinctive narrative farce in a state that routinely skirts the boundaries between fiction and reality anyway.

Properly reinforced, I figured the antidote for this great cosmic irony was to go as deep into the Florida woods as I possibly could on this otherwise Black Day, and then, to return, not frenzied and addled from the Walmart-esque squeeze of overcompensation, but revitalized with authentic discovery, maybe even comforted with nature's very real organic grace.

The method for selecting our annual destination was at once straightforward and complex, a true exercise in optimism that only required us to go with whatever the moment eventually revealed. We would first imagine something in nature that was vibrant and singular and alive—a rare animal or plant or a curious rise or fall in the landscape. Then we would try to find our way to it, zigging and zagging about on mostly unmarked paths and firebreak roads and animal trails until we reached it. On one hand, it was a deeply rewarding actualization of choice and free will. On the other, it was simply a chance to be kids again, and that was pretty liberating all by itself.

In preparation for this year's outing, I closely studied a highly detailed topographical map, looking for features I may have missed during earlier treks in a nearby state forest. It wasn't long before I identified a tiny pond that lay well beyond the range of where I had ever been. On the chart, a little creek overflowed from a circular splotch that was the pond, squiggling its way a half mile or so north to Blackwater Creek, a major tributary of the Wekiva.

Since the rolling karst terrain here is often friendly to the formation of springs, I was hoping the pond itself would be spring-fed, a limestone vent or two pumping up clear water from the aquifer into the pond's sandy bottom. If it were, it would be another divine and mysterious gift of the Florida landscape, a place where we could be reminded of what really does count in a world that sometimes seems to be wobbling precariously on its axis. Our respective nooks in the larger culture might again regain a bit of stasis, and wholeness on this special day would be measured not by the ka-ching of a cash register but in the natural equilibrium of the human soul.

On my topo map, uplands like scrub and sandhill are colored white, waters in rivers and springs are a light blue, and the low swamps around them are pea green, jammed with plantlike symbols to suggest low, moist vegetation. The altitude of the landscape is charted in feet and divided by contour lines to illustrate variations—sometimes depicting ancient shoals and dunes rising forty, fifty, and sixty feet above the low wetlands on this otherwise pancake-flat terrain. Jeep paths and abandoned rail lines are also identified, as are certain country roads. Like most topo maps, this one was assembled from aerial photographs and ground-level surveys. The last time it was updated was 1970.

Florida has lost an enormous amount of natural space since that time. But far-thinking souls who understood the value of nature a few decades ago lobbied for public land-buying programs, from the Keys to the Panhandle. As a result, some 110 square miles of state forests and preserves are scattered about us in this Wekiva River basin. And that's why I figure a map like this could still hold clues to the true spirit of the native landscape, allowing the cryptic and the unseen a place to endure, maybe even to flourish.

In this way, our excursion into nature on the day after Thanksgiving might truly manifest our own very real sense of gratitude for the glories of the natural world around us.

↓ ↓ ↓

Our hike into the forest today started just before noon, when I met Bruce at the cattle gate that usually blocks access to the main north-south road of packed clay and gravel. Earlier in the week, I had called the rangers' office to ask for a permit with the combo lock numbers that would open that gate so we could take my vehicle deeper inside the forest, allowing more time to explore the unroaded landscape by foot. With scant funding for rangers to be on-site like they are in state parks, precautions like this keep the landscape wild and undisturbed. A locked gate dissuades littering and vandalism as well as casual visitors who might want to spontaneously churn about yee-hawing in their four-wheel drive vehicles for no good reason.

As a result, the chances for a true wilderness experience are greater, lots of woods and swamps and uplands where you're more likely to run into a Florida black bear or gator than another human. Once a mile or so inside the gate, I drive more slowly so as not to miss the westerly spur trail that ought to give us the best access to our destination.

I pull over at the first dirt corridor that intersects the one we're on, parking near its mouth. The narrow, grassy jeep path here creates an open trail that should lead us to the distant tree line created by the hardwood forest. The lower swamp will be beyond and below the forest. Somewhere near its edge, we hope to find the pond.

Around us, the landscape gently rolls, leading us gradually up into a desertlike scrub before lowering us back down again into a scrubby flatwoods, a sort of hybrid terrain where hearty drought-tolerant plants thrive atop the seasonally soggy forest of palmetto and pine. In this world, most of the ground cover is stunted and low, restored to its historic incarnation. Before the land was moved into the public domain in 1990, some of the higher uplands had been used to grow pines for lumber and to range livestock. But access to outsiders was restricted even then; it was particularly so in the soggy swamps and marshes, which were naturally secluded in their vine-tangled gloom.

The weather is about as good as it gets for walking through an open flatwoods, and after a mile or so of this, I begin to feel relaxed, more fully at home in this wild and singular place. Early naturalists knew all about this sort of effect, of course. As Emerson once wrote, "At the gates of the forest, the surprised man of the world is forced to leave his city estimates of great and small, wise and foolish. The knapsack of custom falls off his back with the first step he makes into these precincts." Certainly, I had been eager to shed my metaphoric knapsack of socialized ritual and to rely more fully on my own wits. In this way, I could be informed, maybe even comforted, by nature's voice and the be-here-now immediacy she requires. I do carry a knapsack—but it is a real one full of water and granola bars, maps and compass.

The terrain on both sides of our trail seems low and broad for as nearly as far as I can see. By the topo map, we're walking through a stretch of flatwoods that's fifteen feet higher than the distant swamp. Shiny blueberry plants, their sweet fruits recently picked clean by birds and black bears, command the lower understory, with the saw palmettos, scrub oaks, and gallberry bushes towering over them. This natural world is a savanna, a transition between grasslands and forest special to warmer latitudes like Florida. Plants and animals that live here have learned to adapt to the extended droughts and extended rainfalls that characterize it.

For right now, we're in an ecotone, a place where two different plant communities brush up against each other. The cusp in between is enriched, a juncture that is more biologically diverse than the respective habitats of each.

We see one scrub jay, its brilliant blue plumage marking him every bit as thoroughly as the rounded crest on his head, as he flits from one low branch to another. A few late-season butterflies that I take to be "orange sulphur"— because that is the color of their wings—hover around a goldenrod with a new yellow blossom so brilliant it seems to glow, as if electrified. Then a flock of stocky birds materializes around us, moving in the way that birds do when on a mission. I look more closely and see the distinct flashes of dusky orange on their chests and realize these are fellow travelers, migrating robins flying south to avoid the northern winter, likely headed for the Antilles or Latin America. The protected landscape here is a treasured way-stop for them, a link in the corridor flyway that offers food and shelter in their seasonal travels.

As a little boy growing up in the country along the midcoast of the Atlantic Seaboard, I knew robins only as solitary birds. For me, spotting the first one of the new spring was a blissful event. It was not unlike discovering the very first tender green sprout on a bare, winter-scorched branch when I climbed the ancient wild black cherry tree behind our home. I was beside myself with it all, proud with the way it made my folks so pleased when I ran inside to share the news of seasonal change with them. I guess it was only natural that those nascent discoveries later informed my adult sensibilities, igniting a very real sense of wonder in nature that I have yet to outgrow.

And today, seeing the first robin is joyous for another reason because it means that the more pleasant and comforting winter weather of Florida is arriving. My folks have been gone for several years, and I am now older than they were when I was a little boy. Nonetheless, something hopeful and loving throbs deep inside my chest during such moments. A powerful nostalgia takes shape, and I instinctively find myself wanting to run inside the house where my mom and dad and brother and I lived to tell them I have seen the very first robins of the year.

It's warm around us now, and the sun has done its job in helping the plants and trees release their distinctive vapors from their leaves and needles. Many scrub plants are volatile, their biochemicals evaporating at relatively low temperatures. There are the aromatic scents of the wild vanilla and rosemary, an olfactory reminder of the way the plants have evolved to keep themselves from being eaten. They are joined by the subtle perfumes of pine needles and the amber sap, flavored with the herbs and lichens clinging to the trunks and limbs and growing on the soil.

We are deep in now, far from any smells or noises associated with so-called civilization. And so, when a light breeze rises up and wafts across the pinelands, it blends all these scents in the most pleasant of ways. But there is something far more in this gentle wind. I imagine it to be a primal, unconscious memory scent of another time. I think of it as a taste of the wildness that once infused all of La Florida, a heady, archaic fragrance that now brushes up against the pores of my skin, against my very soul, a potency far beyond the human senses of smell and touch. It allows me to feel that hope still exists as long as we remain respectful to any authentic place, and grateful for the chance to be fully alive inside it.

It strikes me that there is a sort of conversation taking place here between me and the natural world—even though a not a single word has been spoken out loud. The writer Linda Hogan has observed this too: "There is a way that nature speaks, that land speaks. Most of the time we are simply not patient enough, quiet enough to pay attention to the story." I'm figuring this language is recorded in the touch of the breeze, the song of the scrub jay, the flow of the terrain, all bound together here in this sweet and timeless moment of solace and light.

Since the tallest feature of this flatwood is the random pine and its bristle of green needles, it's a bit strange to suddenly spot an angular, geometrically ordered structure sticking up from it in the distance. As we get closer, I see it's a homemade deer stand, a sort of miniature metal tower where a hunter climbs up early in the morning, settles in on a small piece of plywood at the top, and waits for the deer to start moving around to feed. A vantage point like this is also a dandy way for anyone to observe nature as she awakens, fresh and new, with the very first ocher-colored glow of the sun as it pushes its way just above the wild green horizon.

We stop to take a closer look at the stand. We are here between seasonal hunts, so I figure we might as well put the empty tower to good use. Bruce puts down his pack, and easily climbs to the top, maybe twenty-five or so feet off the ground. The view up here is great, he says. And when he climbs back down, I go to the wobbly ladder and cautiously step and pull my own way to the top as well. When you're getting used to being hunched down inside a savanna, a perspective like this is oddly enlightening, creating a vista you wouldn't have from inside a low, rolling terrain.

Everything below me seems smallish, flatter than it did when I was down on the ground. I can more clearly see the trail we are following as it winds far off into the horizon toward the distinct line of hardwood trees, the little pond hidden somewhere inside. The tops of the stockier shrubs and bushes look almost like the crowns of an unkempt field of giant broccoli, the only variation in the tones of green, brown, and an odd, tawny yellow. I feel as if I've somehow transcended the human-bound constraints of the land, a rickety homemade pylon providing far more magic than I had ever imagined.

Topography still defines where we are. And while the details of topo maps have always fascinated me, I've also been curious about the use of the word itself. I've made it a point to learn more, discovering that *topographia* is a word from both Middle English and Greek. It means, simply, "the detailed, precise description of a place."

I understand the concepts of both *detail* and *precise*. However, "place" has taken on a broader meaning these days. Writers often search for ways in which the feel of the land exists beyond mere geography. Examining the ways in which nature defines us requires a closer look at how that place also affects the broader culture—the lifeways, hopes, and dreams—of humans who either live in it or who are transformed by it in any meaningful way. The self-identity that can result helps inform the otherwise ambiguous "sense of place."

But there's much more going on here too. Identifying the emotional topography, the contour lines separating the rises and falls—the spatial extent—inside the human heart is far more the domain of poetry than of science. And at what altitude will a tender myth expand and become far more of a comfort than a conjure? And where is the ecotone that marks the terrain where caring truly begins and ends? And how do you know when the boundary of the past meaningfully nudges up against the present—or, when the primeval becomes spiritual? I'm guessing it's all hidden inside of the ephemeral notion of place, a territory inhabited by land and culture and heart, where only the human doing the searching will ever know for sure.

For nostalgic and sensitive guys like me, the emotional world of memories and deep feeling is one vast, lush landscape where almost anything is possible, if you want it to be. And so, my walkabout here on this Black Friday has to do with the hope of discovering new places. But, more profoundly, it has to do with acknowledging the deeply felt truths and dreams tucked away in the sometimes remote geography of my own life.

Down from our tree stand experiences, we again walk across the flatwoods, closing on the tree line just ahead. As we do, I marvel at the size of the forest and of the hardwoods inside of it. Clearly the moist, mesic terrain that slopes down toward the lower swamp has nurtured the trees well, even turning the sabal palms into sturdy green giants. The trail we followed from the flatwoods continues into the thick hammock. But as it goes, it quickly becomes more constricted, as if we're burrowing into the swamp through a foliage warren.

The nearly unlimited visibility we had back on the open uplands disappears, replaced by an abject darkness at the end of our organic tunnel. At first, the blackness is about a hundred feet or so away. But the deeper we go into the gloom, the closer it becomes until it's only a few yards in front of us. The well-crafted webs of the giant golden orb spiders easily fill the ever-narrowing portal, as do the spiky catbrier and the wild grape vines. Back under the sun, the sabal palms seemed tropical and pleasant and nonthreatening. But here in the dim light, when I grasp the fronds to move them out of the way, the sharp serrations along the rims often cut into my palms, and sometimes into my neck and forehead.

Bruce stops every so often to check a satellite map on a GPS-like device he has brought with him. It shows us—identified as a solid blue dot—and it shows the location of the actual pond. On the bright screen, the little pond seems only yards away. But it is another illusion of the techno-world that makes it seem so. Its location is not far, says Bruce, less than a half mile. But the increasingly restrictive nature of this foliage tunnel has reduced our pace considerably. What is left of our trail is barely wide enough for a wild hog to navigate, and the head-whacks of the branches and the strangle-like grips of the vines are remarkable in their natural constraints.

The terrain is falling under us, and I imagine the contour lines of the map are now jammed far closer together to reflect the marked incline. As we near the bottom of this natural earthen contour, the ground becomes soggier, less predictable. As I try to figure the best places to step, my pace becomes far more tentative. I realize my intellect is no match for a landscape that has been millions of years in the making.

Indeed, it is as if we have entered not just a different terrain, but a different epoch. Emerson, like other wise men of the woods, knew of this too. He once wrote, "The tempered light of the woods is like a perpetual morning, and is stimulating and heroic. The anciently reported spells of these places creep on us."

We are making enough noise so that I've rationalized no self-respecting viper would stick around very long. And while we are effectively inside the thick tangle of a subtropical jungle, I realize the greatest danger—the true vulnerability—is more my own instinctual fear of a prehuman unknown, of a reality that has existed long before warm-bloodied mammals ever crawled through the hazy portal of evolution.

Another thirty or so minutes of this, and we are just about sea-swamp level, at the place where—if there is any flowing water from a creek or spring run—it will be here. The canopy of the subtropical foliage is thick overhead, creating a gloomy prehistoric landscape in which bright sunlight exists only as a faint shard of memory. We are squarely inside an immutable fretwork of green, a time-stuck place almost mystical in its isolation. If the ancient spells are to creep on us, as Emerson reported, they would have no better place to do so than here.

Finally, after one last wallop in the head with a heavy palm frond, the southerly, upstream wall of the jungle suddenly falls away, revealing what seems to be an open natural theater surrounded on three sides by swamp. I resist the thought that the palm thwack might have left me briefly senseless, and instead summon up the hope that we are at last where we want to be. It helps that Bruce notices it too. He is standing a few yards ahead of me, next to the edge of this impromptu theater, a clear stream running at his feet. I figure this modest rivulet must be the little squiggly line I earlier saw on the topo map, the one that courses north to the Blackwater from the pond. "This must be the creek," says Bruce, and I smile broadly. It's a sort of kid-like smile that comes not from nominal courtesy or a feeling of superiority, but one that says, *Wow, we did it, bro!*

The stream, only a few inches deep, is barely flowing. But it is clear, as transparent as that of any spring run. The fallen leaves of the sweetgums and maples can be easily seen under its waters. The luminous, open theater that is the sawgrass pond, the encircling hardwoods with their transitional foliage and the wonderfully bright Florida sun, are only a few more yards away. While there are still vines and briers and webs, they have diminished for right now. I walk to the edge of this secluded natural arena with great aplomb, as if I am walking onto a stage. Adjacent to the stream is the rare open mound of packed black earth, and we go to it without hesitation.

We squat down on our haunches atop the gator mud slide at the edge of the little pond. A clutch of cattails is growing next to me, and across the pond, next to the unmoving set of snags that I wish not to be giant gator eyes, is a school of small fish. They are disc-sized, like half-grown bluegill, and they are jumping from the water at once, like fish do when they are being threatened.

We have identified an unknown place on the topographical map, and we have followed the charts that led us to it: the hard-copy chart on paper and the electronic one that Bruce has in his knapsack. The silver-like sheen on the water's surface, the clarity of the little creek that flows out from it, and the slightly higher basin that enfolds it suggest that this round splotch of blue next to us is likely fed by a spring or two on its sandy bottom. It will take another few visits to figure this out for sure. But for now, the knowledge of this is reassuring, evidence that a keen cartographical hope could be ground-truthed in real life.

Covering the distance between the jeep path and the pond has taken far longer than I had imagined. Yet that knowledge does not worry me now. I mindfully think of time and space as useful, friendly notions, dimensions we can use to estimate what it will take to get us back out. I figure we should make it before dark, feeling all the rises and the falls in the real-life sweep of the topography as we go.

I reach out to the closest stalk of cattail and pull it from the water, roots and all. I know the Creeks who became the Seminoles once ate tubers of plants, and I figure the pre-Columbians who were here before them likely did the same. I take out my little Buck knife and peel the outer skin from the white tuber. I cut it in half and offer a chunk of it to Bruce. I swash the remaining lump of root in the clear water of the pond, and then chew on it. It tastes vaguely like the heart of a sabal palm, wild and rich and tender. Bruce notices this too and comments on the similarities they share. In the full recovery of the human senses, I'm figuring anything that stimulates the taste buds is also fair game, another sensory avenue into the immediacy of the now.

I smile again, looking out over the pond to the jungle-thick sawgrass, which is now sea green in the radiant afternoon Florida sunlight. It all seems incandescent, glowing in the very best of ways, and my spirit seems to be doing little childlike flips inside my heart.

When I first studied the topo map a couple of weeks ago, I remembered an observation from the Zen poet Gary Snyder. I am now struck at how meaningful it is at this moment. "There is a tame and also a wild side to the human mind," Snyder had written." The tame side, like a farmer's field, has been disciplined and cultivated to produce a desired yield. It is useful, but limited. The wild side is larger, deeper, more complex, and though it cannot be fully known, it can be explored."

It is this wild side that has landscapes and animals within it that have surprised us, that have enriched me with discovery and hope. It can refresh us and scare us and make us whole, all at once. If we're lucky, we can become fully human again, as alive and aware—as flawed and wondrous, complex and untamed—as we were meant to be.

As I am considering this wild side of the human psyche, the cruising gator turns from its primal business on the pond and once more is staring directly at us. From somewhere deeper in the dark woods, a barred owl wails softly, more of a plaintive sigh than a hoot. It is almost as if the swamp, having held its breath all this time, is finally exhaling. In all honesty, I do not know what will come next. But I am far more exhilarated than distressed.

I do know this: within this gift of wildness, we might be informed with the spiritual ecotones that bind action with deep feelings, might even acknowledge the mystical contours that bridge the cusp between memory and scared dreams.

And this experience might transport us—if only for a little while—to a wild gator pond hidden deep in the swampland, tucked away at the very edges of the human imagination. It is a timeless, everlasting gift of exploration that is hunched down and gloriously alive, atop a compacted mound of black gator earth, in the warm and caring sunlight of the human heart.

6   Alph the Sacred River

What Will Become of It?

> The state with the prettiest name,
> the state that floats in brackish water
> held together by mangrove roots . . .
>
> Elizabeth Bishop

I am somewhere inside the vortex of Blue Spring, way past the "Prevent Your Death: Go No Farther" sign at sixty feet, and far beyond the muted glow of surface light.

The river that Blue feeds has been gradually warming, and the warm-blooded manatees who overwinter here have just left.

Gar in clear run of Blue Spring.

Except for a few snorkelers back up in the shallow run, my dive buddy and I are alone in the spring. The only illumination down here is portable, hand-held. And like the trail of exhaust bubbles from my regulator, it tethers me to the surface with my own limitations. Scuba tanks, face masks, containers of light—they are all reminders of how unsuited we humans are to immerse ourselves in the most primal and universal element of all.

Here, near the 120-foot-deep bottom of this limestone chasm, I am as aware as I have ever been of the pervasive power and magic of water. All but invisible, it arises from a dark slot in the rock, flailing me like a rag doll with its energy.

If underground water fuels the veins and capillaries that sustain our Florida physiography, then I am squarely inside a natural incision, a place where the liquid transports itself to the surface, where science meets myth and culture head on. The naturalist William Bartram sat on the banks of Blue once, and later wrote in wonder of the "diaphanous fountain" that surged just below. He wrote likewise about Salt and Manatee Springs. In all his travels, nothing seemed to touch him as fully. His descriptions inspired the Romantic poet Coleridge to write in Kubla Khan of Xanadu, "Where Alph the sacred river ran, through caverns measureless to man." I would give all I have if Bartram could be next to me today, could feel the full sway of this natural "ebullition," down here inside of Alph.

Looking closely in the soft rock around me, I see subliminal clues to the prehistoric sea that accrued to form first the platform and then the crust of Florida. The clues are fossilized shells, still ribbed like a cockle or cupped round like a clam. They are welded together by the dust of Eocene coral, whale skull, oceanic sand, an assemblage of calcium turned white as bone.

Even the manatees are a reminder of this oceanic genesis. I have encountered them underwater before, have seen the residual but distinct toenails on their front flippers, visual evidence of their own long and convoluted genetic journey from sea to land, and then back again.

But if the fossils and the manatees are an aide-mémoire to the core fiber of both people and place, the most urgent reminder is the fierce upwelling itself. Isotopes of water have been dated in Florida springs. And although a water molecule seldom stays in the atmosphere for more than ten days when hidden in the dark fissures and bedding planes in the rock—as it is here—it may remain so for ten thousand years or more.

It is inescapable. The water that pushes and shoves me around in the throat of Blue once fell on uplands as rain millennia ago, fell on and around the earliest native Americans who lived here. They drank it, bathed in it, were nurtured by it.

How did they regard it? Of the Timucua—here along the St. Johns for at least four thousand years before the Europeans arrived—we know at least shards of their language. Of their words, there were five different ones for trust, six for virtue. But there was only one root word for water. Dew, rainfall, pond, river, lake, lagoon. It is all *ibi*. Perhaps it differed in context or pronunciation or modification. Nonetheless, it is *ibi* going in, and *ibi* coming back out. *Ibi*, a liquid god that rendered this once-arid sandbar and savanna luxuriant, that made it a jungle, warm, wet, and wildly productive.

The Timucua had a reverence for this water, as they did for all of nature. Their deities were woven into it, and not separate from it, not safely contained to a one-hour sermon, one day a week. *Ibi* held fish and snails, fed wildlife, watered crops, floated dugouts, gave life. In storms and in drowning, it also took life away.

So it was, too, for the Muskogean-speakers who migrated here when the Timucua were vanquished. The brave warrior Coacoochee hid out with a band of two hundred in the wild swamps of the nearby Wekiva River during the Second Seminole War. Coacoochee reported the spirit of his twin sister once visited him from the land of souls, offering him a cup of pure water from the spring of the Great Spirit. "And if I should drink of it," said Coacoochee, "I should return and live with her forever."

Water was enchantment, certainly. But it was also deeply respected, feared, and honored, held close to the heart in both mystery and awe. It was sacred.

Water has shaped culture in Florida from the very first moment humans stepped foot on this ancient sea-bottom terrace. When they arrived twelve thousand years or more ago, the peninsula was dry, and nearly twice as large as it is today. Few modern rivers or springs flowed as they do, and these nomadic Paleo-Indians encamped around limestone catchments on prairies and at mouths of coastal rivers, sites now inundated with the sea.

The glaciers began to retreat, the climate warmed, and water from the shallow seas was drawn up into the sky. The great hydrological cycle that sets Florida decidedly apart from other global deserts on this same latitude began to stir. Freshwater springs, charged by the new rain seeping into the soft sea rock upland, flowed effusively. Swamps and marsh were birthed, and rivers snaked through their lush and moist topography. The vast glade of shallow water and plants and limestone south of Lake Okeechobee took form, revealing what the Spanish would one day map as the "Lagoon of the Sacred Spirit."

By 5000 BC, millions of years after most of the North American continent had fashioned itself into mountains and valleys, Florida finally took its present-day shape and substance.

This new peninsula was verdant and biologically diverse, one giant organic marketplace of fish and game—and at last it had stabilized enough to offer sanctuary, to allow time for mythology to arise from the connection between people and place. Nomadic hunters could settle inland on rivers, build mounds, and grow crops. Tools, points, and pottery could become finer, more sophisticated, and tribal cultures and their art more complex.

Leaders could evolve into chiefs and shamans, powerful men who could mediate with the forces of nature—especially the powers we moderns would one day call hydrology.

Perhaps more than any single place on our continent, the new wet landscape of Florida was occupied almost as quickly as it had been formed. It was as if the water-driven terrain and its people grew together, the environment shaping culture as quickly as it shaped itself.

When Ponce de León arrived in 1513, blundering westward of Puerto Rico in search of Bimini, he sailed along the mid-Atlantic coast, landing near Cape Canaveral. Soon the first permanent geographic name on the North American continent was scribbled on his chart—La Florida. It was springtime, flowers were blooming, and he noted this new land was "very pretty to behold."

Pánfilo de Narváez, following the conquistadors' quest for gold and glory, sailed around the Florida cape with ships loaded with horses, provisions, and four hundred men, and landed somewhere near Sarasota Bay fifteen years later. Over the next eight years, the first Spanish expedition to explore the New World by land would be whittled down to four men, and—a decade before de Soto—the survivors would cross the Withlacoochee, the Suwannee, the Apalachicola, and then the Mississippi, building canoes or, when possible, swimming.

There was no gold in La Florida, but there was plenty of water, and, as it does today, it enriched the soil, turning leaf and wood into humus and peat, composting the landscape. For the next two hundred years, Spanish missions were built along major rivers and coastal lagoons, forcing the converted Indians to use the fertile land of La Florida as a breadbasket to fuel Spanish plundering elsewhere in the New World.

The French artist Jacques le Moyne, here for a very brief time with the ill-fated French colony at Ft. Caroline in 1564, left a more complete graphic picture of the same Indians with his forty-two drawings. From le Moyne, we learn the Timucua swam with children on their backs, rode in giant dugouts, performed ceremonies, captured alligators, dried fish, and planted crops—all behaviors made possible, indeed, even encouraged by the liquid nature of La Florida.

It was the ambitiously brutal conquistador Pedro Menéndez de Avilés himself, who after learning of the breadth of Florida's rivers and wetlands, felt sure there was some way the interior could be navigated by his large ships. It was he who first schemed of a cross-Florida canal to allow such a feat.

Meanwhile, with no technical solution to enable humans to commandeer such a soggy place, Florida grew slowly, lagging behind the rest of the dry and maneuverable continent. After all, there were twelve thousand miles of rivers and streams, and no fewer than 7,700 lakes. Some one thousand springs have since been identified—more than any other region in the country. When they settled here, Europeans usually chose natural harbors on the vast coast, and inland, along high river bluffs or atop ancient Indian middens. Florida was one big swamp and marsh—what the author John Rothchild has called "pre-dredged real estate"—and the best and surest roads were its waterways. It was a reality that would not escape the tourist steamboats that arrived in the early nineteenth century. Fishing and boating, pirating and salvaging came with the territory; they are the natural antecedents of what is left of the Florida persona today.

Bartram, here in two separate trips in 1764 and 1775—and who lived on the St. Johns for two years in between—was among the first to see the water-driven ecological connections, to marvel at the strong rivers and the magic of the powerful springs. Our first spiritual naturalist, the gentle Quaker was an unlikely explorer. But he found his way farther into the interior of Florida than the Spanish ever had, sailing and oaring a boat all the way down to Puzzle Lake on the "grand and noble San Juan."

Bartram understood the promise that this gridwork of nature had—still has, even today—to hold mystery close to its heart. Unlike open savannas or mountains, you cannot see very far at all in a jungle, and every tree trunk, every vine-clogged pathway, every bend in the river conceals a new discovery. In contrast with the geological drama of continental mountains and valleys, this is a territory woven into the folds of biological nuance.

For 250 years, Florida had been a region to be exploited by Europeans—a place to be sopped up, trimmed, and tamed. But for Bartram, the man the Creeks called the "Flower Hunter," it was a natural cathedral—a place where we "learn wisdom and understanding in the economy of nature, and be seriously attentive to the divine monitor within."

Perhaps nature as religion may have had a chance in Florida. But when technology finally developed to allow "submerged bottomlands" to be drained and sold for as little as twenty-five cents an acre in the nineteenth century, then Florida's destiny—which was once to flow—began to ebb.

In the long haul, humans have done more to disconnect themselves from Florida's water in the last century than they did in the twelve thousand years that came before. Water has become a visual Muzak, a background to our clever hardware-driven lifestyles, a solvent to be turned on or off, ditched away or drained. Once a noun and a verb, once a giver of life—once a muse to writers, artists, musicians—water in the last century became an expletive. It was called "flood control."

Today our lack of connection to water has caught up with us. The feature that most shaped Florida into a singular place is being transformed. Now lakes are drying or turning eutrophic, the springs declining in magnitude, the coastal estuaries becoming cloudy with sediment. The reefs, those miraculous living berms of color just offshore, are ailing. Even when we have the best intentions, we often forget that water is guided by gravity. We all live downstream in one fashion or another.

And we have a tremendous thirst, a utility far beyond any sacrament

Coacoochee may have imagined. Floridians use 170 gallons a water a day—compared to 110 gallons nationally. The level of our aquifer has been steadily declining since 1935. The magical "ether" Bartram once described is becoming scarce.

For the first time in the history of Florida, the liquid energy that once shaped us is now being shaped by us. We have taken ownership of *ibi* away from the gods. The good news is the sensibilities Bartram once dared to show are gaining new ground. Some Floridians are emerging from the swoon of technology as if awakening from a long, odd dream.

Nonetheless, the purity of the original watershed can never be restored. The *ibi* of the Timucua will never be again. And if water has lost its sacredness, can mere human law ever atone for it? A century from now, will Coleridge's Alph still flow, or will it have become a dry chasm in the rock?

And the liquid enchantment of Florida, what will become of it, and what, ultimately, will become of us all?

7   Emotional Ecotones

From the Windowsill to the Amazon

The "edge effect" in the world of ecology describes the margin where different plant habitats meet. When they do, the variety of animals and plants there increases dramatically since this "edge" functions like a community junction, or an intersection. This particular juncture of richness is also called an ecotone. Florida, where I live, is blessed with a multitude of these ecotones since the diversity of the subtropics meets that of the warm, temperate climate here.

A young boy with a paddle I bought in a village along the Amazon.

But we also have emotional ecotones in our own lives, places where the past brushes up against the present, maybe the future. For deeply nostalgic guys like myself, the past is particularly rich, and sometimes it flows like a wild river, carrying its own energy with it. Sitting here and typing these words is a present-tense activity. Yet those words sometimes reanimate the images and experiences of the past. As for this personal history, I can chronicle a lot of it by simply looking around the room. The two windowsills in front of me are packed with the icons of memory, creating ecotones of sensibilities whenever they're considered.

There's the small hand-carved dugout canoe with its perfectly downsized little paddle. The dugout's about ten inches long and made from some sort of tropical hardwood. It imitates the larger dugouts that natives who live in and near tropical rainforests still use today. I came across this one in a small village on the Chagres River in Panama, far upland from the canal. Villagers still use the dugouts on the upper Chagres for transportation, setting their fishing nets, gathering native plants for medicine, food, building materials, and drug-induced pathways to the spiritual Shadow Land.

I've also seen dugout paddlers in Nicaragua, Guyana, the interior of Brazil, and in Peru upstream from Iquitos, the latter on the rivers whose confluence creates the Amazon. In an adjacent Florida Room, I have mounted one of those life-sized paddles on the wall. It's a work of art, really, and is carved out of a single piece of lightweight tropical wood. Its handle splays out when it reaches the blade, making it nearly heart-shaped. The wide, thin blade then tapers down to a very distinct point at the bottom.

The wide blade is effective at moving water while the point of the blade allows the user to stick his paddle upright in the mud when he returns to shore. No matter how you cut it, it's functional art. It's also a portal into the distant history of Florida, when Native Americans here performed the same chores that indigenous people in Latin America and elsewhere still accomplish today.

I bought the paddle at a village on the Rio Samaria of Peru for three dollars. It wasn't a tourist souvenir, since the remote village of hunters and gatherers had no such gewgaws. When I first asked the owner in my woefully broken Spanish if he would sell it, he said yes. His native language was of a particular "Indian" origin, and he seemed as unsure of his Spanish as I did of mine. I finally figured he was telling me to take his dugout out on the river to practice with the paddle to make sure it worked for me, figuring that, of course, I would have my own dugout on my own tropical river back home.

Like the paddles, each dugout was also a work of art, crafted individually from logs harvested from the rainforest. I'm guessing the process was not unlike that depicted by the French artist Jacques le Moyne, who, in 1590, portrayed the native Timucua crafting a dugout along the St. Johns River of Florida. In le Moyne's portrayal, the log was first cut and then the top of it was carefully burned to make it easier to carve out the wood inside. The bottom of the hull had no ridge or keel to stabilize it, and certainly had nothing resembling a rudder.

The bottom of the Timucuan dugout was simply round, just like the one I would be paddling. When I first pushed my borrowed dugout into the deep, dark waters of the Samaria, I almost capsized. It didn't take me long to figure how to paddle so as not to risk flipping over: I hunched down as much as I could on my knees to lower my center of gravity, and realigned my Norteamericano paddle strokes to allow for the fact I was essentially sitting inside a log.

There were huge caiman thriving in this river, aggressive reptiles that make our own Florida gators look docile. I also noticed that the four red-bellied piranhas the dugout's owner had caught earlier were lying in the bottom of the hull next to my knees. (Piranhas make good eating, albeit with a jerky-like toughness to them.) Capsizing in such a place would probably not be a particularly good thing.

I finally got beyond the village to a place where the river narrowed and I was surrounded by walls of thick green tropical foliage with a fretwork of lianas on each shore. It started to rain because, after all, this is the rainforest and the wet season was just beginning. I noticed that several cracks in bottom of the hull had been partially sealed by flattening out sardine cans and tacking them atop the cracks. Between the heavy rains and the leaks from the cracks, I was soon sitting in several inches of river water. Two of the piranhas begin to flop about, rejuvenated by the new infusion of the Samaria.

Around the next bend, I came on another dugout, this one with two fishermen in it. They were both standing up, which was itself pretty remarkable, given the unstable nature of the craft. And they were pulling in a large net full of odd-looking Amazonian fish I had never seen before. Clearly they had learned how to hold their bodies when standing and throwing nets, and in doing so, had developed an athletic skill and balance special to this place on earth. Had they been living in the tundra of the distant north, they would have likely learned to hunt caribou and fish through holes in the ice. But they lived here in Amazonia, and this place had shaped them inextricably—had speciated them, really, just as nature will do to all of us if we allow ourselves to fully live inside of it.

The two natives were on the opposite shore, and like good fishermen everywhere, they were working the shallows where fish come to feed and to hide. One waved stoically to me, and I waved back, doing my best to not make any sudden moves in doing so. I figured I could have been on any large river in Florida five hundred years ago and seen a vision that was not dissimilar to this one. The gift of that realization was both startling and revelatory. As I paddled on, the fishermen were gradually absorbed into the whiteness of the rain, sharp edges of reality giving way to a soft blur, almost as if they existed inside a photographic vignette.

Soon the rain obscured everything, and I was alone again, just me and the dark river below. I was as close to the shore as I could get now, and a pygmy kingfisher—a ringer for our own belted kingfishers back home—flitted about in the thick foliage understory just a few feet away, barely more than a couple inches in length. Then, just when I figured I was reaching some sort of stasis with this place, shards of fruit begin to unexpectedly rain down on me. When I looked up, I saw a white-faced monkey sitting in a high bough of a ceiba tree, peeling what seemed to be a mango with its hands.

The mango peels joined the revitalized piranhas, which were now in a good six inches of water. The powerful little fish had no interest in me, but snapped at the fruit shards as they fell. I had no real idea of where I was, only that I was absorbed in the wildness and grandeur of this tropical river, and that there was something profoundly vital and alive about it all. A clunky old *Fitzcarraldo*-era riverboat had brought me to this world; my solitary journey in the dugout delivered me somewhere else entirely, a place my overloaded senses could hardly bear. No wonder that those who live so close to the earth need myth to explain what their intellect cannot.

By now, the dugout was actually more stable than ever due to the ballast of the water inside. Still, I thought it a good idea to not let it lower the gunnels any more as they were now just a few inches above the river. I emptied my water bottle and used it as a bailer, removing enough of the ballast to keep me safe, but not so much that it might lose its value as a counterweight.

And then, a hundred yards or so away, the pink dorsal of a boto, the rare freshwater dolphin, surfaced and began to move toward me. I had come to this place especially to see and to study this animal, but I had hoped to do so from the safety of the decrepit riverboat I was living on for a few weeks. Now I was in full solution with it, and this unexpected intimacy went straight to my gut. I was no longer the impartial and intellectual gringo observer who could pick and choose what he wanted to record. A large primitive animal larger than my dugout was moving steadily toward me, and extravagant Western ideas couldn't do much about that.

Without even thinking, I carefully sank the blade of my paddle into the water and held it there, vaguely hoping the dolphin would sense it, and swim below and not into it. When the dorsal was just a couple yards away, it sank under the surface, leaving only a trail of bubbles. The boto was under me now, and the enormous displacement of water actually pushed my dugout up nearly a foot, where I teetered unsteadily for the longest three seconds of my life. (I remembered a manatee once doing the same thing back home in Florida on the Mosquito Lagoon, and I was somehow comforted by this memory.) I looked to the other side of the dugout and saw the boto's dorsal again emerge from the water, watched as it moved steadily away, back into its own time. He could have dumped me and my fancy modern persona in a second had he wanted to do so.

The natives here tell stories that mythologize the boto, giving it supernatural powers, even allowing it to morph into a human when all the conditions are right for that. That mythology had helped draw me here. But now that I was fully in its grasp, the essential power of the Amazon and its myths took on an entirely new meaning, easily dwarfing any gringo pretense I had brought along. It struck me that true "discovery" was more than being surprised by little secrets in the landscape. The full gestalt included fear and deep respect as well, vital information that we Norteamericanos try so hard to excise from our experiences in nature.

I'm figuring the Timucua once knew the full emotional and spiritual sway of all that surrounded them—just as the Amazonian natives fishing from their dugouts do today. It's this wholeness of nature that so often eludes us back home because it requires us to evoke the complex puzzle of myth and wildness again, one careful piece at a time. Objects created to sanctify myth can be imbued with a power far beyond our limited "civilized" range—even if the creators of those icons are long gone from our earth.

Funny, but I was pondering the objects on my windowsill to consider the metaphor of ecotones, of places where the past intersects with the present and the future. And in the evocation of memory, I've blundered onto a moment that's every bit as alive and compelling as the Now. Maybe that's part of the enigma of emotionally driven ecotones—you don't always know the boundaries of where they begin and end.

The dugout paddle with the heart-shaped blade I brought back from Peru is still mounted on the wall, not far from where I am sitting. I'm going to lift it from its mount now, and grasp it again, just as I did when I paddled on the Rio Samaria. I want to see what other stories it might also remember.

8 Wild Hogs, Bears, and Ancient Acorn Memories in the Landscape

It's sunny and brisk out here inside a broad landscape of pine flatwoods, loblolly and slash poking up randomly from the green sea of saw palmetto like skinny utility poles, green fringe bristling from the tops. It's November now, a perfect time to be anywhere outdoors in the real natural Florida that still exists.

Jacques le Moyne illustration of Timucua preparing and cooking foods gathered from the land.

My hiking buddy and I stop to get our bearings about two miles in at the side of the trail—which is not a real hiking trail but a rough dirt road used as a firebreak. There are, in fact, few traditional trails in this massive forty-two-square-mile state preserve, so we make do with whatever gives us a clear and open path. The terrain that sprawls around us is wonderfully diverse, scored with the upland scrub of ancient shoals and edged with blackwater rivers, the characteristic flatwoods tucked in between. We're on our own back here, and I like that idea very much because it means the chance for discovery is great.

We sit on our haunches, me swigging from a bottle of water and my friend checking his GPS to see where we are on the map. When he looks up from the little electronic screen, he glances farther down the trail and then turns to me. In a perfectly neutral conversational tone he asks, "Is that a bear?"

That's exactly the sort of thing I always hope to hear. When I look down the trail, I see something big down on four legs, trotting along toward us in a blur of spiky black hair. We've already passed generous piles of blue-black bear scat, so we know they're back in here, local bears bulking up for their Florida version of winter "hibernation" with fat acorns and berries, maybe the occasional beetle, or a particularly slow-moving armadillo. But when I look more closely at the blur, I realize this would have to be the leanest and fastest bear I've ever seen.

In another nanosecond, I realize it's actually a large wild boar with its head down—following some sensory path only he knows. In his single-minded quest, he doesn't even seem to realize we're here. I often run across signs of wild hogs out in the woods and swamps around Florida, earth tilled up for roots as if a small bulldozer has moved through. Sometimes I see their hoof tracks in the hard sand, and once in a while I'll catch sight of a few of them way off in the distance, running the other way.

But to be on a trail atop a wide, flat landscape under a bright Florida winter sun and see a wild boar moving on a fast trot toward you is, well, uncommon. Since this firebreak road is used by preserve rangers to control prescribed burns, it sports two sets of deeper ruts where a vehicle of some sort has traveled. We are in one rut; the boar is in the other. I fantasize that he acknowledges our existence on some level and is very politely running in the opposite rut from us as if he understands the American style of driving on the right side of the road in order to pass oncoming vehicles on the left.

The first domestic hogs were shipped here by Hernando de Soto five hundred or so years ago for food, and that original stock was later joined by others introduced by settlers. Some hogs were enfenced while most were left to roam wild to feed themselves until the time came for a harvest. But, left to their own devices over the centuries, the survivors turned feral, learning to eat nearly anything that would sustain them, including rattlesnakes, insects, and berries. The larger and more ferocious males have a reputation for attacking when cornered or threatened, using their sharp curled tusks to try to shred the threat—whether human or animal—until it goes away.

As the hog closes on us, I see his tongue is out and he is panting like a dog on a long run. Except for the lethal tusks, he could be a dandy just-pretend Disney animal, one of those animatronics that are programmed to perform entertainingly on demand. But of course he is not. So, I figure I ought to at least get my camera out, since whatever happens next, it should be worth capturing. As I fumble with my camera, we continue to talk. The animal doesn't seem bothered by that, and continues to trot along with his head down. In another ten seconds or so, he should pass us in the opposite rut if he sustains the same speed. I remember wild boars have a great sense of smell and of hearing, but they don't see all that well. The stiff breeze is blowing toward us, so our scent as well as our odd human sounds are lost to the wind.

In another few seconds, he finally hears us and then does a cartoon-like double take—he looks up, skids to a halt in the sandy trail, spins about as if on a lazy Susan, and gallops away in a cloud of dust. The finesse of his movements amazes me, as if I have just witnessed a *grand jeté* or some other ballet move, as orchestrated by a feral hog. The whole experience, from beginning to end, was actually very brief in linear time. I figure it's a testament to how the human senses stretch out each moment to its fullest potential when the immediacy of a brand-new possibility is trotting toward you with its tongue out and its tusks gleaming in the sun. In such cases, our nascent mammalian intellect defaults to a more primal wisdom and to the Zen viscera of the now.

A kayaking buddy once told me that of all the animals, wild hogs will actually hold a grudge, although I'm still not sure where she learned this. I'm pretty sure I didn't do anything to aggravate this particular boar. But then again, I am a human, and from the perspective of a wild hog, we upright walking mammals probably all look alike. Hogs are hunted nearby on the other side of the river, and maybe he had lost a colleague or two to that behavior. Perhaps they were out one moment, strolling through the neighborhood with great porcine camaraderie and glee—and then, the next, the former buddy was being ground up into pork patties in some hunter's garage up in Umatilla.

I'm sorry to miss snapping a photo of our fellow traveler but am also a bit relieved that any grudge he may have carried won't have a chance to be realized today.

On we go, deeper in through the flatwoods. Before we started our trek, we had seen a dozen or so folks back in the grassy parking lot, all decked out in official-looking hiking attire. They appeared to be preparing to stage some sort of structured outing that required actual planning. I figured they stuck to the marked loop trail, which safely encircled itself several miles back. Since the trailhead kiosk for this land doesn't even include a map for these dirt ruts, those on more casual saunters seldom make it back this far. Although Florida often appears tame—the predictable "nature on a leash"—this preserve is really as wild and isolated as it gets, and that's why we're here.

A pine flatwoods—sometimes called "pine barrens"—is exactly what its name implies: a pancake-flat landscape colonized by pines with a thick understory of saw palmetto, maybe some gallberry bushes and seasonal wildflowers like the Catesby lily. Today there's also a mild scent of wild vanilla in the air. The topsoil here is underpinned by a layer of impervious clay, which means the land is usually seasonally wet from the subtropical Florida rains. And the random shallow depressions of sedges will sometimes hold water, becoming ephemeral ponds. I get a kick out of the fact that the most common terrestrial habitat in Florida is more water-driven than not.

As we move deeper in, the sun warms me, seeming to radiate into my bones, replacing the bracing chill. This flatwoods is bordered on horizons to the east and west with great, dense hardwood tree lines, so it seems if we're strolling through a giant natural aisle. The farther north we go, the more narrow this natural aisle becomes, tree lines moving in closer now. We are hoping to reach at least the edges of the St. Johns River, near where the tributary of the Wekiva confluxes with it. The fire roads we are following sometimes splay off for reasons I don't understand. But I figure if we follow any of these paths northward, we'll eventually make it to the river's wetlands.

When I've hiked here after the summer rains, the wetlands edging the river have swept down across this low landscape, making a complete passage impossible. But today is different: we've been without the seasonal Florida thunderstorms for several months now, and if there's ever a chance of making it closer to the St. Johns, it's now.

The once-wide tree lines eventually converge into a thick subtropical forest, and we head off onto a canopied animal trail that takes us northeast inside a thick hammock of live and water oak, hickories, and a few old sabal palms. The ground around us is thick with fat acorns, much larger than I've ever seen them before. My partner wonders if the bitter cold of last winter has inspired the trees to grow bigger seeds, maybe with the notion of nurturing offspring more able to withstand the cold.

Surely a larger acorn is also good for the animals, such as the black bears, who must bulk up on fodder for the winter. Bears, smarter than we give them credit for, have actually been seen shaking trees to make the acorns fall. Native Americans, who invested so much of their intellect and emotion into this landscape and its gods for five to ten thousand years, must have known the particulars of this. Maybe they didn't have a written language, but they knew more luxurious fodder would also mean fatter bears, deer, and anything else that could stave off a tribal hunger.

These "earth people"—as Peter Matthiessen describes indigenous, pre-industrialized cultures—took full advantage of Florida's rich diversity and long growing seasons. They ate wild grapes, hickory nuts, both the roots and vine of the catbrier, turtles, gators, panthers, manatees, pocket gophers, even the inner bark of pine trees.

The simple acorn was so important to the pre-Columbian Timucua of northeast Florida that they actually created effigies to that oak seed, little totems in clay. In the Thursby Mound at Blue Spring downstream on the river, at least four different types of oak effigies—each about two inches long—were found in the massive shell midden there. The symbolism seems clear. Like a hormone-driven college freshman who puts a larger-than-life, airbrushed pinup on his wall, effigy makers visualized the world's fattest, most perfect acorn in the hope that nature would oblige. If you dream it, it will come.

I also think of the singular hair style of the male Timucua as once rendered by the early French artist-explorer Jacques le Moyne. In these illustrations, the long hair of each is bound tightly into a bun atop his head, pinned with carved antler or bone. It looks for all the world as if the heads of the natives have become giant acorns, clasped by a stem at the very top.

It is both darker and cooler back here under the foliage canopy of the hammock. We're walking atop an earthen berm now, one that likely supported a tramway for an early logging rail. It would make sense for it to lead north to the river, since the St. Johns was the highway into the low interior of La Florida: Steamships serviced it, off-loading settlers and early tourists, transporting citrus and local things away. The once-noble virgin cypress, trimmed of limbs, were floated away in great rafts to distant mills, the two-thousand-year-old wood sliced into shingles and boards, useful human stuff.

Large, heavy-bodied birds flit through the trees in a flock, and although they seem to be migrants, they're much larger than the warblers and wrens we've been seeing. Then it strikes me that they're robins, and I instantly realize I have done a reverse acknowledgment of their arrival. As a little boy growing up on the then-rural Eastern Shore of Maryland, I was infatuated with spotting the first robin of spring. And now, years later and many miles away, I'm delighted to see the first robin of winter, getting itself ready for the theater of a northern spring. In such moments, I feel almost as if I've peeked behind some great cosmic curtain, watching the actors rushing to prepare for their next scene.

To the west, I look between the thick line of tupelo and hickory and see the now-dry swamp below. We walk down into it, stepping carefully around the cypress knees, sturdy mahogany-colored gnomes crinkled with age. Sharply defined watermarks on cypress and other buttressed trees here clearly remember when the river flowed four to five feet above the bottomlands where we now walk.

We walk back up on the berm to make better time, and I see several wild orange trees, smooth gray trunks spotted with lichens. We stop and my partner shakes one of them, just as a bear might do. Several oranges come plummeting down, and I cut one in half with my pocketknife and taste it. Unlike most wild citrus, this one is ineffably sweet, not a hint of sourness. I wonder if the trees aren't a relic from an old failed ranch that comprised a small chunk of this land a century or so ago, wild terrain briefly tamed before it went natural again. The rancher was a retired president of a local liberal arts college here in Winter Park.

As an academic, the man was a great success. But as a rancher, he performed on the same level as other brilliant artists who tried to grow crops and domestic animals in the rich basin of the enormous St. Johns River—Delius, Bartram, Stowe, even Rawlings. Perhaps, had they been better planters, the words, lyrics, and music they left behind might have been diluted by their industry. Nearby, a red-shouldered hawk—the raptor of the subtropical swamp—shrieks, communicating what I imagine to be a warning. Within the minute, I hear the wonderfully haunting calls of sandhill cranes clacking from somewhere high overhead.

Finally, the berm of hardwoods ends, falling way to more low wetlands. But this time, the dehydrated swamp is bereft of trees, thick instead with the herbaceous water-loving plants that hug rivers and creeks. The dominant plant now is a freshwater version of spartina, at least waist high, and we follow an animal trail through it that winds north to the river. The soft earth under us in this spartina forest is as dry as it will ever be.

Despite all we've done to it, Florida has sustained an essential natural energy. There was once a fort named "Florida" with a landing just across the river from here, nearly contemporary with the ranch. Yet a century is a long time in a relentless subtropical climate of sun and rain and decay, and today—except for the orange trees—there's little to be seen of either.

We are almost six miles in now, and we stop for a snack near an old shallow logging canal that spindles its way to the St. Johns. The midafternoon air is pleasant, and there is absolutely no sound back in here except that which nature allows. The fat acorns are still around us, some freshly dropped from the tree, some lopsided, half-buried in the earth.

Today I've traveled several miles beyond where I've ever been on this landscape before, finally having a chance to descend into the now-dry swamp, to be surrounded by a new "hammock" of strange and wonderful grasses. I finally catch a glimpse of the river, and I know now that we can probably walk to its very edge. The St. Johns is tea-colored from the tannins here, but it is blue and sparkling wherever the sun hits it.

There are no watermarks of memory here, except maybe in the scant history the Timucua left behind. It was all in the doing, in the gathering of plants and animals and the seeds of the trees, perhaps in the grateful bliss of a sunny winter day that allowed the collectors of nature's gifts to freely roam. The philosopher Thomas Moore once wrote that the human soul needs a "vernacular" life, one enriched by the very real particulars of experience. I'm thinking that such a life collects all the parts that have ever been, restoring wholeness to the natural and spiritual landscape of the human heart.

Funny, but in some very real way, I feel secure just knowing the fat acorns are scattered about in such great abundance. It is a feeling that, best I can figure, is evoked from some shard of collective and unconscious knowledge, a shared commonality of nature and life. Despite all that this put-upon, misunderstood, and maligned state has endured, there is still hope, and it inextricably surges through me now, as real as any transfusion into my blood has ever been.

If I could mold clay, I'd create an effigy that might conjure this single glorious moment of exhilaration in honor of the Timucua and the bears, the wild boar and the warming winter sun, an effigy that would be at once natural and particular, thankful and whole.

It would be an image that would reach down into my heart, and then—with almost no effort at all—soar far out into the heavens, bouncing off planets and stars, until one day, maybe five thousand years from now, it would return and comfort another human, out wandering about in search of wildness and discovery and light.

9   A Journey of Turtle Eggs, 'Dillos, and So Much More

Today, we're looking for some natural waterscape to shoot scenic footage for my friend Michelle's documentary on her solo river adventure, and so we head east from Sanford through the low and subtle tropical "valley" of the St. Johns River. We pass over the long and wide bridge that allows the river to still nip off an end of the massive Lake Jesup, aiming for a track of land just beyond a second bridge that spans the natural channel between Lakes Harney and Puzzle.

Michelle Thatcher shooting on the river for her Alligator Princess *documentary.*

I park at an inconspicuous trailhead for the Buck Lake Conservation Area managed by the regional water management district. No one's around. A sign here warns "Equestrians" to avoid the trails during the winter hunting seasons. I wonder why only horseback riders are cautioned, and vaguely wonder if it's okay to accidentally shoot a hiker or two.

I shoulder Michelle's pack with her camera gear, she grabs the tripod, and we set out across the hard-packed earthen trail into the sprawling tract of marsh and pine flatwoods, a preserve bordered to the east by a narrow ridge of scrub. The noise of road traffic soon fades, replaced first by the call of a hawk overhead, and then by the braying of hunting dogs in the distance. The trail crosses several creeks linking wetlands on both sides of us, vast sheet flows of rainwater that still seep across the oceanic memory of this odd Florida landscape, bright-yellow wildflowers bursting out wherever they've been touched by its energy.

A few hundred thousand years ago, we would be on the shallow sea bottom, moving across a sandy plateau of a substrate, interrupted every so often with higher shoals, maybe an island or two. Add a few intermittent ice ages, and—voilà!—terraces and rolling hills are birthed. Today, the big mother river of the St. Johns courses to the north as a result of these permutations, moving slowly but surely downhill from a headwater escarpment more than a hundred miles south of here. But around us, marshes and shallow lakes that are not directly in the channel flow every which way—to the east, puddling up to form Six Mile Creek and leaking southward to Salt Lake. Or settling in to create Buck Lake to our west, just behind the rim of sabal palms and myrtle and sawgrass that edges the trail.

We take the first chance we can get to reach that lake, veering off onto a trail atop a berm likely created to dike wetland flow when this 9,300-acre tract was privately used for cattle and logging. Loblolly and slash pines appear, their canopies of needles crisp against the cerulean Florida winter sky. After stuffing myself over the last few days with holiday cheer, it feels good to get back outdoors, to stretch my legs and inhale the sweet essence of a real natural place.

A mile later, the trail dead-ends into marshy Buck Lake, giant white cumulus erupting overhead in slow motion just like down in the water-enriched landscape of the Glades. During my first visit several years ago, I watched in awe as a female turtle came out of the lake, lumbered past me on the trail, began to dig two holes with her rear legs, and then deposited more than forty alabaster-colored eggs into them. Each hole was then carefully packed and covered, and the mama turtle, finally satisfied that all was right with the universe, turned and lumbered back past me and returned to the water as if I never even existed.

I thought then of the ancient energy that sometimes pushes us toward our own destinies, thought of how it can be at once so pervasive and so unknown, leading us across a terrain fraught with dangers that we don't even care to see. In that world, reality is a landscape that holds only the promise of determination and of light.

A two-story wooden observation tower has been built since my last hike here, and we climb to the top and set up Michelle's tripod. She shoots the great sprawling lake and its marsh and the wrinkles of fish at the surface, and off in the flat, flat distance, a golden hump that is a cypress bayhead. She walks down the tower and out to a soggy point of land, and I sway the camera on the tripod so that it follows her. It's an intimation of all the moments of decision she faced during her recent solo paddle of the larger St. Johns River system, a courageous effort made with only a compass and a map.

Unlike so many paddlers who obsessively rely on electronic gadgetry and satellite fixes for security, Michelle was driven to take her paddling trip on this sprawling St. Johns River system by a deep, silent grit of determination and passion—one intended to gift others with a shared vision of a rare place, rather than a materialistic souvenir.

The title of her film is *Alligator Princess of America's Nile*, and that name is both meaningful and loaded with irony. Because the St. Johns flows from south to north—like the Nile—early promoters intent on using any excuse to sell Florida to visitors and prospective land buyers inventively called this river the "Nile of the Americas." This domestic "Nile" embodied other exotic ideals as well since it flowed through a basin where the warm temperate climate of north Florida met the subtropical clime of south Florida. Biological diversity was rich here, for both plants and wildlife.

Gators, of course, were symbolic of this exotic river, and early black-and-white photos promoting it often illustrated alligators—after an impressive session of taxidermy—in close quarters with living humans. In a way, it was not unlike Disney World selling its own brand of happy fear today via its just-pretend pirates and quasi-haunted mansions. A particularly stylistic photo from that era showed a little girl in a fancy princess-like white dress perched atop a nicely stuffed gator. While Michelle's one-woman expedition belied the notion of humans dominating this complex and still-wild river system, the image of the little gator "princess" on her reptilian throne was still valid in a sardonic sort of way.

We pack to leave, taking one last look at the marshy prairie that defines the character of this face of the river system, a remote place as geologically young as it is wild, so far off the radar of most Floridians that it is seldom fully seen. The late-afternoon sun is low now, and the pine and palms, ferns and sawgrass around us are soft in the golden light.

At the side of the trail, we see the curled, empty shells of turtle eggs, dug fresh from a nest. Even though I didn't see the plunder taking place, I figured that raccoons were the likely culprit since they are known to dig up food like this whenever they have the chance.

For now, we are content, feeling good to be alive on such a glorious Florida winter day. Suddenly we come onto an armadillo digging away at the edge of the trail. He finally hears us and executes a bizarre leap straight up into the air like some cartoon animal before scampering off into the brush. We look on in quiet amazement; soon the little 'dillo returns to his dig, all the while sniffing the air like a small pig. Once there, he buries his head back into the soft upturned soil, letting out muffled snorts every so often.

This is a strange creature, tiny pinkish porcine nose, shell-like prehistoric armor, possum tail, feet like claws, hair bristling from under its shell, and a set of dull eyes no bigger than pinheads. It looks as if it were glued together from leftover parts of a make-the-animal kit.

Michelle carefully unpacks her high-definition video camera and slowly moves toward the rooting 'dillo. I do the same with my digital. Soon we see what has drawn this strange non-native exotic back to its hole. Inside are not tubers or nuts, but turtle eggs. The "snorts" were actually slurping sounds it made as it sucked the yolk from the new eggs. Broken egg shells and yolk residue now come into a more complete focus for us. The eggs likely were laid by a local river turtle—a peninsula cooter or a Florida redbelly.

We shoot some more footage, getting right atop the carnage. I'm conflicted, knowing that another thirty seconds or so of footage means another turtle egg. Finally, we abandon all pretense of stealth and move toward the 'dillo. The animal looks up once, leaps into the air, and bolts down the edge of the berm, and into the thick underbrush beyond.

I carefully pick out the still-whole shells closest to the surface, and we pack them gently in dirt from the hole inside a soft blue jacket Michelle pulls from the backpack. I figure they'll have little chance of surviving with the 'dillo still at large. Maybe I can incubate them in a hole next to the pond in my own backyard, later gathering them for a return trip to their home lake.

There are yet more eggs undisturbed and deeper in the ground, and I let those be. I then remove all the loose shells, and cover what is left of the nest with soft earth, patting it at the surface as I had once seen a mother turtle do years ago. Before we leave, I sprinkle shards of weeds and dead palm fronds atop the nest to hide it.

Back on the road, we drive across the river valley, watching the sun dip into the broad marsh to the southwest, teetering atop a pine canopy as if uncertain about which way to go. By the time we pull in my driveway, it is full dark. I turn on a little lantern, and we make our way into my fenced back yard. There I dig a hole with a garden trowel close to where my good dog Shep is buried, a few feet from the little pond and its waterfall. Michelle gently takes each tiny egg from her jacket and hands it to me, and I place it into the new hole. "Egg," she says, and then sprinkling earth from her jacket into the hole, "mother's dirt."

And so it goes, for nine turtle eggs being buried into a human-dug hole in the darkness of the Florida night. We are resolute, focused. It is as if there is nothing else around us to thwart our destiny—and here in my own back-yard, there isn't.

There is simply hope, and it is embedded deeply in the natural world we know, buried as surely as it is buried in our own human souls. It is a hope that has led us individually across river systems on far continents, below the ocean onto the reefs of night, inside tropical jungles infused with wonder, all of it rich with the redemptive reward of the unknown. It vaguely occurs to me that, all along, there has been the faith that "mother's earth" would somehow prevail, an essential goodness that might hatch a displaced turtle shell—that might even deliver the eternal wisdom of nature and its ancient rhythms into our modern lives.

10 Laberinto de las Doce Leguas
A Cuban Labyrinth of Many Choices

By night, our oceanographic ship, the RV *Seward Johnson*, has traveled across the open mouth of the Gulf of Guacanayabo, beyond the Cayos Manzanillo and Balandras and the fishing harbors of Santa Cruz del Sur and Manzanillo. In a strategy meeting up on the bridge last night, the captain told us that a winter front was preparing to move through. Winter cold fronts in Cuba usually scour the waters clean, leaving better visibility in their wake, but they can be troublesome, even dangerous, when it comes to driving small boats about for scuba ops.

A typical street in Havana with the classic old American sedans, the last cars to be imported before the extended embargo against Cuba kicked in back in the 1950s.

"We'll get a blast out of the South, maybe twenty-five knots," says Capt. Vince Seiler. "It isn't a big deal. We'll just point our nose into it. Then, after it passes, the wind will then come out of the north and, down here in the lee, we'll be protected."

Cuban national Dr. Rodolfo Claro—likely the most astute of all our marine biologists about the waters of his country—said the prettiest and the cleanest shallow water will likely be found in the last leg of our cruise, between Isla de Juventud and Cabo San Antonio, Cuba's westerly cape. After the meeting, I walked out by myself on the stern below and stood there, gripping the railing as the props churned the black sea into furrows of white just below.

We're on a month-long oceanographic expedition, and have spent most of it cruising the southern shore of Cuba. Roads seldom link this remote coast, so villagers trade and communicate with others using boats instead of cars. We live in an era where a lot of national funding for underwater science in the United States has been diverted to the showier space program. Harbor Branch Oceanographic Institution, which owns and operates our ship and the submersible on it, has leased the entire ship—along with its crew—to the Discovery Channel, which will produce and broadcast a documentary about this particular voyage. This is the largest and most technologically complex expedition to ever be launched in Cuban waters, so the possibilities for real discovery are great.

From the stern, I saw a full moon overhead in a clear winter sky, surrounded by streaks of high cirrus clouds with their icy crystals, interrupted only where they periodically assembled into a lunar halo. It was haunting, a striking contrast to the billowing, water-rich cumulus that we've seen over the last few weeks puffing up in great mountains of white atop the Caribbean terrain. I knew the Cayman Islands were somewhere south of here, far enough to be out of range for even the best scope aboard.

The Caymans, a British Crown Colony comprised of several low, limestone-coral islands, has capitalized on the U.S. embargo against Cuba for the last several decades. Scuba divers who would ordinarily have traveled to Cuba now fly over this giant island for the Caymans, and in doing so have made that set of islands one of the most popular dive destinations in the Antilles. While sport diving in the Caymans is good due to the plunging nearshore "walls" of coral, the topography of the islands themselves is one-dimensional—especially when compared to the great diversity of beach and mountain we've seen in the rolling Cuban landscape over the last several weeks. And while European sport divers still travel to Cuba, the dive infrastructure here is relatively undeveloped compared to the many dive resorts of the Caymans. But what the Caymans have gained economically, they have lost many times over in the ravages that an unchecked diving clientele can inflict on both its reefs and its island culture.

We anchor for the night some fifty miles west of Cabo Cruz, offshore a subchain of mangrove cayos mapped as Laberinto de las Doce Leguas, Labyrinth of the Twelve Leagues. Some 130 square miles of the Laberinto is designated as a marine "protected area" by the Cuban government—one of several "Areas de Manejo Integral." There are forty-odd protected areas around the entire Cuban coast, according to the IUCN, the international alliance of scientists that keeps track of such things. Some are "managed" for wildlife, some for rare and endemic plants, and some for tourism. But the truth is that enforcement is scant. Managers face the same dilemma as marine sanctuaries do throughout the entire hemisphere—lack of funding. Clearly, this southern coast is isolated and difficult to reach by paved roads from the rest of the mainland. In fact, the remote villages we have seen scattered along its shores seem to be bound to each other by the sea, via the traffic of working fishing and lobstering boats, rather than by any direct highway transportation. Its protection, even within its own country, is more a result of its sheer inaccessibility than anything else. If the most interesting places are found at the end of the worst roads, as the writer Paul Theroux has suggested, then this southern Cuban coast surely has some of the most intriguing places in all the world.

Using the results of yesterday's rich hands-on survey of the Cabo Cruz shore, our chief expedition scientist, Dr. Grant Gilmore, lobbied to include mangrove forest in the filming. Mangroves provide storm protection, support for the marine food web, and serve as a genetic storehouse for science. It is the tropical version of the more temperate tidal salt marsh found rimming estuaries back in the coastal United States. Limited by its subtropical range, the mangrove is now concentrated in the generally less prosperous countries of the Southern Hemisphere. Ironically, these are the places where its health is anything but certain since those countries are far more reliant on the vagaries of wealthy North American investment—a factor that often trumps well-meaning but weak eco-laws. Certainly mangroves do have a very particular beauty to them, but appreciating it requires time, and a perspective informed by the greater value of ecology. The truth is that mangrove stands—low, scrubby, and surrounded by soft mud—are the antithesis of the tourist postcard image of a fancy beach with umbrellas and cabanas. When coastal development is proposed, the promised "prosperity" of hotels and resorts more often than not prevails over the native plant community. Savvy ecologists are now teaming up with economists to set a real dollar value on the tidal mangrove wetlands—just as they have on coral reefs after ship groundings destroyed large tracts in the upper Florida Keys. In one equation, an economist from Tufts University figured if wetlands were valued for their "clean water, flood prevention, pollution reduction and recreation," they would be worth 150 times more left intact than if drained and destroyed for tourism development.

Despite Gilmore's persuasive urging to focus more on the complex world of the mangrove "forest," our deep-diving submersible is beginning to turn up more exciting finds—including a spectacular ghostly white nudibranch that Dr. John McCosker recently captured with the sub's mechanical collecting arms and tubes at 1,802 feet as it undulated through the darkness. The nudibranch, a mollusk without a shell, usually hunkers down along the bottom in search of fresh meat, including other marine invertebrates and even plants. But this one seems lifted out of a story by the Cuban surrealist José Lezama Lima, perhaps one of his seductive dancing spirits writhing in slow motion, bulging with tentacles and tiny false heads, ever struggling to awaken from a dream.

The result is that the filmmakers—as well a few of the deepwater biologists aboard—remain unconvinced of the importance of the mangrove story for the larger expedition. In comparison with the Jules Vernesque dazzle of the sub dives and the storybook thrill of sunken wrecks and coral reefs, mangroves and seagrasses seem tame and safe. There is scant danger in these shallow monocultures—little of what the chief underwater producer Al Giddings calls the "sphincter factor," that special dramatic moment when a viewer tenses up with fear.

Still, Gilmore argues for aquatic plant systems as a reliable way to distinguish the health of a "forbidden" Cuba from the rest of the developed and known Caribbean. In doing so, he hastily composes a memo to the filmmakers which sounds a bit like an outline for a grad course on marine ecology.

Entitled "Cuban Mangroves–Seagrass Meadows," Gilmore's paper lists major points of their utility:

Sunlight: Source of All Energy on Earth (Reveal sunlight in association with the tree and seagrass meadows)

Mangrove: A Tree of the Sea, giving . . .

Shelter from Predation

Fallen leaves enhance the food chain of the sea when they begin to decay (the leaves can be carried out to sea, floating on the tide carrying their trapped energy from the sun to the open ocean and deep sea.)

Fertile Meadows of the Ocean Margin

Indeed, seagrass pastures not only nurture small fish and crustaceans, they are a major food source for green sea turtles and manatees, two endangered species found here. Like mangroves, they stabilize the bottom, keeping the vital nearshore coastal zone from churning itself into a mud-driven froth every time a good blow surges in. Where tourism prevails in the Caribbean, seagrass beds are often crossed with scars from the propellers of power boats and smothered with sediment runoff from land. Mangroves are cut down to provide affluent visitors with an open vista of the sea. But here in the Laberinto de las Doce Leguas, both seagrasses and mangroves are largely unscathed, and the inaccessible nature of the place helps make them so.

Topside producer Jim Lipscomb quickly grasps the role of these plants in defining the larger picture of the marine landscape. Giddings remains unconvinced but is game to give it a shot. Now the vital story of the Fertile Meadows of the Ocean Margin just needs to be captured on film with some theatrical verve if it is to be useful to the eventual documentary. Or as the überambitious Suzanne Stone character says in *To Die For*, "What's the point in being a good person unless the camera's watching? And if the camera's watching, it makes you even a better person!" Today we will be in a Valhalla of Cuban mangroves, a virtual maze of wetland plants, and the cameras will be watching. I wonder if they will be better plants because of it. I take care of my online chores by answering another half dozen questions from website readers and dashing off an essay, which I upload with some digital photos. Incoming questions arrive from schoolkids and scientists alike—include a patronizing missive from the in-house Discovery producer back in the United States, who signs it as "The Envious One" because he was not included in the expedition. There is a startling dose of magic surrealism to this entire online reportage in which words and photos created on the geographic far side of the moon can be made available to the world on the Web within hours. Lipscomb has asked if I would print and post my essays on the corkboard in the hall outside my work space, in the belief that—like video rushes—they will provide some context about the expedition for all aboard.

Generally, my shipmates are good sports about this peculiar and self-conscious process of turning yesterday's actions into today's Web news. Since there are eight Ph.D.s and many college grads on board, more often than not, I find enthusiastic editing changes scribbled onto the hard copy of the dispatches. Only chief engineer John Terry, a buzz-cut, eternally grimy man whom I have by now come to regard as the "Pigpen" character in the cartoon *Peanuts* seems to miss the point. After reading one dispatch, he asked me if we were even "on the same trip." Since Terry does not dive or have any interest in the local culture or environment, it occurs to me that his version of the expedition is a myopic voyage that ends at the edge of the gunnels. It is reminiscent of how cruise ship passengers sometimes travel the world, returning with little except the memory of the shipboard casino and buffet table.

By late afternoon, the mangrove contingent is ready to cast off. I climb the metal ladder down into one of the skiffs. The front is on us, waves are already washing over the stern, and anything not secure floats about on the deck. Although the sun is still bright and warm, the sea is as rough as it's been, except during our earlier crossing over the Florida Straits. Both top-side and underwater film crews are along, so we will be taking both boats. Claro told us there is a giant, ramshackle houseboat back here somewhere, a floating lodge used mainly by Italian sport divers who, like other Europeans, don't mind rustic accommodations in order to be near pristine diving conditions.

Several of the *Seward* crew are also optimistic about the idea of encountering female Italian sport divers, whom they have already imagined will be sunning themselves naked on the houseboat deck between dives. Before casting off, we try to raise the barge on the radio, but no luck. Finally, just when it seems we will be on our own in the mangroves, a Whaler-like skiff comes zooming out from shore. It moves alongside, and two men aboard shout to us in Spanish, identifying themselves as Noel Lopez, the boat pilot, and Vicente Hernández, the fishing guide with the floating "hotel." They will lead us back to their lodge. It sounds like a plan, so off they go with their 55 HP Yamaha blazing a white zigzag wake through the thick tangle of green, and off we go, in hot pursuit.

It is low tide, and Seaman Corbin Massey has our motor wide open to keep the boat up on a plane, swerving at drastic E-ticket angles deeper into the stunted mangrove jungle. Although the Cuban boat quickly disappears into the mangroves—where rounding each corner reveals four or five new potential channels—Massey expertly traces its path by following the bubble-froth trail it has left behind. This backcountry looks for all the world like the Ten Thousand Islands of the western Everglades—or the Florida Keys, without concrete and Golden Arches. It seems as feral today as when the Spanish first named it.

The houseboat soon appears. It is a ramshackle two-story barge with a certain *African Queen* appeal. Political scientist Richard Fagen later writes in his journal about our trip: "It was like a high-speed chase from *Miami Vice*; and the old steel barge looked like it would not be out-of-place on the Amazon!" The scent of fiberglass and marine paint makes it clear the barge is under repair. No Italian divers are anywhere, naked or otherwise. The rusty hulls of two metal and wooden Cuban fishing boats are tied up next to the barge. Fagen says they are old Cayo Largos, boats custom-designed to be effective in both catching and transporting seafood. One is a battered lobster boat, wire traps stacked on its bow. The other, I soon learn, is a floating classroom for young Cubans training to be captains of fishing boats. Their school, Escuela Superior de Pesca, is back on the mainland at the edge of the Golfo de Guacanayabo in Manzanillo.

The barge has a sign identifying this, a bit grandiosely, as the "Tortuga Hotel." Although run by Cubans, it is owned by an Italian tour company that offers package deals for up to two weeks for divers and sportfishermen. To do so, they bought exclusive fishing rights to a six-square-mile area around the Tortuga. This sounds more like the sort of bucks-for-resources deal often found in developing countries, but there is a covenant: the sportfishing is all "catch and release." I walk inside the main structure on the lower deck of the barge with Fagen and our Cuban government observer, Ariel Ricardo. Fagen has just told me if relations between the United States and Cuba are ever normalized, Ricardo wants to become the first Cuban ambassador in Miami. "He's a masochist," says Fagen with a wide grin.

Tacked to the walls are sets of shark jaws and varnished blowfish (sans sombrero), and photos of anglers with large jewfish and barracuda. In one picture, a man holds a bonefish that weighs at least ten pounds. A certificate in English declares a "Grand Slam" was accomplished here on May 5, 1997, when a Mr. Silvano Capro caught a 3.5-pound bonefish, an 18-pound tarpon, and a 22-pound permit, all on the same day. An aerial photo illustrates the spur-and-grove reef system that occupies much of the space between the mainland and the cayos. A rectangular hole in one wall opens to the kitchen and the tops of a few liquor bottles, indicating the hole in the wall is also the bar; above the hole is a hand-made sign, La Cucaracha Borracha, the drunken cockroach. Vicente tells Ricardo that everything is indeed released after capture, except Spanish mackerel and jacks and large grouper, which they keep to eat. On the wall is also a large display of anglers' lures—Super Shad Rapala, Sinking Shad Rapala, and a lure the exact color of the flying fish netted during our first night at sea. Under the display of lures is the banner logo of the American company Rapala. "Uhhh-oooh," says our official Cuban observer, affecting a singsong Ricky Ricardo I-caught-you-Lucy tone. "Some-body's been vio-lating the em-bar-go . . ."

Although all dive shops in Cuba are government owned, they are operated as joint ventures with foreign investors, who are often German, Canadian, or in this case, Italian. Visiting sport divers used to on-demand service in dive destinations like the Caymans and Cozumel are warned up front about the lack of infrastructure. As one sport-diving guide advises, "You should be prepared with all spares [backup equipment] needed for diving, as these are either not available or excessively expensive. A well-stocked medical kit is recommended, for although Cuban medical professionals are well-trained, supplies are limited. Dives can sometimes be delayed for a number of reasons, including limited available fuel, Coast Guard clearance to depart port, et cetera, so patience is needed."

This same guide also identifies seven separate dive sites just west at the Cayo Anclitas, on the outer rim of the coral and sand islands sheltering the inland gulfs. It includes coral pinnacles, plunging coral-covered walls, and a deep garden of rare black coral—Cabezo de Coral Negro. Blacktip, bull, and silky sharks are also reported to routinely cruise these sites—but the guide reports they do so because divemasters from the Tortuga release bloody chum in the water to draw them in. Of all the underwater stops along this southern coast, this is the only one so far in which a shark encounter—the sphincter factor!—is guaranteed. But the weather choreographs opportunity here, and if good viz and large marine animals don't appear during our brief stop, then we'll leave both in our wake.

By now, Lipscomb, Giddings, and their crews have disappeared in our launch, back somewhere in the red mangroves. I savor the opportunity to spend a little time with real Cubans. Under the tattered awning of the fishing boat, older men, their faces lined from long days under the Cuban sun, play dominoes. On the other boat, a gaggle of teenage Cuban boys take turns diving off a railing, sometimes sharing a ragged mask or kicking about on a broken surfboard which likely came to them as flotsam. In the water, they look like sleek brown otters. A cook is preparing their dinner, and the scent of grease and jutia—a local giant rodent—fills the air. Once I get a look at the in-progress main course, I realize the jutia is similar to muskrat, a regional food I ate in stew, growing up on the Eastern Shore of Maryland. But there are two major differences: this Cuban rodent is endemic; and, unlike the commonplace muskrat, its popularity as regional cuisine threatens it survival. "Jutias are an Antillean invention," the naturalist Alfonso Silva Lee has observed, since the animal evolved from a South American ancestor that invaded the islands about 20 million years ago. While they can be found in the Bahamas, Hispaniola, and Jamaica, there are ten species of the rodent here and the jutia congo bottoms out at ten pounds—the largest of its kind.

On the battered stern of the school boat, I meet Angel Herrero Pacheco, one of the teachers, a sturdily built, thoughtful man who used to be a fisherman, and who now passes his knowledge along to the youngsters. Angel refers to the kids as "my 17 *tiburones* [sharks]." "The school," says Angel, "doesn't just teach navigation and other skills to future fishing boat captains—it also tries to nurture an appreciation for the sea." "And, also," says Herrero, smiling broadly, "to have some fun."

The students are in the first year of a two-and-a-half year course; their classroom training is reinforced with field trips like this, during which they stay out as long as a month at a time. "Most of these boys come from fishermen families, and we try to show them that life on the sea can be rough—the sailor's and fisher's work is very hard. . . . It is work, work, work." Clearly, Herrero is trying to balance the utility of the work with the romance for his charges. But the reward of commercial fishing can also be far beyond both. In fact, lobster fishermen, as I will later find, fare better than almost any other Cuban because they catch a valuable commodity that can be exported for cold cash—and as a result, they receive a bonus for it.

During their anchorage here, the kids will go to the beach at night to watch and count the loggerhead turtles, as this is the season in which they arrive from the sea to dig their nests and lay their eggs in the sand. Although the endangered turtles are protected by Cuban law, locals still hunt them for both eggs and meat. When possible, hatchlings are caught and taken to a "turtle farm" on Isla de Juventud, where protection from predators—including man—will give the tiny and vulnerable turtles a head start for a couple years before being released to the sea. We had planned to stop near that farm on Isla de Juventud, and I now have an additional reason to look forward to it. "We maybe find six or seven nests on this small island nearby, when the turtles finally come in from the sea," says Herrero. I wonder when that event will take place, and Herrero flashes me a smile. "Only God knows these things."

As part of their training, each student is given the helm of the fifty-foot-long boat at the end of the trip into the field. "We tell them, 'Now, you have to take the boat straight home.'" Most live on islands or the coast, a hundred miles or more away, somewhere between Manzanillo and Santa Cruz. After several weeks at sea, they are homesick and eager to steer their floating classroom to their casas as soon as humanly possible. "They learn a lot, and when the time comes, they are very happy to show they can drive the boat—and very happy again to see their families."

Angel shows me the claustrophobic engine room, dark, sooty, and smelling of burnt oil. An ancient Russian 150 HP marine engine looks dangerously unpredictable. Berths are bunks stacked up against one another in a single, narrow room with a few inches of water under planks slotted over the V-bottom. Back on deck, the "bridge" has four pitiful little gauges, a wind-up clock, and a single, battered two-cell flashlight. "Our ship is very old—it barely goes six or seven knots. We have some leaking here, some leaking there. We must always stop to repair it. We are always asking for a new boat," says Herrero, a bit despondently. "But it never comes." He waves his hand in the air, as if to signify something that has just flown away and may never return. "Our country is not in good condition, you know. Economically. It seems to be a curse." Still, it is not all despair. The boys seem to be having a great time. Sea turtles still come to nest on the beaches, and whale sharks can sometimes be seen just offshore. And there are, says Herrero, tales of pirate treasure buried somewhere in the cayos of the Gardens of the Queen. "Everybody wants to discover it," he says, visibly brightening at the idea. "You never know what you might find . . . if you only try to look."

The film crew returns to the houseboat. There, assistant producer Taima Hervas makes a point to ask me what the story is with the kids. I tell her about the aquatic schoolhouse, hoping the unique aspect of Angel and his *tiburones* might fit into the story line. Lipscomb has joined us; he listens, nods his head. He is intrigued, but not enough to include them into the film. "Maybe if we had them up on the beach, hunting for turtle nests or something," says Lipscomb. "Not much action, otherwise."

Over a cup of espresso, I ask Gilmore how the shooting went, and he tells me a bizarre story of a confrontation between Giddings and Lipscomb— over the jutia. "We're way back in the mangroves, and after Jim found out the jutia was endemic and rare, he wanted to film it. Somehow, one of the guides captured one, and Jim is holding it, petting it. And Al goes, 'No fucking way am I filming a rat!' They go back and forth, and finally Jim tosses the jutia back in the water. Instead of disappearing, it swims in circles around the boat. Al just stands there in his wetsuit, with his arms crossed, glaring at it."

The wind is howling this morning and predicted to get worse—both the temperature and the barometer have dropped, signaling the arrival of a brief winter cold front. Last night as I tried to sleep, it felt as if I were on a water bed mounted on a slow-motion Tilt-a-Whirl. This morning at breakfast, green water was slashing up over the portholes, making the outside look like the wash cycle of a Maytag.

As our ship lists heavily from side to side, life aboard becomes just a little trickier. Cook Jay Grant cut two of his fingers this morning, deeply enough to need stitches—had there been a doctor to provide them. Giddings's film crew made a dive late yesterday with guides from the Tortuga Hotel, trying to find some black coral or sharks in 110 feet of water. Dr. John McCosker reported that the bottom stair stepped away on the outer edge of the keys, first down to thirty feet, and then—after crossing a nine-hundred-foot plateau—down again to one hundred. Native guides Noel Lopez and Vicente

Hernández fed some groupers at the top of the reef, and encouraged the Americans to do the same. Giddings moved in with his cameras on, and as McCosker started to feed a grouper, it promptly bit him on the finger, taking a piece of flesh with it. And they ended up being buffeted by a thrashing current—even at that depth—and little good film came from it.

As a result of the approaching storm, a series of midlevel descents planned for the JSL submersible later today have been scrubbed. Water in the aquarium in the wet lab has sloshed out, so it is now barely half full. Its lone occupant, a redeye gaper (*Chaunax stigmaeus*) taken by the sub at 1,500 feet the other day, looks even more baffled than usual, affecting the eternal bewilderment that its look-alike cousin, the batfish, permanently wears. McCosker had been hoping to find a bioluminescent flashlight fish somewhere at scuba depths along the coast after dark, and this is the first good coral bottom where it might live. But clearly, the weather is not cooperating.

Since we are only a couple days from Christmas, Cuban national Pedro Alcolado, an astute biologist, strung Twinkle Lites around the galley, and assembled a three-foot-high artificial Christmas tree, propping a lead dive weight on its base to steady it after a particularly nasty list knocked it over. The tree is trimmed with tinsel and candy canes and hand-painted Styrofoam coffee cups that just returned from a recent sub dive to two thousand feet. Inexplicably, a rubber arm from a doll baby plucked from a sandy cayo also adorns the tree.

Unlike the inside of the sub, which is pressurized at the atmosphere of the surface, the cups rode along in a mesh bag on the outside. As a result, they were squeezed down to about one-fourth of their original size—squashed by 1,009 pounds per square inch of deep-sea pressure. On the cups were names of our loved ones and friends, tiny links back to a world getting ready to celebrate a holiday without us—emotional icons compressed by the Cuban seas.

Even though winds and waves canceled the sub launch, filmmakers and biologists load gear and prepare to head ashore anyway today, hoping to find enough of a lee in the thick mangrove wilderness of the cayos of Jardines de la Reina to continue shooting more mangrove footage. With no real science to perform, the women aboard ask to be put ashore so they can at least stretch their legs on a beach. The boatman promises to return to pick them up after dropping us off in the mangroves. The most dangerous moments in this entire expedition usually aren't in deep water or the midst of circling sharks, but in the precarious windows of time when we climb from our large ship down into our smaller boat—especially when we must carry cumbersome gear.

As I prepare to do this today, a massive wave hits the hull of the *Seward Johnson*, washing across the stern and, briefly, floating heavy metal boxes and a lighting rig from the sub about us. I dodge the flotsam, climbing down a rope ladder over the edge of the ship to the smaller boat, which is now bucking wildly. As it rises nearly six feet on a heavy swell, I quickly climb aboard and ride it back down like a very fast elevator.

Soon we are off, headed the mile or so ashore to the tight Pasa Pierda Grande, a shallow natural cut that will take us behind the low berm of cayos that stretch across the mouths of the two inland gulfs, Guacanayabo and Ana Maria. We ran this same pass two days ago on our way to the Tortuga Hotel, and I welcome the chance to run it again, for there are hundreds of wild islets back here: some higher ones fringed with snow-white sand and low tropical shrubs, and dotted with the stunted silver palms; others a miasma of the elegantly bowed red mangrove roots and soft ivory-colored mud. In we go, across shallow green water and past flocks of cormorants with their snakelike necks, soaring frigate birds, and roosting roseate spoonbills, their plumage spectacularly pink. It seems raw back here, a place freshly tossed up from the sea, in the lee not just of the wind but of time.

Columbus had a "fairylike fascination" with this natural Cuba, describing it as "the prettiest that human eyes have ever seen." And other observers have followed his lead—including the two modern writers whom Cubans hold in such high regard today, expatriate Hemingway and countryman José Lezama Lima. "Ernesto," as he is fondly remembered in Cuba, pitted man against the sea in macho resolve while Lima explored its more mythic nuances, writing of "the sacred silver of scales and tails that seemed to have been polished by Glaucus." This afternoon, it is the rough Hemingway sea that strands us. When we reach the edge of the cut at Pasa Pierda Grande, we face a stout line of eight- to twelve-foot-high waves rolling in from the sea. Although it is barely a mile offshore, the *Seward* seems impossible to reach, and trying to run through it with the expensive camera gear is not an option.

We head back to the barge, and I find Herrero and the boys and the fishermen still here, socked in by the weather. In our two days away, time seems to have stood still. The dominoes still click, the boys still swim, the old fishermen still laugh and joke with each other. The only disconcerting blip on the screen is our Norteamericano urgency. But even that will be eventually muted by the sudden cold front. Giddings, who is in contact with the *Seward* by hand-held VHF radio, tells Captain Seiler we'll overnight here rather than risk returning through the dangerous seas.

Seiler tells him that's a good idea, especially in that the wind is expected to hit eighty knots per hour. The Tortuga is the only shelter for miles in any direction, and its spartan rooms are conveniently unoccupied. We have only the clothes on our back—or in some cases, wet suits. But the spontaneity of the moment is a heady antidote for such worries—and, after all, we are in the business of discovery.

The science and filming has been shut down for the rest of the day. We have a few hours of daylight left and decide to make the best of it. McCosker, Gilmore, and I arrange to have Vicente take us out bonefishing in the local mangrove flats. We have left our fly rods back on the ship, but the guide produces several light spincasting rigs, complete with lures. Bonefishing is a business of sighting and casting to the fish, which give themselves away with their distinctive "tailing" as they root for small inverts in the sandy bottom.

After a twenty-minute ride through the mangroves, we enter a small cove where Vicente has promised bonefish are always found. A slender, dark-skinned man, Vicente cuts the engine and stands up on the bow and poles us toward the edge of the mangroves. Although rippled with waves, the water is still clear enough to let us see several giant bones—at least ten-pounders—hanging just under the water's surface. But they are skittish fish, made even more so by wind and sudden barometer drops, and they hang motionless near the mangrove roots, trying to be invisible. We cast to them anyway. But instead of gobbling our offerings, they spook, bolting away in a flash of fins and tails as soon as our spoons hit the water.

After returning to the houseboat, Vicente takes us up on the top deck to show us our rooms for the night. Each is austere but clean, identified with a name of a different marine animal on the door. Along with McCosker and Fagen, I'm in Palometa (permit); others are in Macabi (bonefish) or Sabalo (tarpon). Back downstairs, from inside the Drunken Cockroach, Vicente serves us cups of high-octane Cuban espresso. A freshly caught skipjack tuna is cleaned and readied for dinner, along with three spiny lobster. As we are relaxing, we are handed a bill for the bonefishing. It is about three times the price we had agreed upon, the additional padding added by the rental of individual spinning rods for seventy-five dollars each. It is clearly a rip-off, and I want to complain, but Fagen is officious about the cultural differences: "You're in Cuba, man. They do things differently here." I figure fairness is universal regardless of where you are in the world, and to justify it as a cultural disparity is specious. But Fagen remains adamant, insisting it would be politically incorrect to argue the point, and I let it go.

The tropical sun dips below the mangroves, taking the thick golden light of the late afternoon with it. The expedition is on hold and there is nothing we can do about it. And so, with no personal duties calling to us here, in the most distant heart of these southern cayos of Cuba, we gather around a rough-hewn wooden table on the back deck and do what Ernesto likely would have done: we drink round after round of cold Cuban "Cristal" beer, washed down with local rum, Havana Club, dark and sweet.

I soon forget about the bonefishing rip-off, figuring that when money is not at stake, the Cubans are pleasant and affable. But when their lives are given over to profit-making, they can become just as excessive as we North Americans. Herrero generously brings us a couple of guava-colored slabs of mullet eggs that had been drying atop the awning over his bow; they taste salty and piquant, a sea-driven memory. From the kitchen appears a plate of albacore sushi, marinated in fresh lime juice.

We talk some more, and Herrero asks me if I would contact his adult daughter Jehane, who now lives in Boston, when I return to the United States. "I have not heard from her for four months now. Her birthday is soon and I wonder if you would let her know I am okay and also want to wish her a happy birthday." Then, in a dash of Cuban stoicism, Herrero adds: "You know, telephone communication between our countries isn't restricted. It is just impossible." Fully exorcised of civilization, we tell jokes and laugh until the cool Caribbean night consumes us all, scientists and filmmakers, gringos and Cubans. The rising tide swashes gently against the hulls of the barge and the Cayo Largos, and in the mangroves nearby, a jutia scuttles through the shallows, setting off blue-green sparks of bioluminescence.

"The world," says Ricardo, "is becoming a much better place." Overhead, the stars are again stretching across the sky, the oblong splatter of the Milky Way glowing as if it had been airbrushed onto the night. Lipscomb, in his bathing suit and T-shirt with a towel around his waist, stands, clears his throat, and recites lyrics from a poem by John Masefield:

In the harbour, in the island, in the Spanish Seas,
Are the tiny white houses and the orange trees,
And day-long, night long, the cool and pleasant breeze
Of the steady Trade Winds blowing

There is the red wine, the nutty Spanish ale,
The shuffle of the dancers, the old salt's tale,
The squeaking fiddle, and the soughing in the sail
Of the steady Trade Winds blowing.

I am astounded he remembers the lines so well, and am touched by the relevant nature of the lyric. However, the film and ship crew, accustomed to his public declarations by now, have begun to call Lipscomb "the Ancient Mariner."

McCosker has launched into a long, convoluted joke in which sex and fish both play a role, although by the time he reaches the punch line, most everyone has forgotten how the story began. Lipscomb's associate producer Taima Hervas, the only gringa with us, scurries about, at least pretending to organization, although clearly there is little need for it at this juncture. Fagen has now put on a cheap clear plastic poncho to keep himself warm. McCosker informs the esteemed Latin American scholar that he looks like a giant condom. "Noooo," says Fagen. Then, thinking it over, "Really? Do I look like a condom? Really?" Soon, there is dinner, broiled tuna, white rice, fried plantains, and chunks of spiny lobster, swimming in a spicy cream sauce. Dinner could have been Slim Jims and a Budweiser, and this crew would have been very happy. But now—away from a dry ship and with no work to do—they are in bliss.

Sometime before midnight, I climb the stairs and open the door to Palometa. Aboard the *Tortuga*, I have found a copy of José Lezama Lima's *Paradiso*, and I struggle through the Spanish to try to identify a passage that describes the fuzzy magic surrealism of tonight. Finally, I stumble across "For him, every awakening was a discovery of the infinite expansion of each of the starfish's radiations . . . on each of the plates, a fish appeared, its face enlarged." The last sound I hear before I fall into my own vibrant, dream-filled sleep is the bullet-like crack of dominoes being slammed down on the table under the stern canopy below. There is no talking, no laughing, no other sound at all but the smack of the dominoes on the wooden table.

11   Rooting Like a Hawg
in the Understory of Wild

An esteemed professor in environmental studies is down on all fours, like a feral hog. He is crawling through a tightly woven tunnel in an otherwise impassable thicket of saw palmettos, cat-brier, and wild grape vines. Like me, he is making odd exhalations that sound a bit like grunts. The only difference is that my forearms seem to be bleeding a bit more than his.

Hooded pitcher plants in bloom.

We have been winding our way through a state reserve for the last four hours. The twenty-thousand-acre-plus tract of land is one of those miraculous relics of the natural Florida land and waterscape, protected in the river basin here since the early 1980s. But state preserves and reserves are not like "parks"—there are few marked tails, and no rangers present to provide advice or to rescue lost wanderers. As a result, these tracts of land receive far less use than the more traditional parks; the folks who do come are usually seasoned hunters and backpackers who don't mind being on their own. The best we can figure is we're the only visitors out here today.

And so I continue crawling through the labyrinthine weave of foliage, hoping for a clue soon that might help us get back on track. We earlier launched our excursion with the notion of finding a little colony of hooded pitcher plants (*Sarracenia minor*) that live in a bog out here. But at this moment, we've defaulted to the option of simply figuring out where we are. At a small gap in the organic fretwork, we stand up and look around. There are more palmettos, briers, and vines as far as we can see in any direction.

My friend is a rarity—athletic enough to tackle hikes like this, while also curious enough to want to know why the singular Florida landscape behaves as it does. Curiosity aside, we are lost. That could be because neither of us brought a compass today, figuring the bright Florida winter sun alone would guide us by its position in the sky. But foliage canopies are good at hiding the sun, and we have strayed far enough off the known trail to lose our larger topo-context.

It was my mistake. I had figured an animal trail leading off our path might give us a bit of a shortcut over to an adjacent firebreak a mile or so away, as it was initially headed that way. The other road would then lead us to the moist bog where the little insectivores live. Random animal trails like this are constructed by the regular tromping of critters like deer, coyotes, bobcats, even bear. And so they meander for reasons known only to the animals themselves, instinctual beings who don't have to worry about paying mortgages and income taxes and otherwise trying to act civilized. Who wouldn't want to follow such a lead—especially out here in a primal terrain where the "locals" clearly know the lay of the land.

In all candor, these trails seldom lead me anywhere; yet I still nurture that increasingly scant hope they will simply because they *look* like they should. And now that this one does not, I imagine a moment from the classic *Far Side* cartoon in which animals build these avenues not for their own use but to lure navigationally challenged humans onto them. When the upright walking mammal with the oversized brain—properly deluded—becomes lost and entangled in briers, I envision the clever animals sitting back in lawn chairs from some natural vantage point and having a great laugh about it all.

But now, with vines wrapping around us and thorns pulling at our arms and legs and the soft mesic landscape falling away into sloughs and sawgrass, I think, "Well, maybe that was a temptation I might have more carefully considered."

Nonetheless, we keep going. To remind ourselves that we are still cogent, we talk a bit about the essential truth of environmental ethics—of how its realities are inescapable, regardless of the partisan spin that so often afflicts it. Using politics to finesse amendments to local comprehensive plans to allow sloppy, sprawling development can be done—but does that make it right? We consider the probability of having elected public officials in Florida actually pay attention to the true impacts of growth instead of to their own short-sighted, bubba-driven presumptions. We laugh at the improbability of that prospect, and then we crawl some more, sometimes rising up to simply bull through the green stuff.

The air around us smells and tastes pure, lightly scented with the essence of a wild place. Some of it is from the fragrance of winter wildflowers, like the climbing lavender-colored aster we passed earlier, a Gulf fritillary and a giant tiger swallowtail there feeding on the nectar in the blossoms. Some of the fragrance is likely from the sand pines growing in the nearby uplands of the scrub.

The wildlife that created this trail are nowhere to be seen, and I'm figuring that's because we're behaving like humans, crashing rather loudly through this natural fabric instead of quietly weaving our way through it. For now, we see several of the large insects named for what they seem to be—"walking sticks." We also crawl beyond a few black piles of Florida bear scat studded with undigested berry seeds, a mat of fur that likely came from a small mammal, and a number of animal tracks imprinted like calligraphy on the sand.

We stop a couple times for water, and then once for snacks, apples and some wild tangerines. Finally, with our potable water getting as low as the sun in the sky, I start to silently wonder if we will make it back before dark. Just as I do, we blunder out onto one of the firebreak roads that I know will deliver us to the main trail. We are jubilant and smiling. To top it off, we come upon the settlement of hooded pitcher plants that I've been hoping to find. It is nearly winter now, and the plants are far less conspicuous, nearly dormant. But when we stop to look more closely, we're rewarded with the remarkable flair of a plant that has learned to eat "meat."

One of the pitcher plant stems has died and fallen over. I pick it up and open its vascular throat with a pen knife. At the bottom I see a wad of tiny black insect carapaces and tinier legs, all that's left after the plant sucked the life juices out of them. I know that even small anoles will sometimes crawl under the hood and into the rounded stem, the strong, downward pointing cilia blocking its passage when it tries to exit.

The longer I'm here, the larger the aperture of my senses becomes; it's a little miracle that seems to happen in an exponential way when I'm walking about in nature. I figure that simply slowing down has a lot to do with this, as it almost always eclipses any nagging concerns of so-called civilization I have transported in with me. Surely, walking vigorously and breathing real air under an expansive and glorious sky helps too. The worrisome trifles of the intellect seem distant now. As usual, Thoreau nailed it almost 150 years ago: "What business have I in the woods, if I am thinking of something out of the woods?"

Reddish sundews, the little insectivores that often share the same bogs with the pitcher plants, come into focus. They look like tiny starbursts, flattish petals lying open with fine, sticky hairs. Scientifically, these cilia are described as stalked mucilaginous glands. When I look closer, I see tiny drops of moisture on the thin hairs, almost as if the plant is covered with morning dew.

But when an errant insect thinks likewise and blunders atop one for a sip, it sticks to the glands. Gradually, the juices of the plant dissolve the prey until there's virtually nothing left. Unlike the pitcher plants, the sundews are far more difficult to trace through the taxonomic chain. In fact, their genera is *Drosera,* one of the largest groups of carnivorous plants, with almost two hundred species living on every continent except Antarctica.

I find it fascinating that both the pitcher plant and the sundew thrive in bogs that are nutrient-poor since they're able to wrangle their nutrition on the hoof. As a result, neither has to compete with the hundreds of other hardy plants that favor the softer, waterlogged habitats because those other plants must rely on the available nutrients in the soil. With far less energy needed for competition, the little insect-eaters flourish in a rarefied world that's wonderfully apart from the rigors of survival. Over time they become as fully realized as any delicate wild plant can be when it doesn't have to worry about competing with hardier vegetation.

The more I look at the plants and study their design, the more absorbed I become by it all. I smile, thinking to myself that this is what an imaginative young art student might draw when instructed to visualize an ornate—even flamboyant—plant that lives creatively in its landscape.

We speak in reverent tones about the carnivorous plants, and as we do, something gradually seems to shift inside me. Instead of simply crawling and walking into a natural place as tourists, we have become part of it in an intimate and visceral way. I think of ethicist Aldo Leopold's plea for humans to see themselves as an integral cog in the larger ecological world rather than as a creation that is systematically apart. It's only then, he said, that we can make heartfelt decisions about the larger future of the earth. We must do so not as exploiters or as managers, but as an essential living component of it, expressed as tissue, a root, an artery, a clutch of cilia, a central nervous system.

Now that we've found the dirt road, we walk with new vigor, past the rising scrub and sandhills to our west and the swamp beyond the bogs to our east. We breathe, smile, and chuckle far more easily than we did on the way in. Somewhere a few miles away is the path that led us in, and just for now, I'm pretty sure it will also lead us back out.

12   An Early-Morning Paddle
Upstream with the Comforting Grain

Early Sunday is the best time to drive anywhere in Florida, and today it is made even more so because we are driving to a river for a paddle. Into the vast state forest we go, beyond the sandy bluffs of scrub, and then down into the tunnel of hardwoods that transport us across the old concrete bridge.

Bow of the kayak maneuvering through a tight, wild river by morning.

At our launch site just upstream of the bridge, there are a good half dozen men in lawn chairs with fishing poles, monofilament trailing off from the tip of each like a tiny, sure strand of a web looping down into the dark creek. It's still early, but they're knocking back the brewskis, and jawing. They have local accents but seem to know very little about the place where they are. I figure they're more interested in getting buzzed than anything else. The rods and reels are simply props.

I'm with my paddling buddy, Steve, today. His shoulder is still on the mend, so he graciously decides to drive a couple more miles upstream by land and launch where this narrow blackwater river flows past Moccasin Spring. That way, if his shoulder gives out and he has to return early, I'd at least have the advantage of being able to paddle to the springs and then back to the bridge on the river.

As he rambles off on the old dirt road under the thick canopy of cypress and oak and hickory, I unload my single kayak from the roof rack. I carry it down to the edge of the water between a couple of the fishermen and set it there, positioning it sideways so it will be easy to mount. I return to the car for my backpack and Gatorade and paddle. Even though last night was the full moon and the bream have started to bed, none of the fishermen seem to be aware of this.

As I push off, one asks me why I wasn't fishing. I figured they weren't fishing either, at least not in any meaningful way. But, instead of insulting a bunch of half-buzzed country boys, I said something else that was also true: I hadn't been on this stretch of the river in a couple years and wanted to scout it out to see how far we could get upstream.

It's gratifying to paddle out of range, beyond the aura of cigarette smoke and idle chatter from folks who seem as if they have been temporarily grafted onto the natural world rather than woven into it. I haven't used this smaller kayak in several years, and loaded it this morning since its size was perfect for the tight swamp meanders here. It tracks okay too, and soon I settle into an even rhythm in which the white blades seem to rise and fall by themselves on either side of the cockpit, moving the hull forward under their own power. I have paddled enough in my life so that the act itself becomes effortless, almost like walking, and uncaps a deeper energy, freeing it to ignite the senses.

It's been almost three years since I've paddled from here, upstream or down. One of our tropical storms did a thorough job of inundating the shores, and as a result, uncounted numbers of hardwoods lost their grip in the soggy earth and fell into the river, making passage nearby impossible. It's taken all this time for the fallen trees to start to decay and float off or settle to the bottom. As I paddle, I notice that trees back deeper in the swamp have also fallen, and this gives the usually gloomy swamp a luminous quality.

After a mile or so, I realize that the character of this wild river has also changed. With a foliage canopy that is far less dense than it once was, shafts of sun function almost like natural spotlights, highlighting patches of saw-grass and pickerel weed and ancient cypress stumps far back from the shore. The newly illuminated patches glow almost theatrically, as if purposely illu-minated for a special morning matinee. At the edges of the river, exotic wa-ter hyacinths and native spadderdock and button bushes squeeze in tightly to command as much space as they can each get. The bushes are hung with golf ball–sized blossoms, each white and spiky and fragrant.

The shore vegetation is sometimes robust enough to sprawl out into the middle of the river, leaving only a yard or so to push on through. Still, it is easy going so far. I have not yet encountered any logs just beneath the surface, and I am thankful. When they do exist, they often function as a wooden shoal, and you have to use all the effort your torso and your arms can summon to push and hunch your way over them.

Soon I spot Steve up ahead, just launching at the old campsite where the spring outflow from Moccasin meets the tea-dark waters of this southern creek. I have camped here before, once when shooting a nature film in the late spring with a small crew. Then, a nearby bull gator proclaiming his terri-tory bellowed so loudly he made the thick night air seem to vibrate. Another time, I was here for New Year's Eve, cool enough for a fire and a comfy tent with a woman I once knew. These are good memories for me.

The tropical storm had inundated the little spring so that the weight of the tannic swamp water pushed the turquoise spring down inside the soft limestone below. But when the swamp finally retreated, the turquoise stayed hidden, and I wonder when it might return.

Steve joins me in midriver, and we scuttle around a deadfall of a full leafy tree canopy and, on the other side, pass a lone fellow in a camo canoe by himself with several rods. He looks intent, and very comfortable being alone, a human as fully in the moment as he can be. I think of him as the

Zen Master of Bream. I ask if he had caught anything, and he says, "Yeah, a few nice ones." He has his canoe smack in the middle of where the spring run swashes out into the river, and I figure he knew what the brewski boys back at the bridge didn't: spring waters are alkaline and will temper the acid of the tannins, making it more alluring to fish. Then again, maybe it just felt like a good place to be.

The Native Americans knew things like this very well, without ever having to understand intellectual presumptions about the pH of the water or the taxonomy of the animals. The confluences of creeks and springs and rivers were always bountiful, so good they could be considered sacred places, a dimension where humans and other animals could share information that was vital to both. The fish used grunt-like sounds to communicate; the people used myth and story and song. Sometimes these places were so rich in aquatic life that they were called the "Striking Grounds."

We leave the camo fisherman behind, and happily find easy access through cuts in the deadfall, almost like aisle-ways through the low jungle of aquatic plants and downed wood. This river is not heavily used, and it's especially rare to see anyone upstream above where we are now. Several more miles and the river will split, trailing either to Lake Norris or into the transparent Seminole Springs Creek. Many folks dread finding alligators and snakes on vine-hung tropical tangles like this, and that alone goes a long way toward "managing" the resource.

I've unconsciously slowed my breathing by now, and my senses have opened in proportion to that, not unlike the way the pupil of an eye dilates or constricts—not by conscious effort but in response to darkness or light. My peripheral vision always seems to conveniently expand as well. Without a single-minded obsession to blur perception, everything around me becomes fresh, compelling. I begin to see scads of light pink apple snail eggs on the low bark of trees and on the stems of water plants on both shores of the river, far more than I've ever seen here before.

Steve sees them too, and we think on it some. He figures the opening of the canopy over the swamp has made it somehow more attractive to the snails since the subaquatic plants and algae of their diets have flourished in the new light. That sounds reasonable to me. And just as I wonder if the limpkin—the rare solitary wading bird that loves apple snails—might also have been tipped off, I see just such a bird in the tall sawgrass ashore, almost as if I have imagined it to life. He is skittish, more so than most limpkins, and he stalks off into the green after flashing his fawn-like plumage at us.

The narrow, open portals in the middle or at the edges of the deadfall and weeds are becoming tighter, so now I have to duck low to get under branches or pull them back to enter. Usually after a pass like that, a spider or two ends up on the hull of my kayak; sometimes they ride pieces of leaves that stick to my hair. I pull one large twig with several leaves out of my head and see a stunningly beautiful yellow spider with tiny orange eyes. I gently place the twig atop some floating hyacinths, hoping she will find her way back to her home, or maybe create a new one.

Since I can now see hundreds of yards back into the landscape, the effect is almost like peeking behind a thick curtain on a theater stage to watch the company as it readies for the next act. I see flocks of juvenile white ibis flittering about, mottled with feathers of chocolate and white. Walking carefully by itself on its stilt legs is a little green heron. Without any fanfare, a pair of pileated woodpeckers swoop low across the open swamp water, leaving behind their distinctive sharp calls as they go. Back in the river, I bump into a small log, which is now colonized with tiny green mushrooms, each as delicate as a miniature parasol. Giant yellow-and-black tiger swallowtail butterflies begin to appear with regularity, flipping about over the water or atop the puffy white flower balls; they seem for all the world like brilliantly colored folds of origami brought to life in a morning dream.

Steve wonders if the butterflies are attracted inextricably to these plants, the way that gulf fritillaries are drawn to the passion vine, and I figure that they may likely be. Then I stop and carefully move my kayak to a bush where a swallowtail is feeding on a blossom. The undersides of its wings are turned toward me, and even though this position doesn't display its best colors, I am still in awe of the aesthetic weave of the fringe on its "tail."

We pause once to maneuver a particularly tricky passage, and as we do, we disturb a barred owl. She hoots three separate times from somewhere back in the woods and then is silent. We have lost most of the knowledge that the Timucua and the Mayaca and the Ais learned from nature in Florida, but a few myths remain. Owls, great protectors in the nether world, speak in these ancient stories. I wonder what it is that they really say.

Watermarks on the larger trees along the shore are high above where the water level is today, and it's clear that the dry weather has not only taken the flowing river down, but has also drained much of the swamp around us as well. Many of the trees are growing out of mud, intricate root systems as labyrinthine as any chemistry equation. The larger ones seem to splay out from their base with great flair with buttresses, gripping the soft mud for all they're worth. It is what always goes on here, except without the veil of water to hide it. "A swamp with the lid off," I say to Steve, and he smiles.

I paddle up next to a log to take a photo of a spate of apple snails' eggs, and when I do, I notice that most of them have already hatched. Unlike other smaller snails, the apple snail emerges as a fully formed mollusk, a miniature that fits snugly into its tiny shell.

Later, on shore, we will see newly laid turtle eggs that have been robbed from their nest by a raccoon or armadillo, the yolk forever gone. I think of the capriciousness of it all, wondering how a spate of snail eggs or a clutch of turtle eggs is destined to fare, depending on nothing more or less than how the sunlight falls on a cypress knee or the way in which a landscape tilts for the briefest of moments, little miracles the intellect will never understand.

I look again into the open swamp and see the carcass-like stumps of ancient bald cypress logged here a hundred years ago. Once, we pass a large trunk, one that likely sank before it was bled of its sap, and is now forever ashore, the intricate, raised grain of the durable wood on display, as if it were carved for the very best of museums. There is something about this particular wood that seems alive and comforting to me, humanlike almost in its color and in its spirit. And I realize now that it draws on my earliest memories I have of my father, his strong arms and hands browned from the sun, at once resolute and infinitely kind, as if ready to defend me from the worst harm a little boy could ever imagine from the world.

We see no gators, not even a swirl or foamy bubble trail, but we have heard their low, throaty growls from back in the spadderdock, a primal greeting to let us know they are here. I think of all the so-called comforts of civilization we surround ourselves with back in our socialized world of manners—virtual gadgets and behaviors that isolate us from the grit and transcendence of the authentic natural world. In contrast, I think there is no true comfort like seeing the smooth and weathered wood of a tree, fiber as strong as the hands of your father, a memory so deeply embedded that, even today in such a place, it allows me a great and lasting peace.

I tell Steve this is such a different river that I would not recognize it if I didn't know where we were. And he quotes Heraclitus, repeating one of my favorite parables: "You can never step twice into the same river." "Or," Steve adds, "paddle it twice, either."

And of course that is true, as righteous as any life allegory can be. I smile and, keeping with the time-space theme, I say, "Yep, and everything flows . . ." And so it does, and we go with it today, as completely as we can. Suddenly, I feel a light, welcome sprinkle from a single dark cloud, just enough to refresh us as we continue to paddle upstream. In doing so, we push our little boats through the water with deliberate strokes that seem to make the dark tannins swirl like great sluggish vats of syrup, almost as if the river is now moving in slow motion. I realize it is not the water that has slowed; it is my own perceptions, downshifted so they can absorb more of life, one grateful frame at a time.

So it is this way that we go for another couple hours, paddling against the current, dodging the low tree branches, once using all my strength to pull myself and my boat over a sunken log by gripping a branch just above it. I say a little prayer to myself now, one that's thankful for this day, and for having the vigor to maneuver my way through it, and for the nourishing companionship of a good friend who appreciates the same.

Finally, I am grateful for the way the green walls fall away, and the tiny avenue of black water opens up, transporting me onto the crest of instinct. It is a crest I ride with great pleasure, moving with the rarefied hope of a child toward a sort of wholeness of place. It is a fluid place moving now with the calls of the gators and the owls, glowing with the eggs of the snails and of the turtles, alive with the heart-comforting paternal grain of the richly textured wood. It is flowing, always, into the promise of the everlasting light.

13　Saba

A Precipice in a Lonely Turquoise Sea

I am scrunched into a narrow Winair aisle seat when Saba materializes just ahead. It seems like something I once dreamed, steep, green mountain peaks poking up into the clouds, waves frothing where it plunges down into a Windex-blue Caribbean Sea.

In what I take to be a giant leap of faith, our plane soars directly toward the mountainside where a short airstrip opens in

A classic view from the air of the high-peaked mountains and the valleys where the villages were typically nestled in Saba.

a narrow ravine. We drop onto it as if on a carnival ride, taxiing over a pavement shorter than an aircraft carrier. A spire named Diamond Rock juts out of the sea like a giant arrowhead several hundred feet below, and tropicbirds soar into the vapor of Mt. Scenery above.

As one of two nonlocals aboard, I deplane and check in at immigration in the one-room terminal, shoulder my luggage, and then stroll back outside. The immigration officer shuts down his nook when I leave and walks past me to his tiny car. "Enjoy your stay on Saba, Mr. Belleville," he says in a Scotch-Irish brogue, friendly enough so that I half-expect him to invite me home for a cold Carib beer and some johnnycake.

Isolated out here on the edge of the Lesser Antilles, this Saba is a wonderfully strange place. Except for a couple of stretches of dark sand that come and go, there are no beaches, and the steep volcanic landscape is strictly a matter of up or down. There are also no airport hustlers running for my bags, no T-shirt vendors, no pushy cab drivers vying for my attention.

Right off the bat, Saba seems like a retro sort of place not yet afflicted by the aggressive "civilization" that has washed over much of the world. Vertical landscapes and remote geography can do that. If the cultural weave of Saba is uniquely textured, I'm figuring the natural world shouldn't be far behind. And I'm hoping the annual Sea and Learn Festival now taking place will help me figure out why. The festival is a series of seminars and field trips, all devoted to nature and place. Experts study local orchids and birds, octopi and seahorses, lizards and sharks, and then share what they have learned with the rest of us.

I am traveling with the photographer Brad Doane, and when Doane learns there is a "festival" forthcoming, he somehow imagines a sort of Antillean Junkaroo, beads and parades and flashy costumes. I tell him it's mostly designed to celebrate Saba's distinctiveness, above and below the water. An avid hiker and veteran diver, Doane nods and recovers nicely. He can get into that.

We catch a cab to Juliana's Hotel in the village called Windwardside because that's where it is. Eddie, the Saban driver, begins his gear-grinding ascent of the mountain, following steep roads and switchbacks that seem to be glorified goat trails. We pass quaint little white homes with gingerbread trim and red zinc roofs and cisterns rounded like giant vaults.

Although pre-Columbians poked around here as early as 1175 BC, European settlers didn't arrive until 1627. Most were hearty seagoing men who valued independence and transferred their knowledge of boatbuilding to the architecture of their compact homes. Saba is Dutch, but the predominant dialect is a time-stuck English brogue.

As we go higher, palms and calabash trees and pink-flowering coralita vines replace the cactus and scrub of the arid shore. A road sign inexplicably warns, "Prohibited, Falling Rocks When Raining." At the side of the road, a man with a white beard is tossing Turk's cap cuttings to some goats. "Come, come," he says, and they do.

By dark, we reach Juliana's, which is less a hotel and more a lodge tucked into the side of a valley. Johanna, a cheery young Saban who owns the place with her husband, Wim, checks us into the Orchid Cottage, which is perched on the edge of a ravine. Although we have keys, we will soon fall into the habit of leaving the doors unlocked, sometimes even open. As we settle in, crickets and geckos and frogs join in a great welcoming chorus. "Wow," says Doane, of all the harmonious chirping. "At first, I thought that was a CD. It was just the right pitch."

We spiff up a bit and head out for a short walk on the 45-degree-angle asphalt road to the nearby Brigadoon Restaurant. My calves are not used to these angles, and I can already feel them begin to tighten up. Compared to most islands—even volcanic ones—in the region, Saba seems to have cut fewer compromises with its geography in order to please flatland visitors. As I learn more about the proud and singular eccentricity of this place over the next few days, I realize the roads are a fitting symbol for the refreshingly original Saban culture and lifestyle.

Inside a large room in the Brigadoon Restaurant, a big-boned American birder is showing slides of distinctive island birds, punctuating it with the sounds they make, hissing and tweeting with great gusto. The Sea and Learn Festival is clearly in full swing. I learn that the red-billed tropicbird I saw earlier has its main nesting site here on the Saban cliffs. We see photos of the brown-headed parakeet, the rufous nightjar. A bird-watching outing is planned early the next morning at the Ecolodge, halfway up the mountain. "Most birds will disappear around 10:00 a.m. when the hawks come out," says the big birder.

Doane and I soon meet Lynn Costenaro, a cofounder of the festival. She briefs us on diving and Saban customs over a dinner of local fish and crab. Lynn and her husband, John Major, first met in the British Virgin Islands and then moved here in 1989. She was a young fast-track financial analyst on Wall Street; he was a divemaster from the United Kingdom. Now they are part of the diverse expat Saban community, one that blends well with the natives—descendants of Dutch, English, Irish, and Scot adventurers and pirates.

Saba, explains Lynn, is "an active volcano in its dormant stage." If I need a reminder of this fact, I can dive anywhere around Ladder Bay and bury my hand in the yellow-brown sand where the magma deep below still keeps the bottom on a low simmer.

Diving here is considered challenging, says Lynn, since most sites are submerged seamounts just offshore. There are now two hyperbaric chambers here, and bent divers come from other islands to be treated. Yet accidents on Saba are rare—perhaps those who travel here are better prepared for the experience.

Lynn cares deeply about her chosen home, and it strikes me that that's a large part of Saba's spirit—a passion for place, and a gutsy spirit of discovery. "There's an Elfin Forest inside the cloud at the top of the mountain," says Lynn. "And below, we have a marine park surrounding the island. Saba's all about nature—we figure we'd better protect it. It's all we have."

⇓ ⇓ ⇓

Diamond Rock, the arrowhead-like spire I flew over a few days ago, is a hundred yards away from our dive boat, the *Sea Dragon*. Saba itself is nearby, plunging into the sea, all reddish rock and rubble at its bottom.

I do a giant stride off the stern in my scuba gear, right myself, and begin my slow sink into the blue. Viz is close to seventy-five feet, and the sunlight goes on and off, illuminating the coral cover on the steep rock walls as if someone is toggling a giant strobe. The shoal is like an iceberg—far more of it underwater than above. Charlotte, the blond Brit divemaster aboard, earlier advised us to look for the way the rock dissolves into the bottom in "skirts" of ancient lava. The current on the site can be tricky, changing even during the dive, but today it is mild, and the eighty-foot bottom seems like the best place on earth to be. I slowly fin about the edges of the rock, looking up to see the sun backlighting the multitude of tropicals overhead. A school of horse-eyed jacks cruises by, intent looks of determination frozen on their faces.

Pipe sponges and giant anemones punctuate the walls, and peacock flounder flit in the skirts below, formations that look as if the spire has melted into the sand. I fin upward, see the underside of the sea exploding between the peaks above, watch as a hawksbill turtle swims into the frothing white of it all, not unlike a bird disappearing into the cloud forest. I pull my way up the mooring line, and as I do a safety stop near the top, I am surrounded by a school of black durgeons.

When we are back on deck, the boat moves some, but not too much, and then we are down again. This site is Man O' War rock, and it is a fully submerged version of Diamond, except every square inch seems covered in hard and soft corals, sponges, and tunicates. I realize that the rocks we are diving—and all the deeper pinnacles we will soon visit—are little Sabas, everything scrunched up tight next to everything else, ancient lava and not coral defining the undercarriage. Like the big Saba, life underwater vies heartily for space, a densely packed assemblage of marine life imitating the compact homes and little cars and Elfin Forest above.

The fish here are far more diverse and numerous than in most of the Caribbean I have seen. Large Nassau and Tiger groupers, usually missing in action elsewhere, thrive here. I think more about the Saba Marine Park, which stretches out to a two-hundred-foot depth line around the island, and realize that not all marine protected areas are created equal. This one was set up in 1987 before diving was really popular here, so it didn't have to play catch-up, like many parks do. Commercial fishermen, who usually fish the massive Saba Banks farther offshore, seldom harvest the animals here that divers like to see. And the dramatic geography keeps the coastline unspoiled, virtually free of pollution.

Later I will dive one of the deeper pinnacles, this one called the Twilight Zone. It will be dark and bluish, a rock that begins at ninety feet and goes down to below 110, a pinnacle befitting its name. There are places not far from the edge of Saba where the bottom, in fact, will drop away to one thousand feet and more. On the Twilight Zone, we see the larger animals we had hoped for: a five-foot Caribbean reef tip shark, a giant moray eating a spiny lobster, a barracuda as long as I am. There are other seamounts in deeper water, like the nearby Eye of the Needle, hidden places where large ocean-going animals—whale sharks, hammerheads, manta rays—come and go.

Our dives over for the day, we putter back to the harbor at Ft. Bay. I pick up my backpack and head over to Pop's Place for a cold soda and a little paper tray of conch fritters. A wonderfully amicable man is behind the counter of this little open-air pub. I ask him if he is Pop, and he shrugs. "I'm Shuggy. Real name's Frank, but they've called me Shuggy since I was a wee lad." Two little boys crawl up on the red stools, and Shuggy gives them free Snap Pop candy; they squeal with delight.

Shuggy and his wife, Elvira, bought the place from Pop three years ago; a framed newspaper clipping on the wall says so. "Everyone knew it as Pop's, so we didn't want to change anything." Shuggy is a lobster fisherman, still traps them one day a week, and serves his customers lobster sandwiches fresh from the sea. Like many Sabans, he also makes his own version of a customized 151-proof rum by tinkering with various spices like cinnamon and cloves. "Try some of mine," he says, placing a free shot in front of me, the adult version of a Snap Pop. I drink it, and soon I am smiling like Shuggy.

Charlotte, the divemaster, slips onto a nearby stool and we chat. Before the jetties were built here in 1972, everything delivered from cargo ships had to be taken ashore by small rowboats at Ladder Bay and then carted up the island to one of its four villages. Dive boats from three shops leave from the harbor now, and the Saba Marine Park is headquartered nearby. Saba is small, barely five miles in diameter, so any of the twenty-eight dive sites with moorings are seldom more than a fifteen-minute ride by boat, says Charlotte. "There are some natural coral reefs on the windward side, but it has to be calm before we go there."

We ride back up from the harbor with a tall Saban named Garvis, who tells us he never worked at a "lazy man's job," meaning he has never sat behind a desk. He drives a taxi van now and moonlights as a bartender. When he was younger, he operated heavy excavating machinery to help build the road we are driving today.

The road is a thrill ride, winding around the outside of the mountain itself. Every so often, a thick wall of foliage falls away, offering wide, stunning vistas of the valleys called "guts." At one turn, we look out to see a great ancient dome of lava next to an odd flat slab of rock on the coast. "Willy the Whale," says Garvis, smiling at the formation, and a giant whale is exactly what it seems. "On a clear day," says Garvis, smiling to himself, "you can see Montserrat."

By the time we arrive at the cottage, it is twilight, and the cloud atop Mt.

Scenery is rolling down toward us. First it moves across the mountainside, then the road and the patio before finally settling into the gut below, where it simmers like the vapor of dry ice. The frogs and geckos chirp and click approvingly.

Doane and I head up the 45-degree angle road to a bistro called Scout's Place, where the karaoke contest for all of Saba is now under way. We sit on a tiny outside porch that hangs over the edge of a cliff above the fog-shrouded valley below. We talk to a couple of students from the Saba School of Medicine. Juliska, a Dutch waitress with stunning hazel eyes whom we met at lunch the other day, smiles warmly like we are old friends and brings us drinks.

One singer does a really bad Tammy Wynette, and then a guy from St. Martin delivers a surprisingly good Frank Sinatra, Antillean accent and all. The big American birder gets up to do an Elvis song, swaggering a bit too much like Elvis, and he is hooted off the stage by some Germans. "I guess the Germans take their karaoke seriously," says Doane.

It's a "three-goat day" here on Saba, the wind as calm as a baby's breath and the sky full of clouds that look like giant cotton balls. There may be better ways to figure out the day's weather than watching the goats. But in the week I have been here, I haven't yet found one. Here's how it works: The ravine in front of the Orchid Cottage frames the Caribbean Sea a good thousand feet below in a giant V. Free-ranging goats balance on the rocky edges of its slopes. The calmer the wind and the sea, the more goats are out, teetering. A flat sea means lots of goats. A rough sea and strong wind means no goats at all. Goats, whatever else they may be, are not suicidal.

This morning, Doane and I hike to the top of the Elfin Forest with Tom van't Hoff, the biologist who helped set up the marine park and who now runs the Ecolodge. The rocky steps are steep and moist with vapor and mud. We trek upward through a rainforest and into the cloud. Around us is an ancient world with bromeliads and orchids, ferns and liverworts. Vines hang from the wooden skeletons of four-hundred-year-old mountain mahogany trees, stunted and wizened. The peaks here actually "catch" the clouds, says van't Hoff, and function as a giant sponge. "This is a reservoir for the lower slopes," he says. "They gradually release moisture to keep the island green."

Down from the netherworld, we again hook up with the *Sea Dragon* and head out to the sixty-foot-wall of Tent Reef. There I spend most of my dive time shadowing a hawksbill turtle chomping away at sponges. It briefly looks up, and I am struck by the timelessness in its eyes. I must be a nanosecond on its 200-million-year-old evolutionary clock.

By evening we return to the Brigadoon to see a presentation by Roger Hanlon, a cephalopod expert who thinks he may have found a new octopus around Saba. Hanlon, from Woods Hole, wears worn jeans, frizzy hair, and glasses. His T-shirt reads: *Welcome Squid Overlords.* His presentation is entitled "The Wily Octopus: Nature's Master of Color Change."

We learn that cuttlefish and squid are social, but octopus are solitary. Like their brethren, they are also high in protein so everything in the sea likes to eat them. "Some of my irreverent colleagues remind me that I have spent my entire career studying 'bait,'" says Hanlon, who has the confidence to be self-effacing. Octopi have no backbones, but they do have giant brains. To keep from getting eaten, the animals do tricks with camouflage. Their brains turn on chromatophores in their skin like electrical billboards, arranging their color and texture to match their background.

But there's more. Most octopi mimic inert stuff, like rocks and colonial tunicates. But the new octopus actually mimics other animals. When they move along the bottom out in the open, for instance, they swim like a flounder. And the disguise is more than genetic reaction. "This is not a reflex," says Hanlon, clearly in admiration of his species of choice. "It requires some thinking."

The next morning, we board another boat and ride only a few minutes from the harbor with Hanlon. He is accompanied by an entourage of CEDAM volunteers here to help find and film the new octopus. This is called a "muck dive" because it is on a sandy bottom with little coral or other type of relief divers usually expect. And it is shallow, barely more than twenty feet. If an octopus wanted to hightail it out across a wide open space disguised as a flounder, this would be a great place to catch him doing so.

Hanlon came here last year to talk about the specialized "mimic octopus" that lives in the Pacific. After his description, a sharp-eyed diver got a photo of one. Today we will continue the hunt, providing info to help Hanlon prepare a research paper that will describe the new species here.

In his predive briefing, Hanlon shows us signals to use when we spot an octopus and warns us against "wagon training" around it. "We don't want them to have negative associations with divers," he said. With that, we are in the water, Hanlon wearing a cheap pair of yellow rubber kitchen gloves so he can stir the sand in front of him. He has told us that the tiny mimic octopus can burrow into a garden eel hole and, sticking out a tentacle, imitate a garden eel. There are hundreds of garden eels around us today on the flats, and I look for one that might be a tentacle, but with no success.

I poke inside old concrete moorings and under a lost anchor. I see juvenile tricolor damsel fish and a coral banded shrimp. A large stingray swims by with a blue runner shadowing his every move. I look over to see Doane lying on the sand with his camera, trying to get a flying gunnard to fly. Around us, gobies nose-dive into the sand and disappear. Hanlon is in a dust storm of his own making, trying to uncamouflage a cephalopod.

We find no mimic octopus this day. But like everything else on Saba, there will always be another time. Time is a commodity that this strange and wondrous island seems to have plenty of.

14 Inside a Stained Glass Window, Looking Out

I'm searching for symmetry today, as I so often do when allowed to roam about freely in nature. Symmetry isn't the half-mad early-Saturday-morning drivers on a Florida interstate exhaling road rage in repayment for leading obsessively structured lives. Nor is it the perfect geometry of walled and gated "neighborhoods." For me, it's the splendid visual link between what others once saw in natural systems in Florida and what exists now.

Moving from open marsh into a hardwood hammock in the Lake Woodruff National Wildlife Refuge.

My old spiritual bud, the naturalist William Bartram, found both adventure and discovery here when venturing up the St. Johns in his little sailing "bark," sketching plants and animals, sleeping on fine "mattresses" of Spanish moss, and becoming one with this strange new place. I cherish Bartram's approach, not just because he mostly traveled by himself on his second trip up this Florida river, but because he was guileless, forging ahead not for glory or gold—like the conquistadors before him or the greedy manipulators of land and people who came after—but for the sublime unity of purpose revealed in nature and place. Spirituality was woven through it all for Bartram, just as it was for the Native Americans he encountered here.

Our plan today is to enter the Lake Woodruff National Wildlife Refuge from somewhere near Spring Garden Lake, a place Audubon once drifted through on his own Florida excursion, a bit after Bartram. The lake narrows into a large creek, winds around high stands of pine flatwoods and some hammocks, and empties in the enormous Lake Woodruff.

Finally, it sieves about some more land—including Tick Island, where archaeologists have found a mother lode of finely incised pots, bones, and antlers—and finally joins with Lake Dexter, which flows north within the complex St. Johns system. The names here have changed. Today Bartram's "East Lake" is Woodruff; and Audubon's "Spring Garden Spring" is now Ponce de Leon Springs. But so much else remains the same.

When finely detailed artifacts like this turn up, and they do so in great numbers, it's usually a reflection of how naturally rich the place historically had been in plants, animals, and fish. Having a strong-flowing river nearby, as well as a number of creeks, springs, and islands, simply creates the chance for greater diversity of natural riches—a wealth that would attract and sustain early Native Americans. I'm grateful that a national wildlife refuge now protects the natural treasures of a place that, clearly, has been a sanctuary for earlier natives for a very long time.

After all, as Bartram once observed, "This world, as a glorious apartment of the boundless palace of the sovereign Creator . . . is inexpressibly beautiful and equally free to the inspection and enjoyment of all of his creatures." Birds, plants, animals, man. No single one is greater than the other in this grand equation.

Steve is my companion today, and as always, he is intrepid. We park near a trailhead, and, picking one of several high and dry pathways atop berms between impoundments, head out into the wide, generous landscape of wetlands under an expansive blue sky decorated with shifting banks of cumulus. It might rain today, it might not. For now, it is sunny, and by 9:00 a.m., pleasant with an agreeable breeze wafting across the marvelously flat Florida terrain, a mosaic of sabal palms and bulrush, sawgrass in early bloom, fields of pickerel weed bursting with purple rods, and clutches of the duck potato with delicate white orchidlike blooms glowing at the end of stalks inside fat, green spatulate leaves.

The water in the canals is low, far more so than it should be in early summer, and the wading birds are having a field day with the tiny fish that are concentrated in the shrinking sloughs. Large dragonflies, organic little choppers that consume enormous quantities of mosquitoes when hungry, are everywhere. I notice a small dead tree, an artistic sort of snag, really, and at the tip of each leafless branch is a perched dragonfly, as if they have budded here like new sprouts. Dragonfly tree, I say out loud, and Steve chuckles.

We follow a topographical map in and trek across a "Jones Island," likely named for an early settler who once homesteaded here. Like the nearby Tick Island, its relief is mostly from the accruing of shells, bone, and sand over the centuries, a reminder of the presence of the "earth people" who once lived here. At first, the landscape on both sides is open, stretching to sabal palm hammocks in the distance. At the edge of a berm, Steve faces the broad, wet prairie, grasses and sedges and rushes all raging with the chlorophyll of the growing season.

Like so much here in this warm and wet peninsula, the revitalized green seems off the color spectrum, as if a magic surrealist had made up another color just to emphasize the otherworldly quality of this place. The expansiveness of it all is agreeable, welcoming, allowing the soul the tender freedom to roam. Steve once studied in the seminary, and he understands as well as anyone I have ever met how natural places inform the heart. "A marsh like this makes the spirit sing," says Steve, and I think, yep, it sure does.

The morning breeze is light, perfect for a trek without shade. I begin to notice wildflowers, sometimes seven or eight species in just a few yards at the edges of the berms. There is the star rush, a grasslike sedge that looks as if someone has dipped the leaf tips into white paint. There are fields of the yellow daisy-like flowers called tickseed, the fat puffy blossoms of the bachelor's buttons, and a tiny forest of the pipeworts, little white puffs on the end of a tiny, straight stalk. There are vines of white morning glories, a glorious five-petaled blossom I take to be a sky flower. There are even small white flowerets on the saw palmettos. And when the land rises just a bit toward the pine flatwoods, I see that the tight little fruits on the shiny blueberry are now becoming ripe.

When carefully excavating a nearby area, archaeologists once found the residue of eighty-two different kinds of plant seeds, vegetation that could be variously eaten, woven into basketry, or even used for their sensory value in spiritual ceremonies. What we are seeing today is a reaffirmation of that wealth, a very real organic legacy that—if we pay attention—can remind us of the wholeness of the land and the deep imprint it left on its people. Signage is surely handy for interpretation in such places. But seeing, smelling, and feeling these natural signs communicates on a far deeper level.

We walk some more, entering a foliage corridor with a spacious canopy. The swamps on each side of the corridor are dry from the extended drought, but recent water marks from a swift and short-lived flood are still moist on some cypress trunks. Clearly, the sheet flow of water that moved through here not so long ago was at least as deep as our waists.

Finally, we dead-end into Spring Garden Creek, and here we sit atop piles of compacted snail shells the Timucua and the Mayaca left behind. Like the natives before us for six thousand and more years, we drink and we eat, allowing the solitude of mystery and water and place to settle in. We snack on granola bars and sip water from canteens instead of chewing dried strips of bear and deer and slurping creek water from a hollowed-out bone.

Nonetheless, the wondrous symmetry of us being here, resting and refreshing ourselves atop a berm of bleached and ancient shells, takes on an interminable dynamic all its own. Without any effort to direct the moment intellectually, I sense a timeless sort of potency down to the very core of my soul. As I do, I experience a kinship with the deep-hearted affection, love, fear, and awe that others here before me exuded centuries before I ever existed on this earth. Astute writers like Barry Lopez talk about the supremacy of "place" and how, if it is righteously used by humans, it retains a sort of vitality that is never ending. It is a distinct energy, and maybe it can't be measured by our fancy high-tech instruments, but it can sure be felt.

We hike back out through the canopied trail and into the open marsh, which is much warmer now with the late-Florida-afternoon sun. Four sandhill cranes balance on stilt-like legs in a mud slough below the berm, two adults with bright-red head crests foraging for worms while two giant chicks stand quietly next to them—perhaps they are cranes-in-training. The soft unruly down of new feathers of the juveniles spikes every which way from their heads, giving them a slightly bewildered look.

Suddenly, one of the adults looks up and lets out with its wondrous, haunting cry, a deep and throaty exclamation that seems delivered intact from the Miocene, a geological epoch 10 to 20 million years ago, when these ancient cranes first emerged to become what they are today.

We pick up and walk another mile or so on the packed mud trail in the marsh until we come upon great colonies of snowy and great white egrets. Nearby there's a flock of black-headed vultures surrounding a lone roseate spoonbill, a bird so rare here that it's not even on the bird checklist for this refuge. The roseate is young, almost all white, not having eaten enough of the carotene-enriched crustaceans to yet turn it pink. Oddly, all of the vultures seem to be eyeing the white roseate, and Steve suggests it may be injured, that the carrion-eaters are waiting for it to die.

This distresses me, as I want to believe the spoonbill is fine and it's just resting for a bit. I say the vultures are more likely waiting for everything to die—just a matter of time before the nearby peninsula cooters kick off, a nearby gator goes belly up, a stray human hiker bites the dust.

Almost immediately, I am rewarded for my cosmic revelation when the young roseate swiftly takes to the air, only to settle down a few hundred yards away to join a few of its buds atop a bare patch of peat and marl. I tell Steve that all is not lost since the vultures still have the turtle, the gator, and us to ponder, and he laughs heartily at this.

We light out atop the long, narrow berms, sweating now from the sun but exhaling in blissful acknowledgment of all that is good about the world around us, refreshed not just in the solace of our twelve-mile walk, but in the natural equilibrium of all we have seen and felt.

Bartram's sovereign Creator smiled on us today, and I give thanks in my heart, embedding this day in that sweet memory place I once knew as a little boy, sitting in a pew with my mom and my dad and my brother in church. The sunlit stained glass windows around me glowed with a sort of luminosity then, evoking a sacredness and a blessed dimension all its own. And here, decades later on this rare Florida landscape, the water and land and broad, hallowed sky behave likewise, another divine bridge of symmetry and comfort inextricably weaving its way through time.

All that's needed is an organ playing a Bach prelude, and if I listen closely enough, I think I can hear the faintest strains of one rising from the soft murmur of the simmering marsh.

15   A Landscape That Remembers

When a traveler asked Wordsworth's servant
to show him her master's study, she answered,
"Here is his library, but his study is out of doors."

Walking, Henry David Thoreau

The forecast was for rain later today, so I got some work out of the way early on and headed for the woods. The plan was an hour in and maybe an hour back out, no more than five or so miles, but I seldom figure in the dawdling that is so integral to the true art of sauntering.

Walking with my grandsons Will and Ray Crawley and (the late) Shep in the woods. Photo by Beth Crawley.

The trail is an easy one: it splits into a little mile loop through the longleaf to the west, and, to the east, splays off on a series of unmapped firebreak roads back deep in an impressive tangle of palmetto and pine. The latter is always my choice because, from these roads, smaller spurs will often take you away into deeper hammocks, like the one that leads down to the edge of the Wekiva. Another, if you follow it long enough, will deliver you to the shore of the St. Johns, open prairie finally giving way to a canopy of oak and bald cypress, gnarly knees like little goblins back in the swamp.

It's just me today; a few years ago, Shep would have joined me, his boundless sheltie enthusiasm as unbridled as Bartram's own eighteenth-century expression of the wonders that La Florida would gift to our souls. The direction is easy, no compass needed, a trail I have walked before with friends and by myself. The beginning takes me beyond a deep sinkhole, one that's usually empty to its steep bottom when dry. I poke back through the myrtle and sweetgum to see where it is after a few weeks of heavy rainfall, using it as one might use a giant rain gauge funneling down into the terrain. Today it's nearly two-thirds full, a good twenty feet deep, duckweed floating on the surface and a small heron nagging at the tiny fish near its edges.

The dirt road I walk has been packed down by the rain and the tire treads of a park service vehicle of some sort. At trail side, the tiny white morning glory begins to appear, as does the lizard tail, the name of the latter more fully realized now in its own tint of pale white. A tiny pealike orange bud I can't identify pops out of the understory here and there, and then so do scads of what I take to be narrow-leaved sabatia, a five-lobed little wildflower that revels in the moisture of the wet pinelands. It's a flatwoods here, so everything seems to be in place, a little ecological lesson of plants and landscape ready for the listening.

As the last of the hardwood hammocks fade away, I look to the west for the bald eagle nest I know will be near the top of a longleaf and am comforted, as always, when I see it there. It's always exciting when there's a Ma or Pa Eagle about, but just knowing the nest is well maintained is enough for now.

The fragrance of pine and wild soggy prairie is replaced by a strong odor of burnt plants. As I round the next bend, I see the charred remnants of a prescribed burn, the thick stalks of the saw palmettos looking like the arms of some prehistoric animal splayed out across the earth. I survey the burn and see scores of white sand piles—each marking the pitched-up earth from gopher tortoise burrows. Without the vanishing magic of the burn, all I would see would be a vast unyielding field of green.

I take a path that I know will lead me to a slough just behind the main branch of the lower Wekiva. In other hikes here, I have always been able to find a downed tree that will let me ford the little bayou. But today is different: the water is wide and deep, with only a shoal of white sand from an erosional creek interrupting the blur of duckweed that sits atop the mire. I carefully pick my way along the steep banks, looking for where I know a mama gator usually keeps her brood, but today they don't seem to be at home. Farther along on the shore, I see the distinctive bleached white snail shell (*Viviparious* sp.) that makes up most Native American midden mounds along the larger St. Johns.

It vaguely occurs to me that the Native Americans who once lived here would be cheered by the strong, new flow of water, cheered by the animals that would use it, by the way it would open up old creeks and branches long closed by the drought. I won't be able to make it across to the mainstem bank of the Wekiva today because of this, but that's alright.

I turn to go, fascinated by the way the heavy rainfall has inscribed itself in the soft earth, creating a gully to the slough. Small, isolated puddles of tannin lie here and there, tiny ponds with the tea-colored water that leaks from the swamp. In places, it seems the white sand has not just eroded, but has actually melted, flowing layers of soil caught just for now in a freeze-frame of time, perhaps to become sedimentary rock a millennium from now.

Walking out from the gridlock of trees, I feel the first drops of the day's rain. I am sweating now, and it feels good on my skin. Other than a deer track here and there, the only imprint on the packed sand is the one I left coming in. On the way back out, I try my best to retrace those incoming steps.

I think long about those who have walked this trail with me before— all good-hearted women and men. And one little dog who could never get enough of the woods, and the scent it left for him. The visceral knowledge of having been with them all is redemptive, for I have led most of them here, over time. I think fondly of each of them, think of how fully and how differently they were able to respond to the mystery of this Florida landscape. There are stories that remain here, good ones too, and I am grateful for that.

As it was for Shep, the scent is here for me too—except it's not one I can smell. It's one I intuit deep in my gut, a series of vivid memories that allow me to relive each journey I've ever taken on this trail. Ahead, two white tails barely beyond the yearling age spook, bounding away in different directions. I back off, not wanting to scare them anymore, and take a longer trail spur back. As I do, I pass a pile of osprey feathers and wonder what other animal has been strong and swift enough to have done this—an eagle, a stealthful bobcat or coyote?

And just as I'm prepared to cut across an open pine forest of wiregrass and small turkey oak, I see a pile of what seem to be bones and go to it. It's the pieces of a once-large gopher tortoise, its topical scutes pealing back from the heavier calcium, little vertebrae scattered about. I wonder about this animal's story, about its beginning and its end. As I do, I realize once more how the landscape brims with the sacred stories it has to tell us—of its wildlife, its plants and trees, its seasons, its people—from those who once gathered snail shells and slept next to the earth, to those of us who have opened our modern hearts to it all, who cherish the way its lessons settle down on us, as real as any tonic.

It is raining harder now, and I quicken my pace back to the beginning. I am soaking wet, but I am sorry to go, to leave the stories behind. I promise myself when I get home that I will write down some notes that describe my little excursion and the feelings it evoked. Maybe someday it might even turn into a yarn of time and gratitude and thankfulness, a soulful gift generously given by the wild Florida landscape.

16 Producing *In Marjorie's Wake*

Navigating the Territory between the Hero's Journey and a Floating Opera

The golden afternoon light that settles across a water-soaked Florida river landscape seems unlike any other in the world. It particularly does right here on a spit of dry prairie where the Econlockhatchee flows into the much broader St. Johns.

Coproducer and chief shooter Bob Giguere films Leslie Poole and Jennifer Chase in their boat near Puzzle Lake on the St. Johns River as they retrace the aquatic trail once described by the author Marjorie Kinnan Rawlings in the "Hyacinth Drift" chapter of her book Cross Creek. *Photo by Mark Howerton.*

The two women who are cinematically retracing a river journey that the author Marjorie Kinnan Rawlings once made on the St. Johns are setting up their tents for the night. They are doing so inside a hammock of sabal palms, a slightly higher berm of rich earth where slender, gray trunks poke out of the flat delta like giant pipe stems, each crowned with a feathery spray of green. Nearby, the skeleton of a large cow lies almost intact, its white bones picked clean by the black-headed vultures. Three sandhill cranes glide overhead, crying to each other in their haunting way. Finally, they rise so high that they vanish into the heavens, as completely gone as a mirage.

Our film crew piles onto the flat deck of a platform boat and pushes away from the shore, continuing to film the women and their tents and the palm hammock as we go. The sky here in early autumn is wondrous, cumulus billowing out across the wide prairie just like it does down in the Glades. The low, grassy marsh of this upper river has a distinctive subtropical character, revealed in the robust colors of plants and wildflowers that pulse in great waves of ever-changing light. To get here, we carefully navigated through most of Puzzle Lake yesterday, a place Rawlings described as a "blue smear through the marsh" during her own river journey. It is still very much a blue smear, as sublime and enigmatic as it was seventy-five years ago. And in a Florida that has lost so much of its wildness, that gives me great hope.

Our boat carefully follows a shallow, unmarked channel, weaving our way through the walls of sedge and rush until the palm hammock and the tents and the cow skeleton disappear into the landscape, as fully gone as the sandhill cranes.

We close on the large houseboat we've anchored downstream a couple of miles in deeper water; it serves as a sort of floating dormitory, kitchen, and office for our production team. Once aboard, I walk the ladder up to the roof of the boat. It's a rise of only six or so feet, but it's high enough to let me see all I need of a natural world entirely comprised of wild marsh and palms and random smears of blue stretching from one end of the skyline to the other. The sun, low in the sky now, is backlighting the heavy cumulus with great bursts of ginger.

Late afternoon segues into early evening with little effort, and the sun melts into the flat, wet earth, and the bronze light is replaced by scarlet. Soon there is no color at all, only darkness, and it consumes the world around me in the most complete way, creating a very real Florida night unlike any you will experience in a theme park or a tract development or on a highway. It seems as if the dark has even absorbed sound, until, finally, I hear the elegiac call of the barred owl drifting to me from somewhere far away.

Back on the palm hammock campsite, the women have huddled into their tents, using small lights to read and to write in notebooks they have brought along. Suddenly they hear the sound of a strange outboard motor coming closer to them on the Econ. Then a strong male voice calls out to them from the shore, asking if he can come up to visit.

This literary-nature film project, which at first seemed like a lighthearted adventure, is now more real than life itself. If there is a continuum between place and time, between recorded behaviors and human memory, then this unscripted moment in the dark river night is still searching for interpretation.

The purpose of this exercise, after all, is to produce a documentary film. And if any moment or idea or thought is to be made real, it has to be captured in the postmodern realm of high-definition video. Otherwise it drifts away into the ether, as completely gone from sight as the dark prairie and the cow skeleton and the sandhill cranes. Back at the campsite, the request from the shore goes unrequited, the sound of the motor drifts away, and much later, the women finally settle into sleep.

A few years ago, our fledgling not-for-profit nature film group, Equinox Documentaries, was prospecting for a broadcast film idea that would express the best of our intentions. We were looking for a documentary concept that would not just celebrate the rare natural landscape of Florida. It would also address the related, if elusive, "sense of place." In that pre-Recession time, our state was growing at an alarming rate, and we were losing an average of twenty acres of natural land an hour to growth that was more often "sprawl" than not. When the native landscape vanished, the cultural component associated with "sense of place" was in jeopardy as well.

I strongly felt that the dynamic driving the loss went far beyond just poor decisions on the part of politicians who were allowing the out-of-control growth. Three out of every four residents—the people electing these officials—were not born in Florida. From the perspective of natural history and geography, our peninsular state was off the mainland grid for most of these newcomers.

Sensibilities attuned to more solid, geologically understood landscapes back on the continent often had trouble figuring out the biological nuances of Florida's complex system of wetlands, rivers, and springs. With scant emotional obligation to this water-driven peninsula, it was simply easier to allow—or ignore—the sort of growth that was obliterating Florida's singular natural landscape.

Al Burt, the eloquent columnist for the *Miami Herald* who often examined the perplexities of native Florida, nailed it in a piece he wrote back in the early 1990s. Newcomers, wrote the late Burt, too often represent "absentee hearts." When, in fact, "Floridians, new and old, need to take the vows of belonging. Our peculiar dream is alive and real, available to us all, but we need to work at understanding this wonderfully different state . . . to hone our kinship with it."

In more closely examining this "newcomer" equation, I had come to realize that there were plenty of transplanted residents who did "get it." Indeed, many of the writers and poets who had created some of the most insightful works about Florida were not born here. That list was a long one and included earlier "newcomers" such as William Bartram, John James Audubon, Sidney Lanier, Hart Crane, Ernest Hemingway, Elizabeth Bishop, James Merrill, Marjory Stoneman Douglas, Archie Carr, Marjorie Kinnan Rawlings, Patrick Smith, and many more—and that didn't even begin to plumb the long and distinguished list of artists who came here from somewhere else and "got it" aesthetically.

Certainly, being new to Florida didn't routinely exclude an awareness of it. Indeed, I also arrived here as a transplanted young adult seeking my own fortune. Gradually, I came to realize that my new residency status carried with it a heightened sense of responsibility that required me to both learn and to see in new ways. Despite all the myths and hyperbole that had been spliced onto Florida over time, there was still a very real and complex "vernacular" of nature and place at work here.

A few years ago, I talked at length with Bob Giguere, a producer for a regional PBS affiliate, about making films to help folks see Florida in a new way. We figured the best way to do this was to create our own non-profit production company dedicated to that vision. We then chatted with friends and like-minded colleagues who agreed to serve on the board of our grassroots nonprofit. We all agreed that a documentary that simply "preached" would do little to change anybody's mind about the sublime values of

Florida. After all, the intent of creating such a film group was to fill the void left by a mainstream media that often defaulted to the more simplistic black-and-white depictions of our state.

As a guy who made his living writing essays, articles, and books in the genre of creative nonfiction, I instinctively gravitated toward literature with fact-driven narratives to guide our documentaries. I figured that, as humans, we had spent most of our existence as a species telling each other stories, whether we did so around a campfire or, more recently, through the printed word. Indeed, Aristotle examined the need for story 2,300 years ago in his *Poetics* when he considered the worth of an engaging narrative to our lives.

More recently, the mythologist Joseph Campbell suggested the human need for a story was so powerful that it was almost genetically bred into us. Campbell even identified the classic story as the "hero's journey" in which a person leaves the ordinary world and travels to an unknown and enigmatic place, returning with a treasure to share with the world. Metaphorically, that "treasure" could be valuable information—perhaps even wisdom.

Could we identify an intriguing and literate story about nature and sense of place in Florida that we could bring to film—one that would transcend the divisive politics of growth and appeal to the more sublime qualities of both the intellect and the emotions of our prospective audience? If we could, we might be able to set the stage to allow viewers to connect on a deeper level with the realities of the Florida environment. From that more visceral connection might then come a moral belief—one that would be far more resistant to the obsession with pell-mell growth and all its destructive consequences.

One of our new board members had an intriguing idea. It was Leslie Poole, a former journalist who at the time was an adjunct professor in the Environmental Studies Department at Rollins College. A few years earlier, she and a good friend had launched a two-woman boat trip down the St. Johns River in imitation of the excursion that Pulitzer Prize–winning author Rawlings once made on the St. Johns in 1933 with her friend Dessie Smith. Rawlings wrote descriptively and poignantly about that trip. Her chronicle appeared first as an article in *Scribner's Monthly* and then later as the chapter entitled "Hyacinth Drift" in her book *Cross Creek*. Poole and her friend, both veteran reporters, also coauthored a magazine feature story about their own river trip.

The concept of transporting such an excursion to film resonated soundly.

And even though we then had virtually no funding for a full hour-long broadcast-quality documentary, we agreed to again retrace author Rawlings's "Hyacinth Drift" trip on the St. Johns. Except this time we would have video cameras along to record it.

This would not be a feature film or a historic reenactment with participants dressed in period costumes and pretending to be the original literary team. Instead, it would be a real excursion on the contemporary St. Johns by two modern women. Rawlings's connection to nature and her original trip with Smith would be referenced whenever possible. But we would also pay close attention to both the condition of the contemporary river, as well as to the culture it had shaped. There would naturally be room for real discovery in the course of the journey because rivers were anything if not organic in their flow.

I thought there would also be a fine symmetry if our trip participants reflected the personal contrasts between Rawlings and Smith. Those contrasts were grounded in the reality that author Rawlings was a northern transplant who had only been in Florida for five years—and while adventurous and increasingly savvy to the lay of the land and its people—was still considered by her neighbors at Cross Creek to be a raw newcomer. Smith, her companion on the trip, was a gritty native sportswoman who could shoot, hunt, and fish as well as any of the men. Indeed, in a clear acknowledgment of the gulf between them, Smith—a decade younger than Rawlings—called her new friend "Young-un." Rawlings had written that Smith did so "with much tenderness, pitying my incapabilities."

Poole, a Florida native whose family owned an eighteen-foot center-console sport boat, was an avid hiker and fisher who had spent a lot of time on the rivers of Florida at the helm of the craft. In a vague sort of way, she would naturally function as our Dessie. I searched inside my own mental Rolodex for a companion who would be both a relative newcomer as well as a good sport. The most obvious seemed to be Jennifer Chase, a talented musician, composer, and playwright from Jacksonville who had traveled widely overseas. Chase, a transplant from New England, had few of the outdoor skills Poole had developed over the years in Florida, but she was nothing if not sporty and up for an adventure, just as Rawlings had once been.

Certainly it helped that the women each had a good sense of humor, as that would come in handy with the long hours of boating and filming on the river over eight or nine days. And the capacity for good humor provided more symmetry: although Rawlings was afflicted by dramatic mood swings during her adult life, those who knew her reported that she "loved to laugh." Smith also had her own special brand of humor. Once she reportedly sent friends up North what she told them was an exotic, foreign dog. Her friends later responded that they were having difficulty getting it to take to a leash. The "dog" turned out to be a possum.

With our river team in place, we then began to consider the logistics of the trip. We would research as much of that era at the creek as we could, traveling to the Smathers Library at the University of Florida where Rawlings had left most of her manuscripts, papers, photos, and other mementos. We would consult with the Marjorie Kinnan Rawlings Society and more carefully study what Rawlings had written about Florida and the St. Johns vis-à-vis *Cross Creek*, *The Yearling*, and *South Moon Under* in particular.

I had also written a narrative-style book about the St. Johns entitled *River of Lakes: A Journey on Florida's St. Johns River*, so I would also revisit my own research about this stretch of the middle river. We would raise enough funding to pay for a contract film crew and associated production costs, as well as boat and gear rental. We would aim for a national PBS market since the literary-adventure nature of the story seemed most at home there.

As we were more closely examining how we'd construct this river journey, we became aware of a very timely reality: Dessie Smith, at ninety-six, was still very much alive and living over near Crystal River. Poole, who originally had been in touch with Dessie when planning her own river excursion, suggested we do whatever we could to capture Dessie on film as soon as possible. Certainly, Dessie's inimitable memories of her river trip would create a very authentic link for our story, providing valuable footage that could be woven into our contemporary river narrative.

Giguere and I made plans to meet with and film Dessie, and as soon as possible, we traveled over to Smith's Wahoo Ranch on the Lake Rousseau stretch of the Withlacoochee River. Dessie was a remarkable woman, every bit as accomplished in her self-sufficient world as Rawlings had been in hers throughout her life. Orphaned at twelve, she not only survived, but she flourished in the rough and raw interior of Florida's scrub and hammocks. Among other things, she became the first licensed female pilot and the first female hunting and fishing guide in Florida. After serving in the military as a first lieutenant with the WAC in World War II, she returned to Florida to build her own hunting and fishing lodge.

As Rawlings's river companion in the "Hyacinth Drift" chapter of *Cross Creek*, Dessie was a strong presence indeed. When Rawlings wrote that she had "lost touch with the Creek" and became depressed, it was Dessie who came to the rescue by suggesting they undertake the epic river journey. "I talked morosely with my friend Dessie," Rawlings wrote. "I do not think she understood my torture because she is simple and direct and completely adjusted to all living. She only knew that a friend was in trouble."

In "Hyacinth Drift," Rawlings hints that her "trouble" had to do with a man. As the chapter concludes with the women completing their adventurous trip and returning to Cross Creek via the Ocklawaha, Rawlings expresses gratitude for her newly earned perspective: "When the dry ground was under us, the world no longer fluid, I found a forgotten loveliness in all the things having nothing to do with men. . . . Because I had known intimately a river, the earth pulsed under me."

That was the sort of eloquent wisdom I had always loved in Rawlings's writing. In this case, though, it needed to be interpreted with real facts. It was now a matter of record that Marjorie's marriage had been breaking up then and that her college sweetheart Charles Rawlings was leaving—or had left—the Creek. "Losing touch with the Creek" was not merely a writer's construct, but a profound event in Rawlings's life. It was an event that, thanks to the chance for a river adventure, provided context. Learning to immerse herself in the wild, liquid nature of Florida helped the formally educated "Yankee" author to more fully trust her senses as well as the vernacular of her newly adopted Cracker world.

When we arrived at the Wahoo Ranch, Dessie and her caretaker graciously welcomed us with a bounty of food and drink, and we sat around an oversized dinner table made of a large, polished slab of southern red cedar and got to know each other a bit. We figured the most appropriate way to set up the video interview with Dessie was to get as close as we could to the water. So soon we were out on a dock on her property on the shore of the Withlacoochee.

As we prepared to shoot an interview with Dessie in a chair on the dock, Giguere realized that the dock railings obscured the natural background of water and cypress. A much higher stool was located and brought to the dock in order to raise Dessie above the obstruction. Dessie was stiff with age and unable to mount the higher stool, so I bent and put both my arms around her and, as gently as I could, lifted her to the higher platform of the stool. When I released her, she smiled broadly and said, "Ummm-ummh . . . it's been a long time since I had a man around me like that!"

I was both humored and touched by that, impressed with the endearing spirit of this woman who throughout her life had walked a fine line between being a character in a work of literature and a genuine heroine from the rugged Cracker scrub. Indeed, when Marjorie and her husband Charles first moved here, there were barely 1.3 million people in Florida, and the great majority lived along the coast. At the time, Florida was one of our country's most sparsely settled states.

Then the camera rolled, and Dessie talked about the woman she knew as "Marj." When the young Rawlings couple first settled into the Cross Creek farm home with its seventy-two acres of citrus in 1928, they had counted on the grove providing them with an income while Charles wrote his boating articles for outdoor magazines and Marj wrote her poetry and short stories. But the farm had been neglected for several years, said Dessie, and the newcomers—with little experience living off the land in Florida—"were just not going to make it."

Dessie made it a point to befriend them and showed Marj how to hunt and fish and otherwise make a subsistence living as others did at the Creek. Marj loved to cook and entertain, sharing culinary feasts that relied on fresh garden vegetables, farm animals, wild game, and fish. And then the Rawlingses' marriage fell apart.

Dessie knew of the split and saw how it affected her friend's state of mind. As a woman of action, Dessie figured a good adventure would be the salve Marj needed to get beyond the moment. On camera, Dessie explained that she suggested the St. Johns River trip to Marj after an evening of "sitting around and drinking some of Leonard [Fiddia's] good 'shine.' He aged it and it was almost like bonded whiskey."

"We had a couple . . . three of those, and we're talking about fishing. So I said, 'Marj, I've had a yen to go out on the St. Johns from its head to where it turns off there to the Ocklawaha. How about it? Would you like to do that?'"

Marj thought that was a great idea—but then changed her mind in the cold sober light of the morning. "I wouldn't let her back out," says Dessie.

Using a Dutch oven, Marj would handle the cooking chores—"by then, I knew she was a good cook"—and Dessie would drive the boat, fishing or hunting for food when needed.

While the southern edge of Puzzle Lake where the women would launch their wooden johnboat wasn't exactly the headwaters, a two-year drought had made much of the marshy upper river south of there nearly impassable, clogging it with shoals and vegetation. Although Marj studied the USGS maps of the river she brought along, both women soon realized a map wasn't up to the challenge of keeping track of a natural channel that, at Puzzle Lake, was a subtle, shape-shifting contour through a wet and shallow prairie maze.

When they first launched, Dessie explained, a breeze across the water riffled it enough to hide the direction of the major downstream current—and the deeper channel that would be below. So she grabbed a handful of soggy debris and released it under the surface to see which way it would flow. Eventually this revealed the natural channel.

When she later sat to chronicle the adventure in words, Marj attributed the navigational clues to following the drift of the buoyant water hyacinths—thus the eventual river story title, "Hyacinth Drift." In practical terms, the metaphor of the drift was valid either way. It helped chronicle a keystone experience in which Rawlings, the cerebral newcomer, was beginning to allow her senses and the immediacy of nature to trump all else. If the author returned from an unknown and mythical place with a treasure that enriched her own life, she would also share her newfound wealth with the world, thus actualizing Campbell's mythical "hero's journey."

In our particular moment in time here on the edge of the Withlacoochee, it was clear that Dessie had an abiding personal connection with the Florida rivers she had hunted and fished most of her life. Before we left, I asked Dessie what she found so fascinating about rivers. She paused for a moment and then looked up. Her answer was almost Zen-like in its truth and simplicity: "Well . . . I just always like to see what's around the corner."

After the filming on the dock was completed, we returned to east central Florida, buoyed by meeting Dessie and exultant with the footage we had gathered. As it all settled in, I more fully appreciated the flesh-and-blood dynamics of the trip in a time and place where females were seldom exalted for their independence. As it did, my respect for both women increased immeasurably. And then, a few months later, Dessie passed away.

Giguere and I continued to work at our "day jobs" of respectively producing and writing while also meeting regularly to plan for the film. We had now entitled the documentary *In Marjorie's Wake: Rediscovering Rawlings, a River and Time.*

It began to strike me how many disciplines were coming to bear on this project. The list included geography, weather, cartography, navigation, subsistence living, culture, and of course literature. To those essential realities, we were also adding a whole new set of postmodern behaviors—from the use of a GPS and advanced archival research to digitally mastered videography, scripting in a computerized format, and eventually, postproduction editing.

Nonetheless, if there was a single one-word concept that still connected this project to the historic journey, it was *vernacular*—trying to understand the luxuriant particulars of nature, of culture, and of place. Certainly, Rawlings was to gradually find intermittent solace in the comfort of nature, and in her deepening relationship with it. "I do not know how one can live without some small place of enchantment to turn to," she once wrote. "There . . . is an affinity between people and places."

More recently, the Pulitzer-winning biologist and author Edward O. Wilson has described this affinity as "biophilia"—an innate connection humans have with nature. "It's a visceral bond," explains Wilson, "that comes from a long and deep immersion as a species in the natural world over the course of hundreds of thousands of years."

Although often described as a "regionalist" writer, Rawlings disdained that label in a talk to the National Council of Teachers of English in 1939. In that presentation, she drew a clear line between literature that comes from an inner reverence, love, and understanding of people and place, and literature that exploits quaint customs or local color and betrays the people it represents. In short, Rawlings exulted in the vernacular, and by doing so, she was able to communicate the more universal truths we all share. As we moved more deeply into our own film research, I made every effort to "revisit" the Cross Creek and the Florida of sixty to seventy years ago. I wanted to understand that connection on a deeper level, to allow myself the reverence that Rawlings, Smith, and others had for the particulars that enriched their place in time.

Although I had seen much of the St. Johns during the earlier research for my book on that river, I had often done so by motorized boat and sometimes with others, including scientists, who helped me better know the boundaries of the river. Before we launched our film, I made it a point to return to the middle St. Johns and its tributaries by kayak, often with friends, to refresh my own sensibilities. More than ever, I was compelled to experience the river rather than to collect data about it.

In this same way, Giguere and I began to travel throughout the basin of the "Hyacinth Drift" journey by ourselves to shoot what is commonly known as "B-roll" in the film industry. B-roll is a compilation of background images that paint a larger and more complex picture of the A-roll interviews and actions that actually take place during the eventual trip. B-roll in this film included underwater images of fish and aquatic plants at the springs where Rawlings would go to crab and fish, as well as terrestrial animals like wildcats and plants like the native magnolia tree and the exotic water hyacinth.

In the Ocala National Forest, we visited the Yearling Trail to film the very real historic landscape Rawlings had written of in her most popular novel, *The Yearling*. There we carefully walked to the bottom of the very real steepsided sinkhole where the fictional Baxter family went to gather their drinking water. A few miles away, we knelt down next to the small sand boils near Silver Glen Spring where the Jody built and played with his flutter-mill. We also saw the cemetery where the extended Reuben Long family was buried. The Longs, among the last homesteaders in the Big Scrub here, had generously shared stories about subsistence living with Rawlings, telling how a young boy in their clan had once adopted a yearling deer. Clearly, the Longs were the archetypes for the Baxter clan of *The Yearling*.

Despite our extensive prefilming research and planning, the replication of the "Hyacinth Drift" adventure still had plenty of room for interpretation and discovery. We were filming a documentary, so it would not be "scripted" until after real-world action, comment, and dialogue were captured on video. We would take great care to shoot every possible aspect of the theme while on the river over the next eight or nine days. As with nonfiction research in the print world, it was far better to compile too much than to leave anything out.

The author John Barth once wrote a farcical novel entitled *The Floating Opera*. Metaphorically, if an audience remained seated on a shore, the scenes of a theater play would gradually float past them on a river in a great aquatic parade—revealing itself in separate chunks, sometimes coherent, sometimes not. Life, Barth reminded us, often happens in the same way.

We would tell our story by drifting our own rafts of narrative down this real-life river, making in-course adjustments now and then for composition, scale, and coherency. In truth, if the original Rawlings team was more representative of Campbell's hero's journey, our replication was likely closer to Barth's *Floating Opera*. Certainly, on our own journey, we hoped for coherency. Regardless, for our film to work, we needed at least three boats: a houseboat to serve as a barracks and chow room for the crew; a smaller, motorized platform-style boat from which to shoot Poole and Chase; and a boat for the two women.

More often than not, I would be aboard the boat with Poole and Chase, usually with videographer Tom Postel. My role was to provide some context on the natural and cultural history of the river for the women, while Postel's was to capture spontaneous dialogue between them and to record what they saw from the boat. While our presence compromised the adventurous quality of the journey, there was simply no other way to electronically chronicle the up-close-and-personal action when the women were under way.

↓ ↓ ↓

Finally, our journey begins. On day one, Poole prepares to launch her center-console motorboat not far from where Rawlings and Smith began their own river trip off Highway 50 near the dilapidated Midway Fish Camp. At the launch site, Chase comes aboard with her bag of gear after a drive down from Jacksonville.

It is a crisp and clear morning in early autumn, a near-perfect day to be on any Florida river. This is, however, one of the most difficult stretches of the St. Johns to navigate, with its shallow, indistinct channels braided through the wet prairie that is Puzzle Lake. And so, with absolutely no intention of doing so, Poole actually does run aground several times in Puzzle Lake—not in imitation of the historic trip, but because the river here still holds many secrets close to its heart.

That night, Poole and Chase camp out by themselves near the mouth of the Econlockhatchee on the downstream side of Puzzle Lake. We film them setting up camp on a picturesque palm hammock in the early twilight and then return to the houseboat several miles away.

And so the excursion will gradually unfold, a blend of real-world encounters with nature and place studded with some strategically planned prospects.

As the women continue downstream on the north-flowing river and exit the broad Lake Harney, Poole lets Chase take the helm—and Chase promptly comes within a few feet of running into a channel marker at high speed. Later, as they prepare to set up camp along the wild shore of a beach-hammock known as "Brickyard Slough" north of Harney, the women run across some airboating bow-hunters. We chat with them on camera, and then one unexpectedly takes Chase for a ride in his airboat, an event spontaneous enough that it escapes being captured on film. The airboaters return in the evening to show the women a young yearling deer they killed, and the crew is rousted from the nearby houseboat to record the event.

As we continue the journey, we make sure to allow enough time for the river and its singular nature to emerge as a character. This allows our modern sojourners the opportunity to honestly express their feelings about it, to compare what they see and feel with what Rawlings had chronicled.

At Lake Monroe, the women make a point to stop at the marina on the south shore at Sanford since one of the most memorable moments of the original story unfolded here. Historically, the purpose of the stop was simply to refuel. But the spontaneity of that moment took on near-mythic qualities. This was the event in which a rich yachtie offered to help Rawlings and Smith refuel by dispatching his limousine to a gas station. But his "pink petticoats" wife intervened, as she needed the limo to go to church. Rawlings and Smith were refueled—but only after the church obligation was met.

Although we would sprinkle select video moments with Dessie throughout the film, this was the one in which she would retell the entire story herself, explaining how when they finally cast off, the affluent yachtie stood and waved until their boat was out of sight. In the postproduction editing, we switch from the real-life moment of Poole and Chase leaning against a railing in front of a large yacht to our earlier video take of Dessie expressing her feelings to Marj about the encounter: "I bet that rich son of a bitch wishes he were going with us." And then she laughed a hearty, good-natured laugh.

The filming continues in this manner, with a blend of natural happenstance intermingled with a few "scheduled" stops to illustrate relevant aspects of nature, history, and art. Near the mouth of the tributary of the

Wekiva, we stop and meet briefly with Fred Hitt, a retired judge who authored *Wekiva Winter*, a compelling book of historical fiction about the Native Americans who lived along the river during the time of early European contact.

Downstream from there, we next stop at Blue Spring State Park, the natural manatee overwintering sanctuary. On camera, Poole points out that the eighteenth-century naturalist and artist William Bartram had chronicled his own visit here in the 1770s. Indeed, the naturalist expressed deep awe over the mystical Florida springs after visits to Blue and Salt. Those descriptions later inspired the Romantic poet Samuel Taylor Coleridge to write "Kubla Khan."

Our stop at Blue also gives us a chance to examine how art can be influenced by nature in many ways. In considering this, I had earlier contacted the noted Jacksonville landscape artist Jim Draper to ask him to meet us at Blue. The point was for Draper and Chase to organically chat about how the river and its springs have the capacity to inspire. During the talk, Draper describes the essential role of the artist as a "guide" who takes images of nature to the larger community, painlessly introducing people to the aesthetics and encouraging them to appreciate nature firsthand.

While he was waiting for our flotilla to arrive, Draper sketched the mouth of Blue Spring where it flows into the St. Johns. Later he fleshed out the sketch, expanding it into a large painting. That art was later used as the cover image for an album of original songs that Chase composed and sang to express her feelings about the river journey. Like the film, the captivating album was entitled *In Marjorie's Wake*; some of the music was even used to score the film. This was, the best I could figure, a working example of life imitating art imitating life—compounded several times.

After the women navigate their way into the enormous Lake George, they head for the home of attorney Bill Jeter and Deanne Clark on Drayton Island in the northwest corner of the lake. Jeter, then president of the Marjorie Kinnan Rawlings Society, would have a chance to chat about the author's work—and to explain how he was living smack in the middle of the geography Rawlings once used to ground her stories in the realities of Florida's landscape.

The overnight stop on Drayton also gave us a chance to create a dinner party in the very best spirit of Rawlings, who had elevated the act of cooking for her friends into a celebration of goodwill and abundance. As UCF

Professor Anna Lillios points out in the *Marjorie Kinnan Rawlings Journal of Florida Literature*, Rawlings explained her own affinity for selecting and preparing food in *Cross Creek Cookery*. In that book, says Lillios, "Rawlings affirms [the] notion that food is a means of reaching the spirit." Rawlings had written that people are "hungry for food and drink—not so much for the mouth as for the mind, not for the stomach, but for the spirit."

The scholar Carolyn Jones explored that notion even more closely in her *Journal* essay "Nature, Spirituality and Homemaking in Marjorie Kinnan Rawlings' Cross Creek." Jones claims: "Cooking and hospitality become metaphors for spirituality and are moments of self-expression. . . . The memory of food shared and loved reveals the ritual dimension of cooking: that cooking is understanding proportion and creating order."

We wanted to acknowledge that insight as much as possible. And so, within that context, Poole's friend and original companion on her river trip, Heather McPherson, had spent most of the day at Jeter's house cooking an elaborate dinner using recipes from *Cross Creek Cookery*. As a journalist, McPherson had evolved into a food writer and was well known in the region for her own culinary art.

That night, we feast on all that McPherson could find that was local—just as it had been in the kitchen of Cross Creek: blue crab, gator, hearts of palms, and much more. Jeter supplies the dinner party with fine imported wine. Local island friends, such as the writer Herb Hiller and the artist Mary Lee Adler, attend, as does Equinox board member Teri Sopp from Jacksonville. My friend Michelle Thatcher, who helped during the earlier river scouting, drives up to join us from Altamonte Springs. Jeter toasts the evening, and in particular, "Mrs. Rawlings," who would have surely appreciated the ineffable, life-affirming links between the particulars of people and food and place.

In an essay about the event, I later write: "[Rawlings's] infectious laughter would have joined with our own, a river celebration awash in a fusion of art, nature, literature, and time. . . . I sip on a glass of wine and think of others who have been on this island before our arrival, and if the earth spins favorably, will be on it long after we leave."

"And now, later in the evening on the verandah with the warm light of the house glowing from one side and the pitch-black [of Lake George] consuming the other, I think of us all as tiny life shards caught in the slow but inextricable resin-drip of time. Part of the moment surges on. But part of the moment also remains, captured forever in the golden memory light like an insect in amber—the kingfisher's cry, the mythic river celebration of life, friends physically vanished but never fully gone."

The next day, Poole and Chase visit nearby Salt Springs where Chase snorkels in the run and around the limestone vents. Salt also gives us a chance to remember Rawlings's penchant for coming here to catch blue crabs for her table, and to use a wonderful archival photo of the author jigging a blue crab here from a small wooden boat.

Then we head out of Lake George downstream to the mouth of the Ocklawaha. Earlier we had been given a box with Dessie Smith's ashes, and there at the river mouth in a moment of poignancy that could never be scripted, Poole gently releases them to the river's flow. As Dessie's ashes drift off, preparing to round the next corner, Chase—without her guitar or any enhancement—sings "Amazing Grace."

We follow this ancient tributary upstream until it abruptly ends at the Rodman Dam, the reservoir physically preventing us from completing the historic trip route, closer to Cross Creek. We had known the Rodman would conclude the water portion of the trip, and so we load up the boats and return home, planning to drive back to Cross Creek by car in another week.

As explained by Rawlings, the Creek itself is the "flowing of Lochloosa Lake into Orange Lake." Orange Lake is connected by its own outflow to the Ocklawaha. Cross Creek is an actual creek, of course, but it is also the name of the settlement that was once sparsely clustered around it. After we arrive, we unpack our gear and film Marjorie's old farm, now memorialized as the Marjorie Kinnan Rawlings Historic State Park.

We chat on camera with some of the rangers dressed in period costume about the popularity of the site. We learn that the steady but modest flow of literary pilgrims to Cross Creek grew exponentially after the release of the feature film *Cross Creek* with Mary Steenburgen, Peter Coyote, Rip Torn, and others in 1983. The film itself was a ménage of the novels *Cross Creek* and *The Yearling*, intermixed and retold with a good dose of creativity. As visitation to the site has increased, so has the settlement around it. We visit the garden, the rebuilt barn, the tenant house. Poole and Chase sit together on the back porch of the main house and reminisce about the journey and what it meant to them.

From the farm, we have one last stop, but it is a significant one. It is a visit to the home of J. T. (Jake) Glisson. Jake's family were the closest neighbors to Rawlings when she lived at the Creek. As an adult, Glisson wrote *The Creek* in 1993, an engaging memoir about his childhood experiences and his memories of the famous author as a real person.

Except for a brief stint at art school as a young man, Glisson has lived in the Cross Creek area all his life, and he now lives on the far shore of Orange Lake only four-and-a-half miles from where he grew up. Glisson and his wife greet us graciously, and we spend much of the afternoon talking with him about his memories of Rawlings and the Creek. Glisson credits the visit of artist N. C. Wyeth at the Creek when he was eleven as a pivotal moment that led to his own career as an illustrator. The logic, says Jake, was simple. He saw an artist working in real life, and that was more inspirational to him than any intellectual or aesthetic conceit could ever be.

We spend most of our time with Jake out by the fence at the back of his property overlooking Orange Lake. Jake is generous in his remembering, helping us to revisit a moment in time that, in his heart, still endures. As others have written, Rawlings herself had always yearned for a young son, a yearning that in some way was satisfied in print by Jody Baxter and in real life by Glisson and others. Certainly, Jake's boyhood delight in building "flutter-mills" at the Creek was transferred almost intact to Jody Baxter.

Perceptively, Jake explains there are actually "four Cross Creeks." First, he describes the "real Cross Creek" that was far off the grid of both electricity and socialization, an iconoclastic place of hardscrabble, subsistence fishers and hunters, many of whom did whatever they could to survive—legal or not—by catching, trapping, or shooting fish, frogs, and alligators. A second Creek was created by Rawlings with her own "eloquent" perspective on it. A third Creek was born with the romanticizing of the successful *Cross Creek* feature film in 1983. And a fourth Creek exists that's a fusion of the literary book and the dramatized movie. That one is mostly realized by newcomers who now live here in "air-conditioned houses with modern appliances while they try to create a link with a mythological time that no longer exists."

We say good-bye to the Glissons at the end of a long day and finally shut down the A-roll portion of the filming. That night we stay in little cottages near the Yearling Restaurant, the actual Creek itself flowing away into the darkness, only yards away.

After returning to our respective homes, Giguere and I travel together one last time for a day of B-roll filming. This trip takes us up to the Smathers Library's Special Collection at the University of Florida in Gainesville. I had earlier contacted the archivist Flo Turcotte to explain our mission. By the time we arrived, boxes of photos, old letters, original manuscripts, and even home movies of Rawlings were waiting for us. Giguere and I both put on white cotton gloves so as to not inflict ourselves any more than necessary on the organic shards of Rawlings's life. Then he set up the camera on a tripod, and I began gently sifting through the boxes to find graphic archival materials to weave into the film.

At the bottom of one box, I find an astonishing 1938 map of the Ocala National Forest in which Rawlings had scribbled handwritten notes to identify the real places she had fictionalized in *The Yearling*. The map was used in the 1940s to guide the visiting Hollywood film crew shooting *The Yearling*, starring Gary Cooper as Pa Baxter and Claude Jarman Jr. as Jody.

And then I held the original typewritten pages of *The Yearling* and *Cross Creek*, letting my fingers lightly retrace the Courier type and penciled-in editing changes Rawlings herself once made. The experience moved me, to be sure. It was as if the yellowed pages in my hand were far more than processed wooden fragments—for that moment, they became images capturing that ephemeral moment when information passes between the human heart and the human mind and is thrust out by the spirit into the tangible world.

The experience seemed almost ethereal, like capturing the flash of a moment when a spring first bursts forth from the limestone in a flash of water and magic and light. Surely the moment of artistic human satori, of creative realization, is no less than that. It is simply much better at pretending to be unseen.

Finally, I sit to write the script, carefully screening more than twenty hours of high-definition video, excerpting real dialogue and comments, and writing a voice-over narration to fill in the blanks—to cue the audience to the story shards our Floating Opera may have missed.

When I turn it over to Giguere, he edits the A- and B-roll footage (including archival images) to match the scripted story, and then integrates music into the final production, including some that Jen Chase wrote after the trip. An extended "rough copy" of the film is first created, and then that's distilled down to the final ninety-minute documentary. The completed film premiered at an upscale art theater in central Florida known for showing thoughtful foreign and indie films. Afterward, it was released for national PBS broadcast for two years via the presenting station, Florida PBS affiliate WPBT of Miami.

Not long after *In Marjorie's Wake* completed its two-year broadcast run on national PBS stations from New York to Chicago and San Francisco, I received a telephone call. It was from the adult son of Claude Jarman Jr., the young actor who had played Jody so well he was awarded a special child's Oscar for his performance. Jarman's son had seen references to our documentary and read portions of my essays in which I describe the historic landscape at the Creek and in the Ocala National Forest.

The retired actor, now in his early seventies, was visiting his adult son from California. They were in Florida at this moment, and the man who had once been Jody Baxter wanted to revisit the places where *The Yearling* had once been shot. It would be the first time since that film was made that he had returned to those sites. I described some of the real places—Cross Creek, the sinkhole, the spring in the "Big Scrub," and more.

After the phone call, I thought to myself once more about the gestalt of the stories Marjorie Kinnan Rawlings had told, thought about my own time burrowing inside the true nature of Florida, and of the peace it has given me. I thought, too, about Joseph Campbell's mythical hero, and how all of us, if we're lucky, might have a chance to explore the unknown at least once in our lifetime, and then to return with a treasure to share with the world. Despite the re-created character of our story, maybe a few shards of higher wisdom would be revealed—maybe our film could, every now and again, be realized as more of a Hero's Journey and less of a Floating Opera.

And because this is Florida, and life sometimes is oddly theatrical, I also thought of the grand irony in how the "Old Jody" had just indirectly called me to ask where the "Young Jody" had once been.

I wished Dessie could have been here for that one. We would have a great hearty laugh, maybe a jolt of Leonard's good shine. And then we would have gone out on the river to see what's around the next corner.

17 Nurse Sharks in Heat
Make an Awful Lot of Noise

I am in a sea kayak on this oven-hot Florida summer day, strok-
ing away from naturalist Bill Keogh's home on the lee shore of
Big Pine Key. The clear and shallow flats here in the backcountry
stretch to the horizon, randomly interrupted now and then by a
few low-slung mangrove islands with names like Porpoise and
No Name, Little Pine and Water. We are moving across water as

*The naturalist and photographer Bill Keogh takes photos of nurse sharks
mating in the shallows off the Keys from a step ladder that he put on top of
the roof of a small houseboat we used when I was there.*

clear as air, atop schools of tiny 'cuda and solitary rays, beyond a half-grown sea turtle, and a single giant tarpon who remains motionless just above the manatee grass on the bottom. Across the corrugated waters of Spanish Channel we go, aiming for the shark dorsals we see slicing the shallows in the distance like angry brown crescents.

The fins represent male and female nurse sharks—seven- and eight-footers—who have moved in from the windward reef to these knee-deep shallows to engage in a life-affirming behavior. That behavior is sex, and it provides a rare animated glimpse of an otherwise docile, bottom-dwelling elasmobranch that—except for this brief event—hardly ever seems to break a sweat.

But in the throes of reproductive frenzy, these critters will thrash and writhe, twist and flail. Male claspers will go into female uterine horns. The males, holding onto the female's pectorals for dear life, will leave bite marks and white scars behind. Keogh, who has witnessed these events over the last two years, says that on a calm day he can actually hear the males sucking air in great gulps as they try to latch more securely onto the female's fins. "Nurse sharks in heat," says Keogh, "make an awful lot of noise."

They also get documentaries made about them, most notably one in which the nurse shark expert Jeffrey C. Carrier of Michigan's Albion College traveled to flats here and near the westerly Marquesas to witness the spectacle. Carrier, who has been studying the mating behavior of nurse sharks (*Ginglymostoma cirratum*) in the wild since 1992, observed 165 "mating events" between then and when he coauthored (with Harold L. Pratt Jr.) an article about it for *National Geographic* in May 1995.

Given the relative accessibility of the nurse sharks, it's remarkable that so little was known about the critter's courting and mating behavior at the time. From Carrier's study, the world learned "less than 10 percent of the mating attempts end in successful copulation" because the females often flee to shallow water to escape. As Carrier observed, "In the end, only the most aggressive and persistent males are successful."

Keogh, who helped guide Carrier on one of his expeditions here, regards the great, vast flats and the biological stew that simmers atop them with a stoic sort of curiosity. In other visits at this time of the year, he has watched as five nurse males "trained" along behind a female, seen the water explode in a mating frenzy of fins and tails, found massive females resting in a few feet of water, gill covers undulating to circulate water like the metronomic tongue of a panting dog. This self-inhalation is an odd but valuable function of the species, a gift that distinguishes the nurse from its pelagic brethren that must constantly swim to bring in water and oxygen.

"They come up here to pup, and a week or so later, they mate," says Keogh, who is on or under the water almost every day, shooting photographs or just being there, watching the quiet drama of the sea unfold. "Whoever would have thought a nurse shark could get so excited?"

Indeed, nurse sharks may be the Rodney Dangerfield of their breed. Unlike the popular image of a fearsome predator circling through the water in angry scythe-like arcs, the nurse shark spends a great deal of its day simply napping on the bottom. At night, it cruises the dark sea, using the two Fu-Manchu barbels hanging from each side of its upper lip as sensory organs to locate prey. On the prowl, it gobbles small sleeping fish or pushes its rubbery mouth into crevices to inhale sea urchins, crabs, and lobster. The nurse shark's strong, bellows-like pharynx even allows it—when so inclined—to literally suck a queen conch right out of its shell.

The nurse is a magnificent lesson in evolution, sharing a 400-million-year-old common ancestor with other contemporary sharks. In the meanwhile, the nurse has evolved to fill a specialized niche. I can almost imagine the reasoning: let's see, the aerodynamic guys with the sharp teeth cruise above, so I think I'll lay low, learn to undulate my gill covers and slurp with some finesse.

In the unlikely event that you ever get a good glimpse of the underside of the nurse shark's head—instead of the classic downturned Cuisinarting mouth—you'll see what looks for all the world like a catfish with a sloppy Claymation sort of grimace. It's an expression it shares with its carpet shark relative, the Pacific woobegong. Teeth are present, but they are small and roundish and hidden behind the lips, great tools for gripping and grinding.

If this animal is normally docile and slow, it is not defenseless. When unknowing divers and snorkelers reach down to jerk the nurse shark's tail to get it to perform in a Disneyesque manner, its reaction can be unpredictable. Sometimes it swims away. Sometimes it turns and bites the bejesus out of its provocateur. For this reason, the nurse accounts for more shark bites than their higher-profile counterparts.

In one of the most bizarre shark-bites-man tales I've heard, a fourteen-year-old boy was snorkeling on a reef off Marathon when he saw a four-footer lying on the bottom and pulled its tail. Instead of fleeing, the nurse shark turned and latched onto the boy's bare chest, sucking and biting as if it were glomming a giant female pectoral—or trying to suck a conch from a shell. And then, because its teeth were virtually locked into the soft mammal flesh, it was unable to let go. Boy and shark were pulled into a boat and rushed to an emergency room where the hapless elasmobranch was surgically removed.

Although they average from five to nine feet in length, *Ginglymostoma* may reach fourteen feet. Widely regarded as special to the Caribbean basin, the nurse is also found south to Brazil, west to Africa, and as far up the Atlantic Seaboard as Rhode Island. Since it is not commercially fished, its population is much healthier than its more charismatic counterparts. (Ironically, one of its biggest threats is from rubbernecking motorboaters who harass it when it mates, and for this reason a prime mating territory in the Dry Tortugas is now off-limits to humans.)

Like other sharks, this nurse is also immune to devastating human diseases like cancer. Common sense would tell us it's urgent to try to understand why before we give *Ginglymostoma* an anthropogenic smack upside the head, as we have with other now-imperiled species.

For now, we are left to simply reflect in quiet awe, as I am doing at this moment, out here on the distant flats of the wild backcountry of the Florida Keys, a few miles and light years away from the T-shirt Autobahn of U.S. 1.

Just ahead, I see a distinctively gold-brown dorsal dip and settle to the bottom next to a set of bow-like roots of a red mangrove. The dorsal is attached to an eight-foot female, and she is resting amidst the scuttling horseshoe crabs and the black loggerhead sponge and the Cassiopeia jelly, pale après coital scars on her pecs.

It is a primitive world of her own making, one that predates this human and his flimsy little vessel by millions of years—a real Jurassic Park shaped by the reef and the tide and the ever-comforting sanctuary of the flats, a place where a shark with a gummy smile is happy as a clam to be the low elasmobranch on the totem pole.

18   When Blackbirds Glow Scarlet, Just for Now

It's close to 7:30 p.m. and the Florida sun is preparing to set into the western horizon of the big, wide dilation in the river that we call a lake here in Sanford. For one special moment, it balances like a giant ocher spore atop the water's surface, right where the push of the current drives the water back into a tighter channel, a place it will more or less stay until it reaches the next dilation, some forty or so miles north of here.

The southern shore of the St. Johns River where it dilates out to become Lake Monroe at Sanford. Both sunsets and sunrises take on new meaning here, with the vast surface of the water to help reflect both.

I am walking with Buddy, my sable-and-white sheltie, on a small, artificially made peninsula that juts a couple hundred yards into the southern shore of this river-lake, stout old Washington palms with their spiky fronds rimming the walkway that follows the earthen berm out and back. The cane-pole fishermen are packing up, and the waterfront is given over to a smattering of folks like myself who have come to be absorbed by the moment and the water and the spatial magic that is tirelessly recoloring the world around us at this time of the day.

It's early summer now, and the seasonal tilt of the earth and the cosmos has "moved" the sun so that it now sets far to the north of where it descends in the winter. Since its winter orb puts it down behind the ritzy but nearly vacant six-story waterfront condo on shore nearby, I much prefer its friendlier summer descent into a waterscape enfolded by tree lines to both sides, a fine luminous slab of flat, open river water in between.

As the bottom of the sun touches the horizon, the golden sky becomes just a bit more so. A lone osprey carrying a long trail of Spanish moss and twigs in her beak flies low, drops the larger part of it, and then soars up and around with what is left. Am figuring it's a bit late to be nest building; then again, ospreys do return to the same home every year like bald eagles, constructing it just a bit larger as they do. Am figuring this nest-enhancing business must also come in handy when a dwelling wall somehow comes unhinged and falls away. No problem; just snatch a beak-full of moss and twigs, and the repair is complete, no credit card or cash needed.

As she swoops down and then up again, another osprey approaches, and the movement of the first becomes even more animated. Both soar away together, overhead now, and as they do I notice that when the light of the setting sun hits the finely woven feathers of their white underbellies, they seem to glow as scarlet as a roseate spoonbill.

When I look back to the west, the sun is now almost halfway down into the horizon. It seems to have hastened its descent after it first touched the edge of the earth, as it always does. Regardless of how many times—and in how many faraway places—I experience this, I am still astonished at the way time seems to shift, almost as if the solar equation has been blurred by the encumbrance of gravity. If this were true, it would happen this way over both land and sea. But the canvas of open water never fails to accentuate it, primal elements of vapor and light playing their shrewd cosmic tricks for all us languid, earthbound mammals to see.

As if in gracious response for the coming of night, the sky becomes flooded with large starlings, some in small groups, some by themselves. Higher above, a small flock of white ibis flies in unified formation, determined to be near their roost when darkness finally settles in. The shiny black starlings—some so large they could be ravens—continue their avian quadrilles. And whenever one turns its belly toward me, the sun daubs it with a scarlet glow, just as it did for the ospreys.

This goes on for another few minutes, with the flocking starlings becoming even more energized, as if becoming scarlet has somehow made them imagine they are more than a black, glossy bird suspended, just for now, in the darkening twilight of a Florida river sky.

Finally I ask Buddy if he's ready to go, and he wags his tail and we're off. Before I leave the peninsula, I stop at the place where its concrete bulkhead joins the one that edges the waterfront sidewalk. The river-lake is unseasonably low, nearly seven feet from the top ledge of the bulkhead. Down in the corner is a grassy sandbar stretching out nearly fifty feet into the tea-colored river, one that for right now is occupied by several families of mallards. All except two or three are juveniles, not long out of their soft downy phase, and just a few inches shorter than their mammas. They seem as joyful as the starlings and ospreys as they pick feverishly at the snail shells and small worms and other tiny invertebrates that have washed up on their sandy world this day.

Buddy and I leave the river and walk toward my car parked a few blocks away on a brick street in Sanford's old retro downtown. I have already strapped kayaks to the roof to be ready for tomorrow's early call, when I will paddle out to a favorite spring-fed tributary with a good friend. It will be enlivening and fun, and at times, it will feel even spiritual, because that is what nature can do for both of us.

At a street corner, a young elegant woman sitting at a table outside of a bistro sees Buddy and asks if he's a sheltie, but she knows the answer. In one swift and graceful movement, she is up from her chair and squatting next to him, petting his head and folded ears and remembering her own sheltie from her childhood. His name was Benjie, and she says just petting Buddy brings back memories she can hardly describe. Water seems to fill her eyes, almost as if an emotional barometer has sent up a visual marker of the condition of the human heart.

She is sweetness, and Buddy nuzzles her, glorious to be a young sheltie on a small friendly street of a time-locked riverboat town, wonderfully imperfect Augusta Block bricks spreading out around us, just as they have for others for a century or more.

I prepare to go, and as I do, I look back toward the river for the soaring birds with the rays of sun glowing on their breasts, but they have gone for now. Tomorrow's sky and its sun and its evening river birds will be another chapter, one that builds on all those that have come before.

Back home, I assemble a large bowl of romaine and leftover coq au vin, and then add some chopped celery with a sprinkle of ground sea salt and chopped basil from the garden. I have poured Buddy's own dinner into his bowl, and he scarfs it as if he hasn't been fed for a month.

Afterward I check the housing for my underwater digital camera in preparation for tomorrow's paddle onto a river I hope is still clear. It hasn't rained lately, and I'm figuring the same water level that has kept the big river low will also do the same to the smaller spring-fed tributary nearby. With little available tannic water to seep from the nearly dry swamp, I imagine the mainstem will be clear enough to see the sandy bottom. I clean the housing and immerse it in a large plastic bowl of water to make sure there are no leaks; satisfied, I remove and dry it. I visualize paddling my kayak to a still, clear place and, holding the camera a few inches under the surface, clicking off frames, just to see what might appear on them later.

It is at times an uncertain if gentle truth—blackbirds with surreal roseate chests and young women remembering images and feelings particular to another life, one I will never know, and the anticipation of subtropical morning rivers, with secrets well kept, a rare place to paddle and to explore.

The half-moon, now well up atop the horizon to the east, is glowing as if lit from inside, and I feel a subtle but very real grin taking shape on my face, an instinctive reaction that requires absolutely no intellectual deliberation to make it so. Tomorrow may be different, but I won't know for sure until it happens.

19 Laudonnière Meets the Shrimp Lady

Why Is It So?

Interstate 95 swept me away this weekend, carrying me downstream to Fernandina Beach, just south of Georgia. The reason was the Amelia Island Film Festival, an event where our documentary about Marjorie Kinnan Rawlings would be screened, maybe even discussed.

Jennifer Chase (front left) and the author (front right) during earlier filming of In Marjorie's Wake. *At the Amelia Island film party, we had a chance to chat some about the Timucua language and her plans to write a musical play about the French explorer René Laudonnière, who helped lead early French settlers on the lower St. Johns River. Photo by Mark Howerton.*

It wasn't Cannes or Sundance, or even the Jacksonville Film Fest. But it was their first time out of the chute as a festival, and, after all, I always enjoy myself up on this old island with the delightfully peculiar history. Bob Giguere, the cofounder of the non-profit we set up to do nature films, drove up earlier on Friday for a panel and screening, and I meet him and some others here early Saturday morning.

This weathered coastal town is awash with luxuriant tales—including the odd truth that more flags flew over it at different times than anywhere else in the country. The Florida shrimping industry was born here; in fact, there's still a fleet of raw, working trawlers berthed downtown, something you rarely see anymore along the spruced-up Atlantic coast of Florida. Not far from the trawlers, the Palace Saloon occupies one very authentic corner. It is self-proclaimed as the oldest bar in the state, and it sure looks it.

Once in town, I park near the docks and the old trawlers. It's a superb day here on the edge of the Atlantic, easy salty breeze wafting in off the sea, and the compact Victorian downtown a study in a sort of retro glory. The tide is low now, and I figure when it returns the nearby spartina marsh will flood, the tidal creeks will deepen, and the water-fed landscape will be great for kayaking. I suck in a deep breath of salt air and then go inside a building for a panel on filmmaking.

The panel goes okay, with some non–movie folks there like the mayor of Fernandina, who—befitting a town that has an annual "Pirates' Ball"—wears a real black patch over his bad right eye. We all introduce ourselves, a disparate mix of filmmakers, film students, visitors, and some guy who recites a long list of all of his Emmys. (Bob later calls it the "penis resume.") The one-eyed mayor then describes himself as a "rogue hillbilly," which I really like, and says he recently campaigned with the slogan "Vote for Malcolm: He Has His Eye Out for You."

The panel begins to devolve, and I leave, along with Bob and Teri Sopp, an attorney who's on the board of our filmmaking non-profit. Her big, brown, gentle-spirited dog Ginger follows on a leash. We walk across a grassy lot to another street and the courtyard of the Bodega restaurant and sit outside. It's pleasant here, and we feast on Cuban sandwiches and wraps, a waitress bringing Ginger a plastic bowl of water to slurp from. We talk about Florida's recent tropical storm and what it did to the rivers we used to know. On the way out, Bob notices the brick fountain in the courtyard is full of tadpoles, a little world within a world, and we get a kick out of that.

Once outside, we dawdle a bit, finally headed over to an elegant old school building that, during segregation, once housed black students. Now it functions as a sort of community center, and this weekend, it is where the films in the festival will be screened. There will be three flicks shown here this afternoon, our hour-long documentary and two shorts. One short is *Abigail's Spring*, a love-lost sort of feature story filmed up on a couple of real springs off the Suwannee in north Florida. The other is sort of a short documentary about a guy who's a human cannonball. Both are nicely done and arty in a quirky sort of way. I liked the way the guy flew out of the giant cannon in the one film, and liked Scott and Megan, who convincingly played the couple—also called "Scott" and "Megan"—in the other.

Jen Chase, a good friend from Jacksonville, arrives with her kids and her unpretentious Euro-gypsy cool, which I always enjoy since it's such an antidote to our cautious, watch-where-you-step Western protocol. Jen appeared on camera in our film, which retraced a river journey Rawlings once made on the St. Johns by boat. She's also a songwriter, musician, and teacher who composed a CD's worth of music inspired by her experience on the river.

With the movies over, we all go to a reception for filmmakers at the "Historic Bailey House." It is deep in a district of older homes, across the street from a fine old mansion made entirely of tabby, an archaic style that once mixed local seashell and lime dust and water into a sort of Florida-Victorian concrete. The Bailey House has a gracious wide veranda around it, its railing studded every so often with antique horses from some long-ago carousel. The whole thing has a wonderfully genteel feel to it, as if a time might still exist when Floridians had the time and inclination to savor the peculiar wonders of life instead of frantically rushing through it.

Inside, Teri introduces me to an older woman who is the president of the Florida Women's Shrimping Association. She's wired, finely lined from the sun, and wearing a giant silver belt buckle in the shape of a shrimp—which looks a vaguely like a World Wrestling Federation Championship Belt. I graze on the munchies, freshly steamed shrimp, and salmon meat (molded to look like a salmon), and then run into Scott, the guy who played "Scott" in *Abigail's Spring*.

We chat a while about the festival, and then Scott compliments me on our "Marjorie" film. He's a really congenial fellow, and it occurs to me he's a lot like the "Scott" he played in the short film. On one hand, I find this to be fascinating. But on the other, I'm also surrounded by giant silver shrimp belts and antique carousel ponies and cinematic constructs, and a bit confused about where reality begins and ends. I think of the Cuban author Alejo Carpentier, who once wrote, "The Furniture is growing larger." And of the American songwriter Tom Waits, who composed a song with the line, "The piano has been drinking." I also remind myself that I'm in a town that has a "Pirates Club" created especially to exploit the buccaneer history of the island. As a writer who spends a lot of time sorting through hyperbole, I sometimes am challenged with the shape-shifting illusion of it all.

Clearly, my perceptions are not unique. Indeed, flamboyant mythmaking here in Florida is so powerful that it sometimes takes on a life all its own—one that often trumps what is left of reality. All of which was wonderfully satirized in *Sunshine State*, a film by John Sayles. In it, the actor Mary Steenburgen—distraught over challenges her impending pirate fest faces—delivers the classic Florida line, "People just don't understand how hard it is to create a legend." Which sort of epitomizes what Florida has done for so long. When the "facts" of a story are scarce or suspect, they are simply rearranged for convenience into fairy tales: José Gaspar becomes a real pirate; Ponce de León really searches for a "Fountain of Youth"; and elected officials really do care about growth management.

At the Bailey House, Jen Chase and I sit on the railing of the veranda with our cold drinks and chat about the French Huguenots, who were first in Florida more than five hundred years ago via Laudonnière, Ribault, and the rest. The artist Jacques le Moyne rendered the first images of the Timucua in great detail, giving Europe its first real look at Native Americans. I've always figured the French understood these original Floridians a lot better than the Spanish. Certainly they treated them with far more dignity.

A cool, light breeze moves in from the sea. Jen, who is fluent in several languages, explains an idea she has to do a musical play about the early Florida French-Indian relationships. I tell her about a rare dictionary of the Timucua language that might help, and she seems excited by this. The dictionary contains actual phrases as well, and I explain to Jen that they actually provide more insight into the culture since they evoke the ponderings of those Native Americans. From my own study of that dictionary, I remember one Timucuan phrase in particular that asks a profound question. I pronounce the phrase out loud in Timucua, pause, and then add the translation: *Why is it so?*

We think about that some, and the party ebbs and flows around us. I look for the eye patch–wearing mayor, but no luck. Cicadas hum like static from the live oaks a few yards away. It is the perfect background music for the living montage of humans who are now glowing in the late twilight that washes across the veranda. I wonder about the movie characters who are real, and a festival that glorifies pirates who may or may not be. I again think of the lady with the giant belt buckle in the shape of a saltwater shrimp, and I finally give in, allowing myself to ride the affable current of the moment.

And then the night falls completely, the stars glowing way up overhead like tiny laser dots, and on the veranda railing, I shrug, as if to nudge the very last part of the linear world away. I wonder vaguely when the tide will be high, and where, if I look hard enough, I might find a black eye patch.

Swimming with the Dragons
in the Karst

Eric Hutcheson presses his face against the porthole next to his seat in the Dash 8 twin prop as it edges down over the turquoise waters of the Abacos, aimed for Marsh Harbor. A private landowner here had been slicing out a canal from the surface lime rock so he could create a safe harbor for his boats. During the dredging and excavation, workers nicked off a cave-like tunnel that seemed to wind down deeper into the rock.

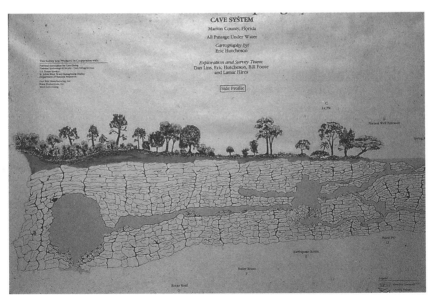

Finely detailed map of Silver Glen Springs in the Ocala National Forest that shows the actual configuration of the spring system inside the limestone under the terrain. Map by Eric Hutcheson.

The landowner knew enough about geology to understand that the soft karst limestone that created many of the cays in the Bahamas—and much of the Antilles—was not dissimilar from that underpinning the Yucatán or Florida. That newly opened cave might lead anywhere and reveal new secrets in the rock. But there were no local divers with the skill to explore its treacherous and winding circuitry as it corkscrewed its way down into the darkness.

Hutcheson was hired to both explore and map this island cave for the first time, and I am along as a writer to watch him do so. Like the ancient cartographers who journeyed to the edge of the earth to chart territory Europeans had never before seen, Hutcheson travels underwater to record the distant reaches of virgin cave systems. In this way, he ventures beyond the known boundaries to those places where ancient mapmakers once marked the end of charted knowledge with fearsome illustrations of monstrous creatures from the underworld. Often they also inscribed a warning in Latin on their maps: *Hic sunt dracones*. Here be dragons.

As the plane dips over Treasure Cay, Hutcheson spots one sinkhole shimmering among the Roquefort-like limestone back in the piney woods of the island. Not far away, in the turquoise swash atop the nearby shallow banks, he sees its geological cousin, a blue hole, which is simply a sink inundated by the sea.

Buoyed by the sightings, and eager to explore the new vein of karst near Man O' War Cay, Hutcheson seems even more animated than usual. At first he wonders if there's a tidal connection to the island cave he'll be mapping. And then his voice rises and his eyes become more intense. He seems like a little kid, enthused about a sort of karst Christmas and the gifts and surprises it might bring. He turns to me and asks: "Wouldn't it be something if there was a flowing spring inside that cave?"

Early the next day, Hutcheson unpacks and spreads out his cave-diving gear on a plastic tarp at the edge of the small harbor. There are two steel tanks bound with the special Y-valve that cave divers use to give each tank two sources of air in case one valve clogs or otherwise fails. Also here are a battery pack and backup lights, a dry caving helmet with clips to mount lights; a pouch full of pencils and sketching materials, two reels of guide line, and plastic underwater writing slates. There are usually two—if not more—of nearly every piece of scuba hardware needed to prepare a well-equipped cave diver with the fall-back redundancy system that's required. When something breaks or jams up far back inside a cave, the diver must rely on his own special training—and wits—to fix or replace it on the spot since surfacing is not an option.

Once everything is found to be in working condition, he then proceeds to either bind it against his body with long rubber strips cut from an inner tube or to dangle it within easy reach from brass clips on a utility belt. The sight of Hutcheson—burdened with heavy cave-diving hardware and preparing to actually descend into a claustrophobic tunnel-like cave—is enough to make a casual recreational diver shudder with the sheer encumbrance of it all.

Finally Hutcheson eases himself down into the water at the edge of the canal. He looks up, grinning from under the battered caving helmet he wears over his wet-suit hood. This is a man who is clearly confident with the notion of pushing the edge of subsurface realities. Then he sinks down beneath the water into an unknown cave, immersing himself so totally in another world that he even takes his exhaled bubbles along.

Once the cave has been tentatively mapped, I'll accompany Eric on a dive so I can more carefully see and understand the full extent of his work here, just as I did on an earlier dive during another project that explored and mapped Silver Springs back in Florida. However, it will take three days and seven solo dives before Hutcheson has enough data to create a working map. Unlike the surface maps left by early cartographers—maps later refined and changed as new discoveries were made this chart will probably be the only one ever made of this isolated little cave system. It is one more intractable piece of the geological puzzle that Hutcheson is helping to unlock inside our earth, one more step to bringing light to a world that for its entire existence has been enveloped by darkness.

Hutcheson spreads out his rough map in the shade of a royal palm tree at the edge of the harbor. A light tropical breeze from the surrounding sea wafts ashore; the emerald-clear waters that help birth it seem to glow from within. The new map shows a pathway into the heart of the island rock, illustrating a labyrinthine alley into territory that just a few days ago was unknown to the rest of the world. Hutcheson looks up, smiling broadly, and taps one finger atop the end of the newly mapped cave sketch. "Dragons be here?" he asks.

↓ ↓ ↓

While caves exist all over the world, the dry ones get the most attention for obvious reasons. In the United States, dry caves and caverns are more widely known because they have been more accessible for centuries. But it wasn't until advanced cave-diving gear and methods were developed later in the twentieth century that some underwater cave systems in Florida and the carbonate islands of the tropics were explored at all.

Eric's finely detailed maps use side-profile perspectives and even simulate three-dimensional formations to help give scientists a starting point from which they can begin to evaluate real-world considerations—like groundwater flow, potential for sinkhole development, drinking-water supply, and even global warming. "Eric has access to a world that few scientists will ever see in their lifetimes," one geologist told me not long after I met Hutcheson.

For his part, Hutcheson thinks the exploration and the illustrative maps from it are exciting, informative—and a lot of fun. "That's why I take these [mapping] jobs," says Hutcheson, who augments his envelope-pushing cartography with a more domestic income from customized plaster work at his home base back in Ocala, Florida. "I want to cover my expenses and support my family, sure. But I want to enjoy what I'm doing."

The cave-diving pioneer and author Sheck Exley was one of the first to sketch such systems with detailed overhead views of the passages he explored in the rich limestone terrain of northern Florida in the 1960s. In the next generation, the veteran cave explorer Wes Skiles expanded that perspective to include side profiles, vivid cross sections that offered cutaway views not unlike those of a tabletop ant farm. Hutcheson, who admits he's more grounded in art than in science, has refined the ant-farm perspective by simulating the three-dimensional world of the underwater cave.

As analogies go, the ant-farm model isn't a bad one for these caves since most of the rocky conduits wind back for thousands of feet below the surface crust, appearing and then disappearing inside the soft limestone karst. Think of Hutcheson, then, as the alpha ant, squirming about inside water-filled conduits of soft rock until he can squirm no farther. Unlike the ant, though, he gets to leave the "farm," bringing back detailed sketches of just how far these labyrinths stretch, providing a glimpse of a netherworld as foreign to the average human as the New World must have been to the early voyagers.

Cave diving is challenging business, even for the most practiced. Since a cave creates the very real restriction of an "overhead environment," the techniques for diving inside of them are far more complex than open-water diving. Surprisingly, many of the actual fatalities in caves come not from trained cave divers, but from experienced open-water divers—even instructors—who simply aren't up to speed on the need for the refined gear and methodology designed especially for "penetrations" into the rocky darkness of our earth.

Oddly enough, most of the caves in Florida are not geographically remote—at least on the surface. In some cases, they may be only blocks away from civilization or, in a few instances, right beneath it. One of Hutcheson's mapping projects has been King Springs, which is smack in the middle of the heavily used manatee sanctuary of Kings Bay in Crystal River on the Gulf coast. And, of course, there is Silver Springs, the iconic Florida tourist spring that pumps millions of gallons of water a day out of labyrinthine limestone fissures while glass-bottomed boatloads of visitors float overhead in the main spring pool.

Nonetheless, there are lots of remote and isolated systems overseas, like Nohoch Nah Chich in the wilderness of Mexico's Yucatán, that do require extra physical effort just to reach the dive site. "It's a two-kilometer hike with gear over some very serious karst terrain," says Hutcheson, referring to that shallow but extensive cave system linked by a series of clear sinkholes, a place imbued with sacramental powers by the ancient Maya.

Although not rediscovered in our modern time until 1988 by the dive outfitter Mike Madden, teams of veteran cave divers already had laid down line in fifty thousand feet of passageway in Nohoch by the time Hutcheson first arrived to map the system with an expedition back in the 1990s. There, the divers descended in small teams to help with measurements and provide other backup support for the cartography, spending hours in water-filled tunnels and caverns studded with stalactites, flow stone, and other ornate limestone formations created when the cave system was dry some fifteen thousand years ago. In many cases, they used hand-held underwater electric scooters to cover more territory than they could under their own power.

"It was so shallow," remembers Hutcheson, "I would scooter four thousand to five thousand feet back and wouldn't use more than one-sixth of my air." The shallow depths allowed the mapmaker to spend from three to four hours by himself in the deepest recesses of Nohoch, resting on a bottom rock and sketching what he saw on plastic slates.

Before it was all over, Hutcheson had produced 140 separate sketches during some forty dives. Back at his studio in Ocala, he consolidated the data and transformed it into a detailed 9' × 3' map that traced thirteen miles of known passageway, helping to establish Nohoch as the world's longest underwater cave system.

In addition to providing the first real graphic data for scientists, the maps also help capture a moment in time before the caves are forever altered by man. "Some caves in the Yucatán are already destroyed by development," says Hutcheson, noting that once-pristine caves near Playa del Carmen have turned milky from surface disruption and runoff.

Of all of Hutcheson's mapping projects, Silver Glen Springs in the Ocala National Forest of northern Florida exuded a mystique that went far beyond the prosaic limits of science. Silver Glen is one of a number of "first-magnitude" springs in Florida that pump out more than 64 million gallons of water from the aquifer every day. Aesthetically, it is the classic artesian Florida spring, bubbling up gin-clear from inside a basin of limestone, tucked away in a bucolic forest of live oak draped in Spanish moss.

But since Silver Glen had been privately owned for years, it had been off-limits to all scuba diving. The five hundred acres surrounding the spring had been used as a rental campground until 1988, when it was bought by the local water-management district and then turned over to the forestry service. Although it remained off-limits to casual sport divers, one of the first priorities of the U.S. Forest Service was to bring in a team of veteran cave divers to survey and map the system, as well as to help catalogue artifacts that had gone virtually untouched in the dark caves.

Hutcheson and veteran cave divers Dan Lins, Bill Foote, and Tom Morris spent nearly seven months exploring and mapping the underworld there. In addition to capturing vital data about the configuration of the caves for the maps, they also uncovered and identified prehistoric animal bones, Native American pottery, and living specimens of albino crayfish. Most spring caves that have been explored in Florida routinely yield endemic freshwater shrimp and crustaceans that are not only special to that cave system but are also new to science. When new cave-dwelling specimens are found, they are shipped to the Smithsonian Institution, where specialists figure out the taxonomy for each, and then conjure new names to fully describe the actual genus and species. It's a testament to how little this aquatic, troglodytic life was known that one researcher discovered that some cave crayfish can live to be two hundred years old.

While the scientific data would be important, the exploring and mapping of the spring also would complete the final chapter of a poetic saga that began more than two hundred years ago. That's because Silver Glen is in the spring-cave belt of the northern St. Johns River visited by the naturalist William Bartram in the 1770s. Bartram, one of the first to describe the springs in the junglelike interior of Florida, was enthralled with the beauty and mystery he encountered. In one description of a nearby spring, Bartram wrote of an "enchanting and amazing crystal fountain, which incessantly threw up, from dark, rocky caverns below, tons of water every minute."

Not surprisingly, it was Hutcheson's strong connection to his own Florida roots—and to his grandfather who made a living with his architectural landscapes of a preurbanized south Florida—that inspired his mission underground as much as anything else.

Although he remembers watching his grandfather sketch as a small boy, he had forgotten about the drawings until years later when he rediscovered them in an old box in the attic after his grandfather had passed away. When Hutcheson unrolled the sketches, he saw the exquisite detail that marked each palm tree, each limestone boulder, each sea grape bush. The drawings captured a natural Miami of the 1920s and 1930s, a bygone era recorded in his grandfather's hand, and then delivered through the years to a grown-up boy still curious about another time.

"I was sort of drifting in life then myself," says Hutcheson. "And those drawings just made it all click for me because that's where I'd grown up. I used to dive there in the lime rock [borrow] pits. I used to play back on vacant land that looked like the Everglades."

As a result, his grandfather's concern for topside detail helped Hutcheson determine what was to be so important to his own underwater maps. Today as he re-creates the individual character of each cave, he looks for a singular design in the scalloped walls, the uniqueness of portals chiseled by a prehistoric water flow, and the special shape of limestone boulders accrued from dead coral and time. "Underwater, I'll sit on a rock and draw everything I see in the cave," says Hutcheson.

Just as his grandfather once captured the time-stuck landscape of a far different era on the surface, Hutcheson is doing the same in the mysterious water-filled conduits under the surface. At the same time, the politically driven, haphazard growth that routinely scars the natural landscape of Florida is now threatening the health of the Floridan Aquifer that fuels the springs. Some major springs are losing magnitude, while a few are actually drying up. Unless a strong movement toward sustainability in Florida prevails, the ultimate future for these magical water-filled fantasy worlds is understandably grim.

While Hutcheson remains upbeat about using good science to rationally manage and abate impacts on our springs, he's a realist. As such, he knows as well as anyone the potential for a far more grim consequence if current trends continue: "A hundred years from now, I can see my great-grandchildren rolling this stuff out and saying, 'Wow! What the hell was an aquifer, anyway?' And then they'll know how it used to be."

21 Inside the Indian Shore

Treading the Line between Past and Present with Puc Puggy

There are bears in the woods today. I know because I see their tracks in the soft white sugar sand, the sign of an ancient animal on an ancient dune, miles from the sea. It is *Ursus Americanus floridanus*, a subspecies of the black bear that is unique to Florida. I look closely and see that the pads of the feet are big

A tree sends out a bundle of roots as it grips onto the "Indian Shore" as once defined by naturalist William Bartram when he explored the river by boat and the shore by foot.

and full. Except for the claw marks, which cut into the sand, the tracks might almost be cartoonish, as if left by a giant, precious toy bear come to life.

But if black bears are precious—in fact, they're threatened with extinction in Florida—they're not toys. They are big, wild animals that need a lot of landscape to roam. When their territory is fragmented, the animals still lumber across these man-made boundaries, just as they've been doing since long before we started building roads and Golden Arches. At one time, the pre-Columbian Timucua and Mayaca—and later, Seminoles—hunted black bears in this river basin. So did the white settlers who followed. Now, the bears' single-largest cause of death is being whacked by cars.

Bears range for the same reasons we do—for food, comfort, and, when the need arises, a warm body. They especially range at the swampy edges of the St. Johns, on this government-owned land off State Road 46 just west of the Wekiva River, and along the sandy limestone scarps that define the low valley of the river. Forested rivers such as the St. Johns are natural corridors for bears, and they wade its swamps and swim its waters to get where they want to be. As long as they stay on public land, they are safe here.

About a half million acres of land have been set aside as a riverine buffer along much of this historic 310-mile-long river, from its headwaters near Lake Okeechobee to its oceanic confluence east of Jacksonville. Thousands more acres are protected inside state and national forests and state and county parks. Though civilization pushes in on all sides, there is still enough wildness left in the St. Johns basin to accommodate the bears.

Hibernation is coming soon, and although it's not the barren winter coma of northern bears, it is a time when the critters simply slow down, sleeping more and eating less. But today the woods on the trail around me are luxuriant and alive—the oaks have dropped chubby acorns, cinnamon ferns have sent up new fiddleheads, and berries are thick on the saw palmettos. Tasty insects, like walking sticks and grasshoppers, are fat too.

It's the most active time of the year for the black bear: a season to roam in search of a mate, as well as to gorge before kicking back. As if to celebrate the advent of this bruin bacchanal, wildflowers are raging—the bright-purple rods of blazing star, the carnival frill of the passion flower, the cerulean blue of the celestial lily.

Last night it rained, and the tracks I see now are so new they must have been made just a few hours—or perhaps minutes—ago. Scat, which appears in great blue-black piles of berries and nuts on the trail, seems just as fresh. I look closely at the trunks of young longleaf pines for other signs, and soon they appear: bark has been stripped off several trees, as if a bear has stood on its hind legs and reached up as far as it could. On one bare trunk, claw marks have been left behind, the signature of a male marking his turf.

I have been searching for bears for more than twenty years along the St. Johns. Like all searches, it has taken me to places I never intended to go, introducing me to an authentic wilderness where I thought there was none. After all, Florida is an odd, discordant state where most tourists are lured into believing that no reality exists except in contrived theme parks or on replenished faux beaches seen from a patio over pink-umbrella drinks.

Where there is no such contrived development, wet forest and marsh-lands may stretch out for miles. For many newcomers, this lowland biologi-cal treasure often seems a puzzle. It was for me, for a long time. When I first ventured deep into this wild Florida, I did so in the St. Johns River valley because that is where I live. Like other artistically minded souls—includ-ing artists Winslow Homer and John James Audubon, composer Frederick Delius, poet Sidney Lanier, writers Marjorie Kinnan Rawlings and Harriet Beecher Stowe—I was moved enough by the experience to want to memo-rialize it in my own craft. Certainly this north-flowing river has been used longer by Europeans than any other in North America, beginning with a French colony at Fort Caroline near Jacksonville in 1564. It is a river with lots of stories to tell.

When I first explored the St. Johns, I "traveled" with a naturalist guide, one of the best there ever was. His name is William "Billy" Bartram, and in his *Travels*, published in 1791, he convinced me of the magic hidden here. Although Bartram roamed throughout the Southeast during his journeys in the 1760s and 1770s, he seemed infatuated with the St. Johns and its gothic, vine-hung mystique.

During Bartram's era, the St. Johns and its cypress-rimmed, tea-colored waters offered the only sure route into a soggy, predredged peninsula. Dur-ing most of his explorations, Bartram sailed and rowed up and down this "grand and noble San Juan," sleeping on "couches" of Spanish moss under the canopies of massive live oaks and magnolias. His childlike enthusiasm is a fine antidote to modern weariness: "How happily situated is this retired spot of earth!" he wrote after a night on Drayton Island. "What an elysium it is!"

Before the naturalist-artist returned home to Philadelphia, the St. Johns had taken him into a wilderness that not even the fierce conquistadors had been able to fully penetrate. Bartram's charmingly baroque narrative in *Travels* simmers with his guileless affection for the "grand and noble San Juan" and all that lived in and around it.

Although much of Bartram's grand and noble San Juan has changed, a lot still remains. Once the avenue for steamboats and winter resorts, the river lost its allure when railroads and then highways siphoned tourists to the coasts earlier in the twentieth century. Its lack of status helped keep large chunks unpopulated. River valley land was cheap enough so that even tragically underfunded environmental agencies could afford to buy in, protecting vast tracts as a public legacy. As a result, there is ample space to imitate the wanderings of Bartram. And when I have questions, I turn to him as if to a trusted friend.

But there is another reason I am grateful to this Billy Bartram. He was more than just our first American naturalist; he was a gentle Quaker who saw humans as a part of the larger community of nature and not as masters of it. It's not a stretch to say he was our first spiritual naturalist. As such, he left me with the clear idea that God—in whatever form we know him—can be found in the details of wild places. Later, others would absorb *Travels* and be forever influenced by his notion of communing with the wilderness, instead of clear-cutting it.

Bartram wrote lovingly of emerging Ephemera [mayflies] and the coloration of Carolina parakeets, of "tygers" [panthers] and bumblebees and the distinct snorkel-like snout of softshell turtles. And plants, which grew in great profusion in the temperate-tropical habitat mix of the St. Johns, fascinated him. He drew them and collected them and named them. "Perhaps there is not any part of creation," he wrote, "which exhibits a more glorious display of the Almighty hand, than the vegetable world, such a variety of pleasing scenes, ever changing throughout the seasons." The Seminoles called the gentle explorer "Puc Puggy," which means flower hunter.

There were perhaps twelve thousand Florida bears in Bartram's time, and with little demand on the land by humans, they were free to range widely. The Seminoles hunted them for their meat, hide, and fat, which they rendered into grease. Skulls and claws were used in ceremony, because the bears—like the panthers and eagles—were powerful symbols of magic, a link to the wisdom of animal spirits. Today there are some 3,000 left, but those are fragmented into five population "islands" on public land, isolated by a sea of development in between.

My hike this crisp fall morning has taken me squarely inside one of these islands, which stretches along the western edge of the St. Johns. This is the territory Bartram called the "Indian Shore" to distinguish it from British East Florida. It was untamed, more remote, and, unlike terrain east of the river, not yet in the "ownership" of Europeans. Most of the great springs that feed the St. Johns—Wekiwa, Salt, Silver Glen, Alexander, Juniper—flow from the bottom of the western scarp here, winding out to the river in clear veins of ether.

This Indian Shore has kept some of its quiet. As a result, it offers sanctuary to escape the shrillness of "civilized" Florida, a transcendent place where wilderness can still lay itself down on your soul. There's still plenty of opportunity to get wonderfully lost here, room to hunt for wildflowers—and wild bears. There is room enough to be transformed.

Visitors who allow themselves full immersion in the St. Johns have been affected by it for centuries. Few came away without sighting a bear, or at least the residue of one—tracks, scat, great claw-marked slashes on the pines.

Bears are vital to this river basin not just because they are furry throwbacks to another time, but because they are an "umbrella" species that requires thousands of acres over which to roam. If we can keep the bear in the landscape here, we get a virtual Noah's Ark of other animals and plants in the bargain. Bartram's softshell turtles, his passion flower, his grand and noble river might still endure, throwbacks to a more gentle time.

There are tricks to be learned here. Of them all, the most essential is the trick of the quiet, the art of opening freeway-dulled senses to natural enchantment. It's a technique Puc Puggy, reaching gently through time, can still teach us.

22 — A Jungle Tram

The Stirrings of Wildness in the Modern Soul

> There are some who can live without wild things,
> and some who cannot.
>
> Aldo Leopold

By early morning, we're on the low shore of a subtropical river and the four-wheel pickup that brought us here is preparing to drive off down a long tramway that bores like a tunnel through the thick hammock of hardwoods and palms, mosses and vines. It is a trail that stretches away for miles. We thank Amy, the biologist and the driver of the official state DEP vehicle, for her effort in transporting us. And—in an odd, ironic moment—we thank her for leaving us behind.

The dirt road that follows the path of the old logging tram.

Before I get out of the truck, I look one last time through the windshield down the dark, canopied path. At the very end, it seems to glow brightly, creating a classic light-at-the-end-of-the-tunnel effect. I figure it's illuminated by a clearing where the sunlight briefly penetrates the interwoven crown of foliage. "Well, I guess you'll be driving off toward the light," I tell Amy. "And Steve and I will be left mucking about in the darkness." I had meant that as a joke, but no one laughs.

Steve and I are, indeed, planning to walk out through the dark and muted landscape. The strategy is to follow the old tramway that had once delivered squat, muscular iron locomotives and flatcars to the very edge of the river for the sole purpose of retrieving trees logged here—just as other engines did on other rivers throughout Florida.

The historic tram is a berm of earth that rises a few precious feet above the hydric hammock that surrounds us. When the workmen finished logging almost all of the first-growth bald cypress, they pried up the rails and ties and took them away with them, leaving only the earthen berm behind. When I look out to the edge of the river, I see there are still eight or nine weathered, rotting pilings marking the route of a bridge that once carried the tram across to the distant shore.

The forested wetland here is, in the simplest of terms, a primal swamp. Aesthetically, it seems to be a vision lifted nearly intact from the gauzy, baroque art that reimagines the geologically young landscape of the Devonian period, when early plants grew like lush green spores, experimenting with leaves and true roots and seeds. It was an era when the newly terrestrial earth was experimenting with different styles, not unlike the way teenagers continually shift-shape, trying on new behaviors to see what works. In that epoch, mosses and ferns grew into bushes and small trees, insects like dragonflies sported wingspans two feet wide, and mammals were only a glint in the eye of the cosmos.

The engines and flatbed cars that once rode this tram seventy-five years ago did so to haul enormous logs of ancient cypress out of the wild Wekiva swamp, eventually transporting them to the deeper and wider St. Johns River where they would be floated in giant rafts, downstream to Palatka.

We have with us a copy of a map Steve found somewhere in the obscure archives of a library when he was researching a book on the Wekiva. The map was originally drawn by loggers and train men, and it charted where the main rail line ran north for several miles from where we now are, toward

Crows Bluff and what had been the landing of Hawkinsville on the St. Johns. For reasons still unknown to us, that main tramway was known as the "Buffalo Tram." I guess at the origin of the name, figuring it was "Buffalo" simply because the engines on it were bulky and strong and powerful like the animal itself.

Our point in walking out by ourselves today is to explore the eight or nine shorter berms on the map that splay off deeper into the swamp from the main rail. Our rudimentary chart has no scale on it. But in comparison to the length of the Buffalo Tram, each line diverging from the mainstem must be at least a half mile or more in length. I have started calling the shorter lines "spurs," thinking that rails would actually carry the train deeper into the swamp to retrieve the mammoth logs. But Steve reminds me that laying track in the swamp was difficult, time-consuming work. The shorter "spurs" were likely not for rails, but were simply higher ground where mighty cranes powered by the engine's boiler would use a giant iron cable to drag out logged cypress so they could be loaded onto the Buffalo Tram.

That practice was called "skidding," and the cranes and cables were known as "skidders." Some of the ground under the spurs used by the skidders might have been naturally higher land. But I'm figuring that most had been built up by felling and stacking less desirable trees—sabal palms and shrubby or immature wood—atop it and covering it with mud and moss and sand.

Bald cypress, a slow-growing tree known as "eternal wood" for its durability, was logged so thoroughly that virgin cypresses are rare in the basin today. While younger trees do grow here, they are usually survivors that were too small to be worth logging at the time   or, that more recently reseeded naturally when their parent grew to maturity. While I have always admired the fortitude of the working loggers, I realize that the owners of the timber companies went about their business with no regard for sustainability. Once the prize hardwoods were logged, the soggy land was of no more use to them and was cheaply sold as what the author John Rothchild once called "pre-dredged real estate."

The protean jungle around us today seems to commandeer nearly every shade of color within the spectrum of green, as if an artist had mixed blue and yellow and then spilled it across the canvas, rendering nearly everything emerald, jade, virescent. When a stray shaft of sunlight penetrates, the green sometimes seems to glow as if electrified from inside. Even the large pines that grow on slightly higher ground have a patina of shiny green on their thick, flaky bark.

I have read about jungles and people in them from a very early age. Unlike folks who are discouraged by the idea of snakes and hanging vines, the infernal hum of insects and the nearly impenetrable jungle web, I have been enthralled by it. When I am in such places, I am eight years old again, imagining my mother and father and brother and I to be the Swiss Family Robinson—living contentedly in a tree house surrounded by the dim light of the tropical forest, friendly shadows buttressed with enchantment. The joy this imagining still brings to me is immeasurable.

I guess it hasn't been a surprise that, as an adult, I've searched to understand the source of my deep and visceral connection with nature. I sometimes think it may be so powerful that it dwells at a molecular level in the human spirit. The scientist E. O. Wilson writes that "wild nature and human nature are closely interwoven . . . the only way to make complete sense of either is by examining both closely." And, so I do.

Certainly, men and their machinery had worked in this swamp once, creating a sharp Industrial Age clanking of metal upon metal, frightening the deer and panther, bear and turkey deeper into the hammocks. But the signs of their existence have been nearly obliterated by the ever-expanding braid of the jungle. I look around a bit to see if anything is moving in the über-green tableau on both sides of the tram. And then I do what I've been doing ever since I was a kid teetering on the edge of wildness—I forge ahead into it with barely contained excitement, stepping over fallen logs, around holes created by rotted palms, ducking under the ambitious webs of the golden orb spiders, and purposely cracking branches, just to let the vipers know that the clumsy upright walking mammals have, briefly, returned.

Oddly enough, our first—and largest—discovery from the tram era is fewer than one hundred feet from the river itself. It is a huge, rusting metal vehicle once powered by thick metal treads, like a tank. Anything that would hint to its purpose has fallen away or been removed long ago. Most of it is shrouded in vines and moss, the standard-bearers of verdancy. Since it needed no rails, we could only guess it had either been brought here after the track of the tramway had been removed—or perhaps it had even been used to help remove those rails and ties. Maybe it mechanically failed, and at some point was simply left behind to rust and decay, a gradual dissolve into the swamp itself.

We take a few photos of it and then search more closely around it for any relics that might have been related to its existence. Near the actual tram, we find one and then another railway tie lying haphazardly where each had been left. Back atop the tramway we continue to saunter away from the river through the tunnel of green.

Despite the spate of recent rains, the swamp on either side of the tram—although thickly gridded by vines and briars, rotting logs and spindly trees—is spongy, but relatively dry. The more we walk the tram, the more we readjust our senses to the lines on the historic tram map. Topography is relatively easy to read in a swamp; any land to either side that's as high as the actual tramway is likely a historic "spur" used by the skidders. Even a decade in the warm and wet terrarium of such a place can spark lush growth—that is, after all, why biological diversity of both plants and animals spikes here in this basin. So altitude is defined less by foliage than by the earth under it.

When we see the first narrow peninsula of higher ground splay off from the Buffalo Tram, we take it, even though it's heavily colonized with trees and brush. Not surprisingly, plants that benefit from slightly higher ground and drier soil have flourished here, a reality that distinguishes them from everything else that must learn to be seasonally inundated by the river and its swamp. Animals clearly use these spurs to travel the river basin, creating rudimentary trails as they do. Here and there, we see sabal palm fronds that have been chewed by animals, and on a slab of particularly high ground, we spot a large pine with its bark scraped clean by a bear, sap still fresh and flowing at a speed that only the most patient of land tortoises might ever realize.

As we test out each spur along the tram, I notice the sweet little native wildflower known as the wild petunia celebrating itself with its bright-blue petals. The pungent white flowers of the sweet bay magnolia tree are sprinkled throughout from eye level on up. Closer to the floor of the jungle, mosses and ferns and fungi are busy consuming every available space that hasn't already been claimed. It is warm enough so I have already sweated through my T-shirt. The scent of the swamp is piquant, somehow both sweet and sour, an olfactory life force that predates anything else I know. I'm struck by the notion that if I stood still for a few hours, I'd be covered from head to toe with spores of green. All we are missing to complete the time leap back into an earlier geological epoch are giant dragonflies with two-foot wingspans.

Back on the main tram, we approach one spur that is more brightly lit by the sun than the rest. It is tight at first, and then opens expansively to reveal deep, open sloughs on both sides. One of the bogs is covered with floating duckweed while the other is filled with a long, spindly grass, punctuated with the native duck potato in its glorious orchidlike bloom. I wonder if the sloughs are actually deep enough to breech the top of the groundwater reservoir here, just as some of the smaller springs and seeps do deeper in the forest.

We see lots of anoles—including the increasingly rare green-skinned native—hear the call of a giant pileated woodpecker, and once spook a red-shouldered hawk who cries sharply at us. Ivory-billed woodpeckers once flourished back in here too, until the old-growth cypress hollows where they nest vanished. The Timucua, who wove nature into their spiritual world, believed that a barred owl who calls out when disturbed is a harbinger of a coming calamity—a war or a storm—and I am secretly glad we have not disturbed any of them today.

Each spur has a life all its own and at some point either tapers and falls away into the swamp or throws up a wall of foliage so thick it's impossible to penetrate. Just as I am preparing to turn around from one such cul-de-sac, something bright and blue catches my attention on the ground. It is a party balloon—one set loose during a moment of childhood gaiety—that after an extended soar through the sky, slowly leaked its helium and sank here in the deep swamp. I have seen other "dead balloons" like this in the backcountry throughout Florida, and I am always a bit amused by the incongruity of it all.

The brilliant poet Stephen Dunn once wrote a poem in which his neighbor saw a man dressed as a clown at the edge of the woods next to his home. Had the clown been anywhere else, he might have fit in. But at the edge of the woods, the vision was so odd as to be startling. It was, Dunn wrote, "a clown without context." And, while the dead balloon doesn't startle me in the least, its presence back here in the primal, neo-Carboniferous swamp is surely "without context."

Steve picks up the lost balloon, and we continue our exodus down the Buffalo Tram, gathering closer to the juncture we hope will lead off to a modern trail in the Rock Springs Run State Reserve, some miles to the north. As we have traveled, Steve has explained more of the logging history here, a tradition that actually started thousands of years ago when the earliest Native Americans migrated into what we know as Florida. The massive longleaf pines were felled first for giant dugouts by the Timucua and Mayaca, while the harder-to-carve cypresses were used later by the Creeks.

Early European settlers cut trees when they were needed too. But when the Industrial Revolution created machinery to do the chores efficiently and commercially, the pace of logging grew rapidly and the natural grace of sustainability was forgotten. Forests along rivers that were naturally deeper and more accessible elsewhere in the Southeast were the first to be cut. It wasn't until the Wilson Cypress Company bought a mill in Palatka that the tributaries and forests of the St. Johns were no longer seen as the bucolic and sacred woods chronicled by poets like Sidney Lanier but were regarded instead as natural treasury vaults of lumber, measured financially in board feet.

The Wekiva swamp, once so wild it gave Seminoles refuge from marauding federal soldiers, was one of the last to be exploited. Logging machinery was not unleashed on it until 1935. It was as if its ferocious wilderness had saved it. Even today, most who venture into the vast swath of public land preserved around this river system usually stick to the main river and the well-marked trails, just as most do who enter the Everglades. The rest of the subtropical swamp and its animal trails remain largely an enigma, visited now and then by biologists and sportsmen and eccentric, deeply earnest lovers of wildness.

We finally approach the cutoff trail from the tramway that will lead us a few more miles back to where we need to be. As we do, I think again of E. O. Wilson's take on the duality of the human and natural spirits. The experience over the last several hours has offered, as Wilson has wisely observed, a juncture where we can more closely examine "wild nature" and "human nature"—and then revel in the wholeness each gifts to the other.

On one level, the last six hours have been a walk in the primeval woods. On another, they have been a glorious immersion in biology gone riot—pervasive, untamed, a precious shard of the hidden unconscious of nature herself, revealed for just now in a Jungian satori, jade-tinted and wondrous. As I walk away, finally, into the brighter light of the known world, I listen closely for the stirrings of wildness that are still nestling with great joy in my soul.

23 Woodland Park

*Keeping a Promise "Where the
Mound-Builders Lived"*

Long before there was Disney World or Wet 'n Wild in Florida—even before the retro Monkey Jungles and Cypress Gardens—there was Woodland Park.

It was built in a place that was the counterpart to today's Orlando—an interior town on the juncture of major transportation routes. These routes were rivers, and they predated the

A vintage advertisement for Woodland Park nicely illustrates how popular the early water theme park became. Photo courtesy of the Sanford Museum.

modern highway and railroad system that later helped settle the peninsula of Florida. This town in the interior was called Sanford, and it prospered in part by being the last major settlement squarely on the shores of the St. Johns River to be serviced by the luxury paddle-wheel riverboats. It was the route snowbirds rode long before the turnpike and I-95 and airplanes took them to Orlando and Miami and St. Petersburg.

This Sanford was 160 miles from the sea in the buggy, soggy interior of the peninsula. Yet it dreamed of greatness. It called itself "The Gateway to South Florida." As it grew, it became "The City Substantial." It was only natural that this small town with big ambitions should host the archetypical tourist theme park in the state.

This park would be different from most of the early Florida attractions, which involved steamboats transporting tourists to "healing" natural springs. It would incorporate water into its theme, natch, because that's what Florida was all about. But in this case, the water would be manipulated inside a more energetic recreational format. In this way, Woodland Park was the forerunner of the more complex and sophisticated "theme park" attractions that would settle down onto the landscape later in the twentieth century.

The dream began sometime in the early 1880s when a local farmer and entrepreneur named Victor Schmelz bought six acres of woody, swampy land near the shore of Lake Monroe, a few miles downstream from Sanford. It's unclear if he envisioned his tourist attraction from the get-go. But he did see the value of the tons of ancient, bleached shells that comprised massive Native American midden mounds there. After all, the geological sandbar that was Florida didn't have the sort of hard rock resources found back on the continent. So the durable composite in the middens—freshwater snail shells, animal bone, even pottery shards—found its way onto early roads as pavement. It wasn't gravel or brick, but it was surely better than sand.

After mining tons of the shell midden, Schmelz found himself with a large hole in the ground. Perhaps if it were full of water, people could recreate in it as they did in more sophisticated swimming pools. But the water for the pool couldn't be tea-colored like that of the St. Johns and most Florida rivers. It had to be every bit as clear and enchanting as that of the natural springs.

Fortunately, the surrounding land was also graced with a rich hydrology, courtesy of the characteristic Florida landscape. The porous uplands captured rainwater and allowed it to seep down into the sand and limestone below. The weight of this water pushed its way toward the lowlands near the river, traveling laterally just under the surface—the same way that springs elsewhere in Florida come to life. But while the groundwater here was not far under the surface, it didn't seep or flow from the ground naturally as a spring would.   Nonetheless, the pressure pushing the groundwater was powerful enough that a man-made breach in the earth could result in a naturally flowing artesian well. Indeed, this was part of the same hydrological system that was then supplying the irrigation to the prosperous celery and row crop farms that were being developed in the rich delta of the St. Johns.

The hole in the ground may have also hinted at its own destiny by holding a bit of groundwater when the shells were excavated. However this notion was born, it came more fully to life when water spouted generously out of a pipe driven into the ground nearby. And this wasn't the dark, tannin-stained water of the river, but the clear, cool water of a spring—a commodity that had already been proven to be attractive in natural settings throughout Florida.

Florida—like most true hardscrabble American frontiers—relied heavily on local resources for its "vernacular" style of life. For instance, the distinctive Cracker-style homes were built from heart pine and cypress because that wood was cheap, durable, and widely available. Clay was scarce and imported bricks were expensive, but the unmined shells left in the middens could play a role as the essential ingredients in a rustic and localized southern cement called "tabby."

Tabby is a building material made of crushed shell, sand, lime, and water that was used by the Spanish in St. Augustine and English colonists in Charleston, South Carolina, from the colonial period until the 1800s. The shells from the midden were crushed and burned to create lime and then blended with sand and water and whole shells and poured into wooden molds. In the case of Mr. Schmelz, the molds were large ones built to create free-standing walls around the large hole. The mixture went into the molds and in the bottom of the hole, and when the tabby became hard, a large swimming pool with waist-high walls was created inside what had been a hardwood swamp of cypress and palm and sweetgum. It was truly a woodland park, and when it opened for business in the early 1900s, that became its name.

Woodland Park was a true original, a lighthearted respite in an otherwise demanding reality. But, today, Woodland Park is a nonplace, even more obscured from memory than the Mayaca who built the midden that served as its foundation. It's not listed in guidebooks, and newspapers rarely if ever mention it. It is as if Woodland Park never existed.

↓ ↓ ↓

Searching for the remains of an obscure nonplace has always held a certain fascination for me. I was eager to find what was left of this prototypical Florida theme park. But before I did, I wanted to see what it might have looked like back in the day.

I drive to the Henry Sanford Museum farther upstream on Lake Monroe and walk through a front door flanked with stone columns sprouting fancifully into the green leaf crowns of giant celery stalks. When I explain my quest to curator Alicia Clarke, she disappears into a back room and returns with a box of files. In the box is a wonderful old brochure with photographs and descriptive copy promoting Woodland Park. I learn that this was a place that featured a large dance hall with a "self-playing orchestration," along with "see-saws, swings and other amusements." The dance hall was built on stilts and stretched all the way out into adjacent Lake Monroe, long before that water body was bulkheaded and backfilled as it is today. This Woodland Park was promoted as "A Real Playground Where the Mound-Builders Lived."

At the heart of this theme-park precursor was its gigantic tabby pool. To keep it clean, the pool was emptied at the end of each day and then refilled every morning with its artesian well. In between, according to its promotional advertising, "the sun and air thoroughly disinfect the empty basin." Around the edges of the pool were a toboggan slide and springboards and a diving stage that was almost twenty feet high. There were forty-six dressing rooms. It cost five cents to get in, and another ten cents if you wanted to swim.

A club called "The Eagles" held their annual "Picnic and Fish Fry" here during one of the park's last seasons. Some 1,200 people attended, and according to the brochure, they were entertained "without over-crowding and everyone was happy."

Old photos show an enchanted site of palm and cypress and live oak, moss-draped boughs swooping above a tin-roofed gazebo trimmed with scalloped cornices.

Visitors were encouraged to have fun, but there were to be no shenanigans. "No rowdyism will be allowed," warned the brochure, "a fact well understood." And, "Woodland Park is in a class by itself and should not be confused with the so-called amusement parks." Archival photos show men in suits and ties and hats standing about outside a white wooden fence under an entrance with "Woodland Park" spelled out in an archway of carefully cut and trimmed tree branches. Inside, kids in black old-fashioned neck-high swimsuits play in the pool; women in long dresses and large brimmed hats watch them protectively. In a state that was trying so hard to be grown-up that it sometimes forgot to have real, spontaneous fun, Woodland Park seemed an oasis of frivolity.

As I sift through other information, I learn that patrons came by car or jitney from Sanford, rumbling their way atop shell-hard roads to get here. I also learn that Schmelz and his son, Lester, who ran the park until 1920, also built a small dock on Lake Monroe to accommodate those who arrived by a daily boat launch.

By now, I'm really eager to see what remains of Woodland Park. Curator Clarke had recommended talking with a couple of old-timers who collected antique bottles from places where people once lived. She regarded them as clever, intrepid, and as knowledgeable as any local historian about local places that used to be.

I track down one of the bottle collectors, and after promising several times never to reveal the site to others—who might take advantage of it and ferret out any bottles he had missed—he gives me good directions to the site. Once I am inside the low, thickly wooded hammock that has re-colonized the area, my best lead to the exact spot is to listen closely for the water that still flows and gurgles from the old artesian well.

Thus armed, I drive to the road nearest the site, not far from Lake Monroe. The road itself leads to the Central Florida Zoo, which is several hundred yards away. At a final turn toward the zoo, a lone historical marker roadside modestly identifies the site of the old theme park. There is, of course, no trail to it and no directions that would encourage anyone to try to find it. In this way, it's not dissimilar to more modern Florida theme parks that closed later in the twentieth century—Marco Polo Park, Tropical Wonderland, and so on. When moneymaking dreams are orchestrated to evoke frivolity and merriment and fun, their demise in Florida seems peculiarly brutal, almost as if their failure reflects somehow on the integrity of commercial illusion making.

Beyond the edge of the road, the woods descend into a wet, green swale of duckweed and ferns, punctuated with mahogany-colored cypress knees and shoals of hard mud. Although it is warm, I have on a long-sleeved shirt, jeans, and boots. It is a good Florida swamp outfit, one to buffer briars that scratch the skin and tiny insects that welcome a good, fresh meal on the hoof. I pull out my compass and walk down into the swamp, ducking under swags of giant webs spun by golden orb spiders and stepping gingerly around cypress knees. Moss hangs heavy in the trees overhead, just like in the brochure. By myself back in here, I still feel somehow safe, more at home than I ever do on the busy highways of Florida.

Despite the fear most have of Florida swamps, it's uncommon to encounter venomous snakes in wetlands like this. Unless you stumble directly onto them, most try to hide or to move out of your way. With this in mind, I step cautiously and slowly to allow them to do so, watching leaves and sticks for any sign of movement. But all I see are little anoles scampering for cover.

After an hour of wandering, I am beginning to wonder what really does remain of this place. There is no gurgling from the old pipe in the woods to call me to it, as I was told there would be. It is as hot as a sauna back in here, and my long-sleeved shirt and pants are soaked with sweat.

Finally, I notice the low ground under me has begun to slope very gradually upward. I look closely and see why: it is the edges of a midden packed full of thumb-nailed sized, bleached white snail shells. My own excitement is almost instantly rekindled, and I imagine that in some way it's a quiet intimation of the giddy expectancy kids a hundred years ago once had when they, too, approached the place "Where the Mound-Builders Lived."

In the distance, atop the highest elevation of the mound, I see two sides of the tabby-walled pool rise from the floor of the jungle, burnished with reddish lichens and dark algaes, like an old Spanish fort. The original pool was 80 feet long by 30 feet wide. This is all that remains.

I walk up to the closest waist-high wall and run my hand along the top of it. I see the knobbiness in the tabby is created by the ancient snail shells collected by the founders of Woodland Park from the midden itself. On the ground nearby is a single slab of tin, likely a remnant of the gazebo. But that's it. The park closed in 1920, and as with other abandoned structures in Florida, locals salvaged whatever they could to build or repair their own places. This was, after all, a time when recycling wasn't performed out of a conscious ethic, but out of an essential need for tangible supplies. I figure the remains of wood that weren't removed simply rotted into soft, organic humus in this warm and wet environment.

Just to the south, the rusty pipe that once filled the pool with its artesian flow is broken off near the ground. I shine a little flashlight down inside and see the surface of still water a few feet below, too tired to bubble or rise. It explains why I didn't hear the sound of gurgling as I approached.

Central Florida has been experiencing a drought over the last few years. But when rain does fall, it doesn't seep easily down into the earth as it once did to replenish wells like this. Local fields once covered with celery and winter vegetables are covered now with roads and culverts, while the low porous hills that once recharged this groundwater are full of stores and apartments and parking lots. The water that made Woodland Park what it was, that filled it anew every morning with hope and anticipation, has stopped flowing.

I stand here alone, inside one tabby wall, trying to imagine the pool as it once was, full of the great raucous joy and exuberance of children a century ago. A small aquatic turtle ambles nearby, across the thin layer of cement that was once the floor of the pool, dodging the thick trees that now grow here. The guileless fun and energy that once drove the park are vanished, gone to that same place as the spirit of the mound builders, swept away with the ever-moving blackwater current of the river itself.

When I earlier researched Woodland Park, I was at first perplexed that it closed in 1920 just as the tourist and building boom of that decade was kicking in. It didn't take long to also discover that the prosperous local farms were busy relocating to the newly available muck lands created by the draining of the Everglades in south Florida during this same era. Certainly, locals with a nickel to spare had been regulars at Woodland Park. But the Yankee tourists who traveled south every winter by steamship into Florida's interior were also being funneled off to the sunny and balmy coasts by new railroads and highways.

This one-two punch affected much of the commerce of Sanford, and its novel allure began to fade. The final act had a respected mayor and banker ravaging the bank accounts of his customers, a behavior that earned him a conviction of embezzlement and a prison sentence. Finally, the city itself claimed bankruptcy. It was a series of blows from which the "City Substantial" was unable to catch its breath for many decades. Surely, this all left little room for frivolity and for the attractiveness of places that—even at a nickel—were whimsical luxuries. Given this reality, it is understandable why Woodland Park waned as it did.

I walk down off the relic mound, back through the swamp and woods. I look over my shoulder only once, when I think I hear a last, long cry of joy from the playground where the mound builders once lived. It is a pileated woodpecker, high up in the mossy boughs, a bird that was here when the Mayaca first colonized these woods.

Its call is at once poignant, timeless, and full of the sort of hope that transforms itself over the centuries. I take that as an evocation, an audible sign that a promise, once made, can still endure in one form or another. After all, it was promise that brought me here.

24 Sacred Caves That Hold Fast to Their Secrets

Diving with the Gods

Hundreds of years ago, the native people known as the Taino came here in great numbers to the sacred cenote of La Aleta in a dry tropical forest on a peninsula off southeastern Hispaniola. They did so to honor their ancestors, to keep their *zemis* apprised of their worship of them, to drink freshwater, and to share in the fellowship of it all.

A member of our expedition to La Aleta during a visit to one of the dry caves of the area in the East National Park of the Dominican Republic. For the pre-Columbian Taino, caves—wet and dry—were portals to the underworld where the gods dwelled.

The Tainos were an elegant, gentle people, and I imagine they will be grateful that someone cares enough about the shards of their life to wish them into existence again. In this case, the "someone" is an archaeological expedition that has been plumbing the depths of the massive cenote over the last several weeks.

Whatever La Aleta was, it has become the wealthiest repository of Taino artifacts in the entire Caribbean basin. The Taino were a people who migrated through and into the Caribbean, island by island, up through the Lesser Antilles, from the northern rim of South America a few millennia ago. Because the language they spoke was Arawak, they are often described with that term.

Here, like the animals and plants of the islands, they speciated from what they had once been, isolated from their brethren back on the mainland. In the Antilles, they became something else, a new civilization created by the distinct island biogeography that shaped other life forms in the Caribbean. They invented flat griddles called *burens* to cook cassava bread over fire, hammocks to sleep and dream in, canoes to fish from and travel by. We know because we are recovering parts of all of these things—save the hammocks, which we have brought ourselves—from inside the cenote.

Yesterday, a diving archaeologist pulled a three-foot-long wooden pestle from the depths of the deep, water-filled limestone hole. It had a finely tapered handle and hammer-like head to squash the root of the *guyaba* into the mash from which cassava could be made. It was carefully carved and shaped from stone tools, and as I looked closely at it, it seemed as if the craftsman had just yesterday chipped the magnificently intact tool from the trunk of a reddish tropical hardwood.

When I first dived into La Aleta a few days ago, I went there as the others did—by strapping on a harness and being lowered into a seven-story-deep hole through a gaping "eye" in the limestone floor of the jungle. At the bottom of the hole was a great vat of water, and atop that clear water, a small Zodiac raft with scuba gear. Climbing in the raft to join other divers, I suited up with tanks and mask and then made the slow descent on a line that led to the 110-foot top of an earthen mound below.

There, all was dark, with the scant illumination coming only from the dive light I'd brought along. As I watched, divers encircled the soft mound, stopping to hover next to it and then periodically plunging their arms inside to see what they could find by *feel*. This is the reason that I have come to think of this particular work as archaeology by Braille.

Sometimes they would pull out whole clay pots so wonderfully complete they looked as though they might have just been molded and fired. At other times, wooden *duhos*—a chair of honor for a *cacique*—were recovered, as was finely woven basketry. Gourds that would have rotted up in the tropical heat a thousand years ago were recovered intact, incised with words and images from the Taino long ago. The darkness and mud and lack of oxygen have been very good to the residual clues of the pre-Columbian culture that remain here.

I am here to do the sort of unconventional work I have chosen to make a living. As a writer who dives and who is incessantly curious about the enchantment of the unknown, I am here on behalf of a large documentary network and a magazine. When I'm not diving or writing or poking about in the surrounding jungle, I closely examine the shards of everything that has been recovered that day. Sometimes I painstakingly translate Spanish abstracts that describe the history of the Taino and of this place. Other times I look on as the few terrestrial archaeologists sift through the earth atop the ceremonial lime-rock plazas that once extended outward from La Aleta.

By night, we all gather around a campfire and eat freeze-dried swill and, sometimes, sip a bit of dark Dominican rum. The archaeologists talk about what they'd found that day, and what might be discovered the next, and what it might all mean. Archaeology has long fascinated me, and when it's practiced underwater, it has a very special allure. Part of that, certainly, is in the adventure of being underwater while the relics of another time are being recovered. But relics inundated by both fresh- and salt water—and especially those covered with a moist organic "blanket" of soil—are often in far better shape than those on dry land. Indeed, once hidden away in situ for centuries, organic materials like wood and reed basketry that wouldn't last more than a few years on the surface sometimes seem to be freshly carved, woven, imagined.

I am dropping directly below the surface of the earth today, snug in my cable-rigged harness, watching the reflected sunlight from the assorted "eyes" of La Aleta bounce off the clear cenote water onto the white lime-stone walls, dancing a merengue of pre-Columbian celebration.

As for the world I leave behind, there may be no more perfectly colored cerulean sky than the one seen through the crevices of a cenote, from inside looking out. It is a vibrant Kodachrome spectacle, one that diminishes as I fall away from it, until finally it seems like something viewed from the wrong end of a telescope. As eager as I am to dive in this sacred well, there is surely something in the genetic memory of surface mammals that makes a part of us mourn the loss of light—especially when we are traveling toward a giant vat of dark water at a good clip.

I continue to drop toward the surface of the water below, and as I do, I suddenly hear something splash under me. I look down and see it is a wooden bucket dropped from the surface at the end of a long rope by one of the Dominican rangers. This site is, after all, inside a national park, and a small team of rangers live here nearly year-round. This one is gathering drinking water from the cenote, just as the Tainos once did, and as I continue to descend to the raft, the bucket passes me on the way up, two contrasting worlds—one sloshing with ether-clear water, the other breathing heavily. Surely the Tainos, who appreciated the duality of life, would have gotten a kick out this.

After I reach the surface, I trade my harness for some dive gear and begin my slow descent down into the depths of the cenote. The archaeologist who is to be my dive partner splashes in a few minutes after I do, keeping his distance so we do not collide. Despite the clarity of the water, I click on my underwater light within yards of the surface, as the surrounding walls and ceiling of limestone have blocked most of the bright tropical surface light. At a water depth of twenty feet, where the clear water ends and a strange chemo-cline of mineralized silt begins, it seems as if I'm forsaking the boundaries of the crisply focused, tangible world for one that is not nearly so. Once I emerge from the bottom of this odd clime, even the scant ambient light from the surface has vanished.

I continue to descend slowly to the top of the earthen pinnacle below; as I do, two divers pass me, heading up the line. They are returning from a deeper penetration—nearly 180 feet—and one is carrying a spectacularly intact Taino pot in his arms. Unlike other pots, this one is squarish, leaving the scientists to figure how it fits into the cultural timeline.

By the time I reach the top of the pinnacle, my dive partner and I are the only ones left in the cenote. Our lights seem meager in the overwhelming darkness, emitting just enough illumination to keep us from being absorbed by it all. I adjust my buoyancy and hover atop the center of the mud-limestone peak, while the other diver slowly sinks deeper next to it, looking for clues. As I have done before, I say a silent but heartfelt prayer asking permission from the *zemis* of the Taino to be here, explaining to them once more that I will do no harm to the sacraments or to their sacred memory. And, as before, my anxiety level drops dramatically, and I seem to become part of the cenote and all the memories and dreams it has held over time. I said far more in my little prayer and—because of the extraordinary nature of the experience—I would ordinarily remember it all. But my mind doesn't retain nearly as much when nitrogen is leaking into it at the rate it is now.

There is one thing I will always remember about this place, though. I have heard other divers characterize this sinkhole cave as mystical, intense, powerful. Long before the Spanish arrived and begin massacring the Tainos on the island of Hispaniola, La Aleta was a vital force in the life of the people who lived here. Sitting around the campfire just yards away from the cenote a few nights ago, Dr. Geoff Conrad, a Harvard-educated anthropologist who has studied the Indians of Peru and Mesoamerica, casually mentioned that this was the most sacred site of all to the Taino. After all, it is a place where the sky met the water, a foyer between the powerful supernatural magic of the underworld where the gods dwelled and all the rest of life above.

Squarely back into my cenote moment now, I see my dive partner fanning the sediment in the earthen cone below, watch him as he pulls up a large pot shard with ornate incisions. After bringing it over to show me, he puts it back. There have been some one dozen whole pots already recovered here, and pot shards—even those five centuries and more old—are to be left behind at this point.

My air pressure gauge edges slowly toward the red, and we head up, stopping in shallower water to blow off nitrogen before we break the surface. Our bottom time is slight enough to allow us to bypass the tank of oxygen tied to the line there. Instead, we fin curiously about the edges of the limestone chamber, shining our lights under ledges and rocky shelves. I slip back under one such overhang that juts out nearly horizontally, scraping my tanks as I go.

For the Tainos, life began and, quite literally, ended in caves. It especially did in the isolated, cavern-riddled peninsula that holds the enormous unroaded karst wilderness that is the East National Park of the Dominican Republic, in the heart of the last great Taino chiefdom of Higuey. A creation myth helped the Taino believe that they first came to life in a cave. When danger threatened, or they wanted to become closer in spirit to their ancestor gods, they retreated to those same dry caves. The caves were their genesis as well as their sanctuary and refuge.

If you were a Taino, you believed your ancestors came up to earth in a grotto called Cacibajagua. It was a labyrinth from which some of the Taino wandered out one day and, under the power of the sun, were transformed into stones, trees, and birds. Here, a mythos was born from the same realities of the environment that shaped the culture of the Taino. It was a belief carefully and precisely molded into existence, as surely as any potter shapes her vessel with the pinches and thumb taps of clay.

Scholars who have studied the culture knew this much, thanks to an account by Father Ramon Pane written in 1494. But it doesn't take a scholar to understand that the Tainos placed an extraordinary value on the subterranean chambers tucked away in the limestone. And why should they not? These are geological wonderlands, secret compartments and passageways and vast coliseums boring down into the earth, surreal places with half-melted ceilings and walls, still growing drip by careful drip.

The centerpiece of this sprawling archaeological site is what we generally know back in Florida as a "sinkhole." But the cenote of La Aleta de la Manatial is so much more. It's a cave, except with water—which made it both sacred and practical to thirsty natives living in a dry rainforest. With the help of divers and archaeologists, La Aleta is just beginning to tell its stories, to shake itself awake again after being forgotten for all these centuries. In this way, the cenote is an unassembled mosaic of culturally embellished clues— pots, gourds, wooden tools, weapons, and bowls. Together they are creating a complex narrative that will be pieced together in the years to come.

Today I am walking with others atop a trail across the jagged karst terrain that leads to a particularly spectacular dry cave. It is named Jose Maria, and, as I will see today, it has its own stories to tell, tales that are still graphically projected as pictographs on its walls. In the context of what we know about the Taino, these images are heartbreaking intimations of the last days of this civilization.

The hike to Jose Maria takes me and most other expedition members through the same dry tropical forest terrain where I have spent most of my waking hours—and a good chunk of my sleeping time—over the last fourteen days. Treading over the coarse limestone that covers most of the trail is like walking a concrete road that someone disked up into sharp bits and pieces. We have only a few hours to get in and out by dark; our pace is brisk enough that if I stop for only a moment to look at anything but my next step, I stumble over rock or the tree roots that crawl atop it like slender snakes.

After an hour, we reach the mouth of Jose Maria, a narrow, dark tunnel that bores down into the side of a wooded escarpment like a rabbit warren. The archaeologist John Foster, who has studied cave art here and in the American West, says the 1,200 pictographs found throughout this cave mark it as "a university of cultural history and mythology." Foster, like the rest of us, is dressed in old pants and a T-shirt, ready for the slip-sliding inside Jose Maria, over floors and chutes covered with layers of blackened bat guano. "Sometimes," says Foster, "there are entire panels that tell a story. If you shine your lights on them, some actually seem to move, to take on a life all their own."

Into the rabbit warren we go, down a rope, over blackened limestone ramps, from room to room, stalactites and columns everywhere, some glistening with sparkly minerals. Jose Maria was only "discovered" in 1980 by the Dominican archaeologist Abelardo Jiménez; it is a testament to the pristine wildness of this region that other such caves are still here, still unknown. Not so far away, Cueva de Romanita was discovered a year after Jose Maria and was then promptly lost again; no one is quite sure where it went.

Today, as I make my way carefully through the labyrinth, I am surrounded at every turn by cave art—frigate birds, turtles, bats, red crosses, a hurricane god with curls to represent movement, a cacique with a crown of sun rays. One scene shows the sun and moon emerging from a cave—a Taino depiction of the beginning of the world.

Back in the deepest reaches of Jose Maria, yards of wall are consumed by the panel I have been hearing about ever since I arrived in this country. It is the "tribute" to the conquest. It illustrates a 1503 treaty briefly forged between the Spanish and the Taino, one in which the Taino produced cassava bread to feed the conquistadors. In turn, the Indians were spared their lives. The panel shows the *guayagi* being grown, grated, baked into cassava, and then delivered to the Spanish caravel, sails forever billowing back here on the dark cave walls.

"The Taino thought this would be their salvation," says one of the archaeologists. "But the treaty lasted less than a year. . . . A Spanish soldier turned one of his dogs on a cacique who was directing the loading of cassava onto a ship. The dog ripped out his intestines. It enraged the Indians, who rebelled. The Spanish tracked down their chief and hung him in Santo Domingo. After that, it was pretty much all over for the Taino."

In the darkest reaches of the cave, beyond this panel, there are no more pictographs. What is left are the bats, who—with owls—were believed by the Taino to be associated with *Opias*, the souls of the dead. Trapped in the caves during the day, they emerge at night to roam atop the landscape of the mysterious Taino. Perhaps they still roam it today.

And, too, there are the Taino words that still remain, terms we have all adopted. Say them out loud in their Taino form and hear their resonance echo from time: *hamaca* (hammock), *iguana, manati* (manatee), *canoa* (canoe), huracan (hurricane), *barbacoa* (barbeque), even *tobaco*. They all figure prominently here in the tropical climate of this region, even extending to Florida and beyond.

Archaeology reveals the tangibles; careful introspection and observation create the rest.

By helping the world to more fully understand the Taino culture, archaeologists working here at La Aleta and other sites I have seen are doing far more than practicing science—they are releasing the Tainos from the dark lock of time, freeing them to roam the dry, enchanted forests of their chiefdoms once again.

You can listen for them now, stepping softly in the shadows, singing songs of their ancestors. Before I fall asleep in my tent, I listen carefully for those hymns, eager to communicate with the spirits who remain here, if only in the most imaginative of ways.

↓ ↓ ↓

We break camp today, and wait patiently for the Dominican army's brown-green Huey chopper to come and take us back to the coastal resort town of

Bayahibe. There we'll check into modern hotel rooms. There will be show-ers, a coastal breeze, even a bed without the segmented worms I would rou-tinely find in my sleeping bag.

Although the relative luxuries of this sound comfortable, I am sad about leaving. To have visited the depths of the sacred cenote, to have walked out on the ceremonial plazas under the pale moonlight, and to have slept and dreamed in such a sacred place is as close as I can come to connecting with the rich and vibrant spiritual energy that once fired this ancient civilization.

From everything I've read and have learned, the Taino were a genuinely kindhearted people—but they were something more. They were a people who could not lie. When confronted with Spanish duplicity designed to trick and slaughter them, they fell like dominoes. When enslaved, they com-mitted mass suicide in a swoon of despair.

In our modern, efficient Space Age culture, a lie is such a common thing it's hardly even called out anymore. But to the Taino, it was an eternal blun-der, one that kept them from joining their ancestors in the cusp where the sky meets the water and the earth. Neil Young sings about searching for a heart of gold; the Tainos were the ones who found it. Indeed, they were the ones who also embodied it.

It is clear from the work here over the last few weeks that hundreds, if not thousands, of Tainos regarded La Aleta as a sort of mystical energy center, a place to recharge their spiritual vigor and life. Poking about in a dark cenote and sifting through dirt in the jungle are both great ways to find historic ar-tifacts that no one has ever seen before. But what is uncovered is more than just a message about a culture that's now extinct—it's a timeless lesson in the history of compassion and deep-hearted honor.

Afterward, the thwack-thwack of the brown-green Dominican army Huey will resound overhead in the forest canopy, and I will pack my dive gear and clothes and computer away so I can go climb aboard it.

But I will be packing away so much more from my month here. I will take with me the clues of a civilization that could not tell a lie, a time-stuck ethic once sanctified with its own honest caring for a heart of gold. Although I can sometimes be obtuse, my mind and heart have been deeply touched by this all. I'm figuring La Aleta still embodies a supernatural love. It's one that has been tangibly embedded in its deep and dark abyss of limestone and water, mystery and light.

Not surprisingly, there is also a great irony present. While the early Spanish vanquished the Taino, the contemporary Dominicans who invest in large-scale commercial tourism are also obliterating other Taino sites throughout their country, places that are not protected in national parks. Encouraged by the Miami Beach–style tourism sweeping across the Caribbean—and often cheered on by their American partners—they seem to be again vanquishing most traces of the natives from their terrain.

There is little duality in all this. Westerners, after all, want the final say in most things, and bulldozers seem far more single-minded than any rain or wind god could ever be. But that is now. I wonder what, in five hundred more years, will be found of the hotels built here on this Caribbean island, and how—ultimately—the power of the *zemis* stack up against that of a pink-umbrella drink.

I don't think it'll be much of a contest, not in the long haul. And if anyone's keeping score, I'm casting my lot with the hurricane gods.

25   On Getting to Know
the River in Flood

After more than a week of walking to the edge of the St. Johns to see it "in flood," I finally had a chance this morning to launch my kayak to become more intimate with this new waterlogged weirdness.

I drove with my friend Michelle into downtown Sanford, and we cruised the streets that run toward the river—Park, Palmetto, and so on. Water had already covered most of Seminole, the road that winds along the bulkheaded shore. Now it was starting to slowly drift up the feeder streets and toward the historic downtown.

Michelle Thatcher paddles atop the submerged Riverwalk along Lake Monroe.

We stopped near the Civic Center, planning to launch on a flooded road there, but a gaggle of very intense gawkers soon gathered and began taking photos, circling us like sharks. Oddly, no one asked questions; they just stared as if we were a Disney attraction that had somehow become untethered and strayed beyond the safety of the park gates.

"It's like we're some sort of bizarre eye candy," said Michelle, figuring it quickly. The whole thing sort of creeped me out. So we drove to a more remote parking lot a few blocks down, unloaded our two kayaks, and promptly stepped into a fire ant mound. After doing our respective fire ant dances to shake them off, we launched the 'yaks right there at the edge of the inundated street curb.

From there, we paddled out and over the River Walk, and then scuttled along until we came to some of those nifty bench swings under one of the waterfront pavilions. I shot some video of Michelle for an independent film she's working on about a trek she made on the entire St. Johns. But once I put down the camera, I realized how wonderfully bizarre it was to watch her paddle atop the submerged River Walk, between the palm trees, benches, and ornate railing. The earlier gawkers, in contrast, didn't seem so strange after all.

Once we were both in the water, we kayaked out to where the natural river usually flows. I saw some odd splashes about a quarter mile offshore—almost like large fins floundering about—and wanted to get a closer look, thinking it might be a manatee in distress. By now the easterly wind was cranking pretty steadily—fifteen or twenty knots—and the river was surging along with rolling waves and whitecaps. The sun had come out and was illuminating the tea-colored tannins in the water; even the whitecaps were tinted a dark amber.

We got closer to all the commotion and saw the giant "fins" were actually the brownish waves splashing on the top of a houseboat that had sunk in the storm last week. Michelle warned me not to get too close or the turbulence of the swollen river might draw me into it. I asked her if I looked like the sort of guy who went around paddling into thrashing aquatic chasms. She replied that I had pronounced "chasm" incorrectly.

The river was really running well by then, and we followed the current back toward shore, moving from lake to sidewalk to road. Soon we were right down by the riverside pizza shop, which, like the adjacent Marina Island, was surrounded by water. I noticed a dorky-looking guy with a bright-red beret standing out front, trying without much success to look fearsome. The inscription on his black T-shirt read "Guardian Angel," so I guessed he was here because of the wonderful eco-mayhem that floods create. Perhaps he was preparing to fend off menacing kayakers who, if given half a chance, would surely loot the pepperoni and parmesan cheese.

We ran into another kayaker in a smaller red boat who had a large pizza box with him—as if preparing to deliver it—and folks were busy snapping his picture. He was a big guy with a good sense of humor. "Domino's delivers," he said, repeating an often-heard commercial line—even though the pizza joint wasn't a Domino's. He seemed to get a kick out of the attention, and I had to admit, it was a nice sight gag.

Michelle paddled around some sandbags and onto the road, where trucks and cars still splashed through to get onto Marina Island, maybe to tend to the boats moored in the marina there. The traffic lights and street signs and sloshing vehicles and kayaking pizza man—coupled with a growing crowd of onlookers happily shooting photos of us shooting photos of them—created one of those special out-of-body Florida moments.

Back on the lake, we aimed our bows into the waves again and paddled around the inundated Marina Island and all its moored and docked boats. The three- to four-knot current aggressively pushed us to the west, leaving us with little more to do than try to steer closer to shore. The City of Sanford actually approved three nine-story condo towers out here, but the recession has kept them on the drawing board for now. The towers were absurdly out of proportion with the rest of the old historic district, but the city—hoping for a quick shot of prosperity—caved. I wish the potential buyers could be here, scuttling in the floodwaters around this ephemeral, man-made island, to see what their future might have in store for them.

We slipped into the lee on the west side of Wolfy's, a waterfront pub, and now in calm water, drifted over to the smaller Memorial Park peninsula, where the giant American flag flies. About a third of it was also underwater, and on the high ground that remained, wood storks were milling about near a flock of black-headed vultures. The vultures were everywhere, waiting for all the decaying bass, mullet, and catfish killed by the runoff toxins to wash ashore.

I bumped into a partially submerged "wall" that rims the perimeter of the peninsula and saw a tiny stingray sitting on it, a half foot or so under the surface, his image tinted sepia by the blackwater. We'd already seen a larger dead ray back on the road in front of the pizza place, and this little guy was likely trying to get as close to the surface as he could to absorb more dissolved oxygen. Very little of the melodramatic reporting that had gone on here over the last week or so had considered how pathogen-enriched storm water affects the ecology. When the river finally begins to recede and the current slacks, I thought, the newly deposited toxins and the reduced oxygen will spell the end for lots of fish as well as the wading birds and ospreys who hunt them.

Sure, Sanford and all of the river towns and cities have had flooding for centuries after tropical storms and hurricanes. But there are now simply more human contrivances crowding out natural lands, marshes, and swamps. When intact, wetlands in a river's watershed have an amazing capacity to absorb and clean rainfall. And, with a historic population that was so much smaller—and less chemically obsessed than we moderns—storm water flowing from the land into our rivers was far less dangerous.

A government report I read when researching a book I was writing on sprawl told of how one-hundred-year "flood events" would happen every five years if only 25 percent of any watershed were compromised by impermeable surfaces—roads, rooftops, parking lots. When that hard surface ratio increased, so, too, would the frequency of flooding. God might have created Noah's flood, but the city and county officials who routinely permit the destruction of wetlands have surely enhanced this one all by themselves. I also realized that as corporations transform thoughtful journalism into a print or electronic version of a Happy Meal, stories like this will be reported less and less in the world of Media Lite.

We said good-bye to the little ray and the wood storks and paddled back into the wind, headed upstream to the street where we launched. People were now lining the riverfront, snapping photos and taking video of us. I told Michelle that it seemed as if we were aquatic floats in a very odd parade. To cap it off, an ice-cream truck playing repetitive kid-type happy music pulled up to service the festive crowd of onlookers. Michelle said, "Wow. I haven't been in a float in a parade since I was in the daffodil festival for my Brownie troop."

The ice-cream truck was playing "Mary Had a Little Lamb," and I thought to myself that if this impromptu storm parade and its stingrays and sunken boats had a drum major, it might be the Latin surrealist Gabriel García Márquez. Surely he would appreciate the magic realism of it all.

And so we continued to navigate this strangely engorged Florida river, drifting down that increasingly thin line between fantasy and what remains of dry land reality here in the Sunshine State.

26 Riding the Food Chain
to the Bottom of the Sea

After I land an assignment from a national magazine to do an article on shark diving, I enthusiastically share this great news with my friends. Their reactions are less than encouraging. "Isn't that, ah, fairly dangerous?" asks one, a marketing VP. "You'll be inside a cage, right?" asks another, an editor. Last, from a left-brained attorney, "Sounds like a death wish to me."

A shark swims nearby while the author waits patiently on the bottom of the tropical sea.

My tack has been to smile inscrutably and explain that sharks are generally shy, that a cage won't be necessary—and, indeed, I am more likely to be attacked and bitten by a domestic pig than a shark. *Jaws* did this to us, I remind them, portraying every sleek, dorsal-finned creature as a demonic eating machine with a pea-sized brain. In fact, I say, "Snouts" would be a far more realistic danger. No one laughs.

To reassure myself, I call up a more reasonable and informed friend, Dr. John McCosker at the California Academy of Sciences. McCosker, a renowned ichthyologist, has coauthored a book, *Great White Shark*, on the most dangerous of the breed. He sets me straight.

"Sharks have a lot more to fear from us than we do from them," explains McCosker. Worldwide, they are overfished for fins, meat, and sport. Out of 368 species, only four—the great white, bull, tiger and oceanic whitetip—have been involved in unprovoked attacks, and then only on the rarest of occasions. Worldwide, says McCosker, there is an average of one hundred attacks on humans yearly—with about thirty of them fatal. But most of those are on swimmers or waders in shallow water, and most are cases of bite-and-run in which the human was mistaken for a more tasty seal or sea turtle.

McCosker also tells me it was probably a great white—instead of a whale—that swallowed Jonah. "The good news is, he was spit back up." I lodge all this comforting information safely inside my brain. Outside my brain, in that little place in my mammalian stomach that secretly replays the theme to *Jaws* every time I imagine a mouth full of sharp teeth coming at me, things are still a bit uncertain.

I admit it: I do have an underlying, visceral reaction to this whole notion. Maybe it comes from the prospect of entering the ocean and getting bumped a couple of notches down the food chain by another species that's faster, stronger, and, on occasion, even more merciless than humans. More to the point, I'm also a genetic victim of the fight-or-flight syndrome. We battle fear in great explosions of adrenaline, or we run. That was a useful reaction when we lived in caves or hid back in the tall grasses. But now that we are civilized, a more rational response is required. If I could deal with my most dramatic fear of all—the prospect of being eaten—I could learn to cope with most anything.

I pack my scuba diving gear, toss in some clothes, and head for Fort Lauderdale, Florida. There I will hop aboard Island Express Airlines for a flight to the southernmost edge of the Bahamas and a rendezvous with my aquatic, dorsal-finned destiny.

⇓ ⇓ ⇓

The twin-propped Cessna 402 from Island Express taxis to a stop on the runway at the international airport at Long Island in the Bahamas. The off-white plane, apparently in the midst of being repainted, has been spot-sprayed in bursts of green, as if by a kid on a rampage with an aerosol can. It didn't fly yesterday because of mechanical problems.

The runway is a narrow, rutted strip of asphalt thick with black tire-skid marks, including a few that our own earring-studded pilot just left. The airport is a two-room wood-and-stucco hut split in half by a patio. A wind sock flies at the edge of the runway, not far from the turquoise sea. I'm clearly in a Jimmy Buffett song.

A large, black-skinned man comes out to greet me and picks up my gear as it's off-loaded from the plane. Like other Bahamians, he speaks in a lilting patois, a blend of African and old English flavored by three hundred years of island living. He piles my two bags onto a wood bench marked "Customs." I hand him my passport and he smiles, no mon. He is a taxi driver.

Off we go to a local German-run resort, my shark-diving base for the next few days. While there are more than 150 scuba operators around the world who engineer shark dives, this Long Island lodge is the granddaddy of them all—and that is a big part of why I am here. If you're going to swim with the sharks, you might as well do it with someone who has experience.

The place exudes an efficiency not always found in the wider Caribbean—must be the Germans. Over the three-thousand-acre estate, there are enough rooms for only 120 people. It is a place of seclusion, a retreat the upwardly mobile use to emotionally decompress from hectic, fast-paced, mainland lives. It is Margaritaville, coiffed up and extravagant.

Here, everyone chills out in different ways. Some rent cars and drive around the seventy-six-mile-long island, past the ruins of colonial cotton plantations and villages like "Burnt Ground" and "Glenton's," maybe dropping in at a native restaurant for a meal of fresh spiny lobster. Others learn to scuba dive. If so inclined, a few swim with the sharks. Shark-wise, the results have been good: in more than one thousand dives in twenty years, there have been no skirmishes between sharks and divers. Shark attacks must be messy, emotional affairs; I figure the Germans simply have no time for them.

My room is one of four in a spacious, ranch-style stucco-and-wood house perched on the edge of the limestone island next to the frothing green surf. A sign outside shows a cartoon dolphin leaping over the words "Haus Delphin." The air here is clean, flavored with the scent of tropical blossoms and the sea. The United States is not all that far away geographically, but it's light years away in ambience. There is no room key, no telephone or television. It is me and my regulator and the turquoise sea. It's hard to be buttoned-down in an environment like this.

I unpack my gear and reflect on tomorrow's dive. Going underwater is like visiting another planet, one where you have to carry your entire life-support system on your back. I've found that the experience has the strange effect of sweeping the emotional slate clean, leaving you to pursue new challenges with a fresh perspective.

And if my diving adventures—in the Caribbean, the Bahamas, and on Australia's Great Barrier Reef—have buoyed my psyche, they have also made me more attuned to the complex world beneath the waves. The sea, that great vast unknown, has become a lot less unknown for me.

Still, a piece of this puzzle is missing: sharks, skittish and cautious in the wild, have eluded me. Underwater, I have only caught fleeting glimpses of them as they dashed away in a blur of tail and fin. With scant firsthand knowledge of them, my subliminal human fear grew out of proportion to the danger they represented. Now I would finally have the chance to meet the fear head-on, to look it right in the beady little eyeballs. The ones set back on either side of the head right above the mouth that seems ready to Cuisinart everything in its path.

It is 9:00 a.m. sharp, and a flatbed truck with two benches full of smiling American and German tourists is beeping its horn at my door. It has come to take me to the sharks. I climb aboard with my gear, comforted that so many others have also chosen to overcome their shark anxieties with me today.

We drive down a dirt road paralleling the sea, past coconut palms and papayas, flowering bougainvillea, and a rubber tree the size of a small house.

When we reach the marina on the leeward shore of the island, everyone but me and a sturdy blond German woman piles off the truck and onto an immense sixty-five-foot boat. Off they go, headed for a series of deserted local beaches, giddy with their snorkeling gear and coolers of cold Kalik, the Bahamian beer.

The two of us then climb aboard a smaller, thirty-one-foot inboard cruiser. I turn to the German woman, whose name is Helga. "Looks like just you and me and the sharks," I say, adding a nonchalant smile. "No," she corrects me. "Just you. I ride on the boat and look at them from where it is safe." Gulp.

Bahamians Omar Daley and Christopher Carroll Smith—"Call me Smitty"—are our boat captains and underwater guides. After sojourns in Nassau, both men have returned to their remote native island. Omar is a quiet man with an athletic build, and Smitty is lean and congenial, if a bit wired. A dark rain cloud moves across the horizon, and our boat tries to outrun it as we head for "Shark Reef." Smitty, in his Reebok cap and workout jacket and khaki shorts, is upbeat. "'Dis is my island, mon. I know the rain and the sunshine. We will have no problem."

Soon we are over the shallow, thirty-five-feet-deep site. "Here, you have the fish and the coral and the sponges," says Smitty. "Every-ting we need for the beau-tif-i-cation of the reef." Then, as an afterthought, "and here, especially, we have the sharks."

Smitty gives me the shark-wrangling history of Long Island. Years ago, a French documentary team arrived here to film sharks. But since sharks are pelagic—strong, streamlined swimmers who generally hunt in deeper, open waters with only brief forays into the shallows—finding a subject willing to terrorize the picturesque coral reef wasn't easy. And, except for the rare unprovoked attacks, wild sharks generally avoid humans. Indeed, the exhalation of scuba bubbles may even spook them.

So locals obliged the French filmmakers by spearing bloody fish on the reef—a guaranteed Pavlovian dinner bell. Other photographers in search of dramatic images heard of the Long Island sharks, and the shark baiting continued. Adventurous divers later joined in on the action. And today there is a simple formula: Divers descend to the bottom, a chum bucket is dropped into the water overhead, and the fun begins.

Honestly, the notion of baiting any wild animal to get it to do something it wouldn't ordinarily do generally doesn't sit well with me. I don't like to see animals encouraged to perform just because we want them to. Alligators fed in Florida's urban lakes lose their fear of humans and learn to associate them with food—swimmers, fishermen, and poodles find a spot on the menu. But here, I figure the sharks have been at it long enough to have developed a routine. Whatever happened to get the ball rolling in these parts predates my appearance by a couple of decades.

Smitty finally says out loud what I have been thinking since I first packed my dive gear. "Yea, mon, it is a fear for most people. Seeing these big animals with teeth like they want to make dinner out of you. But it is not just about the sharks; it is about facing up to fear. You do it, and later, when you see a shark, you don't have the fear." Surely, self-help authors have written entire books elaborating on Smitty's tropical gunwale-side manner.

I slip into my wet suit, hoist on my scuba tank and weight belt, and sit down on the stern of the boat. My feet dangle in the water as I put on my fins. I look into the clear sea below and immediately see great, brown-gray shapes moving in slow circles under me. They have been lured here by the sound of our motor and swash of our hull. It seems the show has already started.

Omar settles down beside me in his scuba gear. I can't help but notice that he is carrying a large metal pole in his hand. "Ah, Omar," I ask, as casually as possible, "if this dive is so safe, why are you carrying that big stick?"

"My CYA stick, mon," explains Omar. "Cover Your Ass." Then he puts his regulator into his mouth and slips under the sea, into the phalanx of circling fins. Like a true believer, I wordlessly follow, ablaze with newfound trust. This will work, I tell myself, because Omar has done this many times before and he doesn't seem to be even mildly anxious.

Then again, he has the stick.

Underwater, I count seven or eight Caribbean reef sharks circling me like giant, steel-gray torpedoes. I concentrate on trying to move slowly and deliberately, as I would ordinarily do if I were here on the reef without sharks. I check my air-pressure gauge, neutralize my buoyancy, and—reminding myself that this is perfectly natural—settle down on the sandy bottom not far from a towering mound of Technicolor corals.

As soon as I'm on the bottom, a lone seven-foot shark swims straight toward me, his mouth in a fixed grimace, looking like Peter Falk's Columbo after a hunch didn't pan out. For a split second, my senses freeze—along with my sphincter muscle. I want to run but I can't, and for the most fleeting of moments, I have a sort of out-of-body experience, as if I am watching myself watch the shark.

Remembering the old adage of not showing fear to a mad dog, I stay my ground. At a distance of three feet, the shark turns abruptly, as if someone has pulled an invisible chain. This happens several more times, before the sharks tire of it and resume swimming in circles just above.

I figure that if I am really going to swim with the sharks, I need to get off my butt and head up to their level. I do so, rising ever slowly upward. The circling sharks swim just a wee bit wider to avoid bumping me. Some scientists suspect that sharks, with their heightened sense of smell, can even detect adrenaline. I think of the little twits with backward baseball caps who weave in and out of traffic back in Florida with NO FEAR decals on the back of their jacked-up pickups. A Caribbean reef tip shark would peel that decal in a nanosecond.

More than anything I've ever done, there is a be-here-now element to this experience that commands the full attention of my senses. At the same time, whatever shards of cerebral concern remain from my topside life vanish. Breathing, something I take for granted back on the surface, becomes a conscious, auditory event. In comes the good air in a long, relaxed suck; out goes the bad in a series of gently exploding exhaust bubbles. Around me, the bubbles become domes of mercury and drift up to the surface. To control myself, I control my breathing, turning it into a Zen-like exercise. As I do, the environment seems to absorb me. I become one with it.

And then something magical happens. I see the sharks more clearly. Gill slits, eyes, and mouths come into focus. The grace of their swimming awes me. I watch how little they twist their body to make a turn, how small the energy investment is compared to my awkward surface-mammal gyrations. Instead of mindless eating machines, they become elegant, smooth-skinned beasts—giant underwater panthers. I begin to admire them. As I do, my fear dissolves with my exhaust bubbles. I settle back down to the bottom on my knees, next to Omar and his stick. He gives a signal to Smitty, who is watching the action from back on the boat.

Down into the water comes a PVC can full of fish heads and guts. New sharks I have not seen before dash to the bucket from somewhere just beyond my range of vision. There must be thirty of them in the water now, and they are fired up. The bucket is theirs.

The sharks attack the chum, slashing and biting at it. The bucket drops to the bottom in slow motion, sharks slamming into it from every which way. As it settles onto the sand, the commotion they kick up creates a storm of dust. The storm grows, spreading toward me, sharks veering in and out of it with fire in their eyes. When the edge of the storm is only a couple of yards away, I back away gingerly, careful not to thrash about as I do.

As quickly as the frenzy started, it is over. The chum bucket, now scored with teeth marks, is empty, lying next to me on the sand. The timing is excellent as my air is also starting to run low. I carefully ascend, moving deliberately. Midway up, I pause and raise an underwater camera to snap photos of the remaining sharks.

As I do, I listen closely to my gut for sounds of alarm. But I hear none. There is only the rhythm of my steady exhalations now, and it is more comforting than it has ever been.

27 Welcome to Our Tropical Winterland

And so for me, the deep freeze that whacked much of Florida this winter came down to this: anoles—those native lizards the size of a magic marker that dart about in the foliage understory—didn't fare well. The hardest hit seemed to be the nonnative Cuban anoles, the little tropical brutes that have quietly slipped into Florida over the last few years and have been bogarting their way into the local habitats ever since. These larger, huskier exotics not only swagger about in their special reptilian way, but they also eat their local counterparts.

An anole takes refuge in a hollow shard of bamboo in my backyard as the temperatures prepare to drop well below freezing and stay there throughout the night.

Am figuring it's less troublesome to think of the Cuban anoles in more of a fictional way—perhaps like the sci-fi "Blob" in the vintage flick of the same name. The Blob was a sort of supernatural, adhesive entity that moved across the landscape like a giant ball of Silly Putty gobbling up everything along the way. Apparently, only Steve McQueen could stop it. And he did so, how? By freezing it.

Maybe the Cuban lizards are annoyed that our native counterparts have the capacity to turn green, which is something they can't do. So they get all draconian about it all. Guess you could blame it on Castro—God knows we've tried to blame everything else on him. But before El Jefe forcibly came to power, Cuba was already rigidly dogmatic—largely thanks to our own U.S. government, which propped up a brutal dictator by the name of Fulgencio Batista. But as with modern China, he was "our" totalitarian and thus immune from the laws of morality—or even from the context of history. Geez, we sure can fool ourselves when we want to.

But we're talking about freezes here. And during this last one, some guy in south Florida actually videotaped a cold-sensitive tropical iguana falling out of a tree. Iguanas didn't sneak in on some container ship like their diminutive Cuban brethren. Instead, they were sold as pets. And, at some brief point of clarity, an owner of that pet grew bored with watching what is essentially a hunk-o-meat with scales lie around most of the day and do nothing except eat. And so the iguana was banished to the Great Outdoors of Florida—which is already overrun with orphaned plant and animal exotics from the tropics.

In honor of the iguana's dramatic response to low temperatures, one out-of-state newspaper ran the headline: "Snowing in Florida: Freezing Iguanas Falling Out of Trees." Which sort of suggested that lizards were raining from the sky like giant banana-shaped slabs of frozen meat, a *Wild Kingdom* episode with a modern and bizarre Florida twist.

I've also noticed that the other Cuban herp immigrant, the Cuban tree frog, has been missing from our local landscape lately as well. These guys have the same sort of appetite that the Cuban anoles do and are putting a nice dent in the native Florida tree frog population (especially the greens). And larger mamas—which can grow to five inches—have even been seen eating southern toads. I'm figuring anything that would eat a large toad surely has an enormous capacity for almost anything. Ralph Waldo Emerson, likely shivering in a New England winter, once described Florida and

Cuba as the "happiest of latitudes"—but this was long before globalization started moving all the ecological chess pieces around.

In fact, all the exotics that have been quietly sneaking away from indoor cages and glass tanks to the hammocks and islands and marshes of Florida's remaining native landscape over the last twenty or thirty years seem to have done quite well. The most recent catch during the last freeze was a giant green anaconda, living in a drainage pipe down in Osceola County (not far from Disney) and feasting on ducks and geese in a nearby pond. This one may be the most dangerous snake of all, given its ability to grow large and eat really big animals. Worse, it may start breeding with other exotic reptiles to create a "supersnake" that knows absolutely no bounds. The freeze sort of stunned it, at least long enough so that many of these particular anacondas could be captured.

Add to this the arrival of other exotics—the meat-eating tegu lizard that looks like an iguana on steroids. (I once saw one lumber across a dirt road when I was riding in a four-wheel-drive vehicle through a rainforest in Guyana. He moved with a certain aplomb, like he was the Bad Leroy Brown of reptiles, and our Land Rover wasn't a worry to him in any way.) And of course, there's the monitor lizard, which, like the tegu, is also doing quite well eating local critters in southwest Florida.

I have been sort of expecting an exotic slam down—or whatever those extreme pro rasslin' matches inside chain-link cages are called. We already know that pythons are thriving in the Everglades, have even seen them rassling with our own native alligators in photos and videos shot there. So am figuring that matching up a native species with an exotic ought to be good for a Pay TV event. Add a green anaconda and a carnivorous tegu to that mix and you've got yourself a dandy tag-team match.

Water-wise, Florida rivers like the St. Johns dip down into the forties during these events. As a guy who was once scuba diving in water almost that cold, I can tell you it's a numbing experience. A Florida spring with its year-round 72°F waters upwelling from our limestone aquifer seems quite toasty in comparison. And that's why the warm-blooded manatees make a beeline for any place that's warmer than the river—including natural springs, as well as the artificially heated thermal effluent from utility plants.

Over the last few years, manatees have been joined by another strange exotic in the springs, the Amazonian suckermouth catfish. There are actually two species of this fish thriving here in Florida, both of which were released via the aquarium trade. In fish tanks they grow to a few inches and eat algae and are peculiar looking, and that's fine for an aquarium. But out in nature, they grow up to a foot or more in length, breed copiously, dig little tunnels in the side of riverbanks, and clog up the springs with their Amazon-iness. Worse, they now appear to have acclimated so they no longer have to seek refuge in our warmer springs and have expanded their range to where no Amazonian catfish has gone before.

When in the Amazon upstream of Iquitos once, I actually saw one of these fish lying atop a water hyacinth (another Florida exotic), out soaking up the sun on a particularly pleasant day. Later, we sat around in the evening on our old riverboat and ate the catfish, which had been shucked from its tough shell. The meat was white and good, and while it didn't taste like chicken, it certainly could hold its own with our own native Florida catfish, cuisine-wise.

Maybe the fish has a marketing problem, and if more folks knew how tasty it was, we'd see fewer of them around. Am figuring our corporate chain restaurants like Red Lobster can pick up the slack on this one, maybe calling it "Lobster Fish" or "Tropical Wonderland Filet," as they've done with the deepwater fish that biologists call "Slime Head," renaming it "Monk Fish" as if consuming it might allow some peaceful culinary supplication.

The other notable moment that happened in central Florida when it got down to close to 25°F one night was that the birdbaths in my backyard froze solid. Not just at the surface as they've done in years past, but all the way to the bottom, four inches or so of solid ice. One of the birdbaths actually cracked from that experience, and when I told one of my northern friends of this, he laughed, since he had learned years ago to empty all the birdbaths before the first serious freeze headed his way.

Well, my little cracked birdbath wasn't that big of a deal since it was easy to fix. But the event was a sort of microcosm of what's happening on a larger scale to our Florida earth. Some northerners call this phenomenon a "frost quake." One of the ways to try to keep crops and plants from freezing is to put a light layer of water (which quickly turns to ice) atop them. But all that groundwater pumping can drain the upper portion of our aquifer, allowing sinkholes to dimple the landscape. (At last count, we had ten new sinks open up just during our frigid January.)

While groundwater pumping from an already overstressed aquifer will cause this, frost adds another stressor to the equation: the top of the ground freezes by night and thaws by day. The effect is not unlike that expand-contract thing that causes birdbaths to crack. When the ice forms, the earth sort of expands, just as the water does in the birdbath. But when it melts, it then constricts back to normal and settles a bit. (It does so usually much faster than it takes to freeze and expand.)

With each successive freeze comes the squeeze-settle push on the terrain, and soon all this sand and soft limestone that are just under the surface— that is, the top of our aquifer—begin to react as well. And then one sunny morning, the earth thaws one last time, and *voilà!*—instant sink.

I stopped writing there for a moment to let all of this "sink" in, and realized I have created a story for a classic comic book that could be entitled "Extreme Wintertime Distress in Florida." In it, South American tegus and anacondas rassle gators and bears, giant flat-tailed marine mammals stack up in springs like cordwood, tiny lizards and frogs battle each other to the death—and if this isn't cartoonish enough, the actual ground under us falls away in great chunks as if it's made of a giant confection and all the sugar-craving kids who ever dreamed of being Charlie in the Chocolate Factory are gnawing their way through it.

Well, I guess there's not too much else to say about the freeze. Except this: February is historically our coldest month, even here in the "happiest of latitudes." All that's gone on could just be a scrimmage for a grander championship game—or a rehearsal for a theater play. And, as we know from reading the comic satirist Carl Hiaasen—or, on a darker note, William Kennedy's *Ironweed*—there's hardly anything you can imagine that hasn't already happened in real life.

28   Steamboats Meet
        Solastalgia Head-On

Sherie is clipping away on my hair at Dave's Barber Shop in a nineteenth-century brick storefront in downtown Sanford, Florida. The wall facing the chairs in the shop is crammed with photos of vintage TV and movie cowboys—Tom Mix, Roy Rogers, Gabby Hayes, and so on. Johnny Cash is singing lullabies from an LP on an old turntable. Sherie is effusive, having fun with the moment.

Dave's Barbershop in downtown Sanford, complete with flag, one-speed bike, barber pole, and my friendly down-home haircutters.

The three worn barber chairs swivel and creak as patrons come and go, some with a friendly country greeting, some with a joke as worn as the chairs. If there's any styling mousse around, it's well hidden. I pay eight dollars for my very good haircut, tip Sherie, and leave. Outside, a large American flag flies next to the swirling barber pole. A clunky one-speed bike leans against the brick exterior here, and when the day is done, Dave will ride it home.

A few years ago, I had seen a superb black-and-white photograph of the front of Dave's in an art show, one-speed bike and all. At the time, I figured the photographer had staged all this stuff, just to evoke nostalgia and a longing for another time. Everything seemed too real to be true.

I walk across the worn old brick street and stop to say hi to a fellow who used to be a local county commissioner. As I do, the photographer for the semiweekly *Sanford Herald* comes along. For a few moments, we all lean on the back of a pickup truck bed and chat, nothing profound, just hanging out.

From here, I walk another block in the heart of the downtown to an independent bookstore next to Magnolia Square. A fountain flows in the square, and a pedestal clock that has been in town since at least the 1920s keeps time. The store is named Maya Books & Music, and inside, owner-operator Yvette Comeau graciously fields questions from customers, scrolling through her head when someone asks about a title, instead of scrolling through a computer inventory.

Layla, Yvette's large black lab/shar-pei is curled up near the art section on the worn hardwood floor. When Layla sees me, her heavy tail metronomes gently on the wood. I bend to rub Layla behind her ears. Books are both shelved and piled high in stacks, leaving only a bit of space here and there for patrons to walk. I always find at least one title that grabs my attention, and when I do, I sit in a comfy chair and thumb through it before I buy it.

On a wall nearby, a framed inscription from the spiritual writer Thomas Moore reads: "A magical (book) store has its own character and spirit, and the browser gets the impression that the store will never reveal all its mysteries. To me, a bookstore should be more like a haunted castle than a government information center."

From here, it's a short stroll out to the edge of the St. Johns River, once the major aquatic highway into the interior of this low, subtropical peninsula for steamships, and earlier, Native American dugouts. Interpretive signs along the shore remind me of the natural preeminence of this transportation corridor. Like most real places in the South, the riverboat town of Sanford came to be because it was near a natural system that was highly useful for human needs. Once here, people farmed row crops and grew citrus and set fish traps, maybe ran a hotel or boardinghouse for the nascent tourist trade.

The traditional relationship locals had with the geography was undeniable: it defined who they were far more than any sophisticated marketing ad for a walled and affluent development ever could. Over time, this bond of nature and people forged a palpable sense of place.

But the steamships that once helped shape the southern lifeways of river towns like Sanford have gone away, their utility lost to railroads and then highways. As swamps and marshes in the floodplain have diminished to accommodate growth, this blackwater river itself has been degraded.

Still, Sanford has sustained its own authentic charm. While the river no longer brings tourists to its shores, the intimate and familiar nature of this relic village does. Merchants and residents and visitors unimpressed by the flashy, self-conscious opulence of some Florida cities come here seeking a genuine sense of community. As Moore has also observed, "The soul needs a vernacular life," one enriched with the particulars of place. "It feeds on the details . . . on its variety, its quirks, and its idiosyncrasies."

Dave's Barbershop and Maya Books and the *Sanford Herald* will hang on as long as their owners are able to make a living. And the town's details, quirks, and idiosyncrasies will hang on with them. But a giant mall out by the interstate is a harbinger of an aggressive, corporate-driven world that is marching lockstep across the horizon.

One study by the "1000 Friends of Florida" predicts the state will double in population by 2060 if the current growth rate continues. A regional analysis, "PennDesign," figures the seven-county east central Florida area will grow even faster, exploding by 136 percent by 2050.

Before the recession, natural lands that were retrofitted to accommodate the incoming were being lost at the rate of twenty acres an hour. If this growth is revitalized, the pervasive sprawl of newcomers will continue to slice and dice the natural countryside, transforming most everything it touches. "Build out" in Florida will happen on all land not protected as a public park or preserve by midcentury. Historic preservation laws will save some districts, such as downtown Sanford. But they can't save the untiring move toward gentrification that inflates rents and depersonalizes interactions.

Florida, known as a bellwether state that helps introduce economic models of faceless efficiency to the Sunbelt, will likely see its own templates for superhighways and chain stores and corporate "prosperity" sweep across the larger region. Of the fifty fastest-growing metro areas in the entire country, twenty-seven are already in the South, according to a 2008 report by the U.S. Census Bureau.

No matter how much spin is put on this caffeinated growth, a few pesky truths endure: the rural character that historically defined the American South relied on an abundance of open space. And that extravagance of landscape—farm fields and ranch lands, wooded hammocks and bottomland forests—is vanishing.

Perhaps even more profoundly, rapid growth can overwhelm the native grace of any place. Swaggering with short-term profits, it's usually too heavy-handed to allow for the more sublime qualities of individuality and "community." If brick streets and friendly shops become more symmetrical and sterile and crowded, how much do we really gain as thoughtful and feeling humans?

Not so long ago, I asked Jake Glisson about all of this. As a little boy, Jake and his family were the nearest neighbors to the Pulitzer-winning author Marjorie Kinnan Rawlings in Cross Creek in northern Florida. Perhaps as much as any writer, Rawlings captured the details of the very singular rural Florida culture in books like *The Yearling*. Her chronicles of "sense of place" relied on an expansive geography, one with secrets still tucked away in the creases of its landscape.

"Well . . . everyone in Cross Creek was a character," said Jake. "You had room to spread out, room to be one." He pauses, bringing his hands nearly together, palms inward. "If you tried to be a character today in a condominium with walls only six inches thick, well, they'd ask you to leave . . ."

In celebrating individuality, Rawlings also praised the natural places that helped create the conditions for it. "I don't know how anyone can live without some small place of enchantment to turn to," she wrote. Enchantment is fueled by a sense of the unknown, a near-mythic condition where not everything can be scientifically examined and collated. It really is more like a haunted castle, less like a government information center. Unlike taxonomy that classifies organisms into families and classes and phyla, enchantment may be elusive—but it's undeniably heartfelt and particular and human.

Odd, but it's taken a professor of sustainability in Australia to coin a term to help us understand the loss of such qualities. Dr. Glenn Albrecht studied abrupt environmental changes taking place in a remote southeastern region of his country. In doing so, he found natives there were anxious, unsettled, even depressed—as if they had already been displaced to another land.

In one essay, Albrecht named this dysfunction "solastalgia" and explained it as a "form of homesickness one gets when one is still at home." As the *New York Times* reported in a Sunday magazine article, solastalgia "is felt increasingly, given the ongoing degradation of the environment."

The issues Albrecht considers are also found in the growing field of ecopsychology, which attempts to remedy our increasing estrangement from the natural world. "As our environment continues to change around us," asks Albrecht, "how deeply are our minds suffering in turn?" Solastalgia, then, becomes a profound yearning for a true sense of nature and place and all the emotional comfort it affords. The loss of this quality is every bit as real as the loss of a river, a spring, a neighborhood.

The malaise of sprawl in Florida really gained traction in the last few decades. Without responsible adult supervision, this giddy pell-mell development will not only build out the Sunshine State as promised in forty or fifty years, it will continue to sweep throughout the larger region.

And while everyone's busy congratulating themselves on the material benefits of short-term prosperity, that intangible—but very soulful—quality of "place" will quietly slip away. The unfashionable barbershops, the weekly newspapers, the independent bookstores where both the owners and their dogs are genuinely happy to see you.

They will transmute and then vanish. If they are remembered, it will be in stories and on historic signs that, for a brief moment, chronicle what it means to live in a community that has a functioning heart.

Epilogue

*Keeping Heart Is Far More
Important Than Keeping Score*

I am figuring that by now you've waded, dived, slogged, paddled—or sauntered—your way through this sampler of widely diverse water-imbued experiences. As promised from the get-go, the stories here aren't drenched with pontification about the value of water to our lives. Instead, they're intended to soak the imagination a bit with the possibilities of it all.

One does not need to dive with sharks—or with the spirits of pre-Columbian Gods—to more fully actualize the water experiences available to us. Certainly, we can have high adventures, if

Soaking in the peace of blue on a log during a river paddle.

we want them. But we can also take a casual stroll—or even a hike—next to a lake, a river, a lagoon. And if we feel comfortable doing so, we can paddle across or around the edges of such a place. If we want more emotional information, we might slip into a dense hardwood forest or a fretwork of mangroves that cradles the less-seen margins of fresh- and salt waters. Or we may simply crank up the routine of our saunters so that we are more often in a place where we can be near a natural cache of water.

Surely it helps if we familiarize ourselves with the possibilities of geography. As you've seen, the places here are scattered about Florida and the bioregion just beyond—sometimes they even exist in the sweet wellspring of memory itself. I'm guessing that any reader with an imagination who has been stirred in the slightest way by these journeys can find their very own water-infused experience almost anyplace in this country, on this earth. For those of you who have already been doing so for much of your lives, you have my greatest congratulations.

I've been careful to entitle this book *The Peace of Blue*. The pun on "peace" and "piece" is not a small thing. This surely is one man's take on his particular water-themed wanderings in the larger world—and, in that way, it is my "piece," my own singular reportage of life. In the very best of worlds, I might also achieve a certain "peace" from the experience if I pay close attention to the moment.

The point here has been to make the stories "available" in an effort to invite folks to come along with all the possibilities they can summon to engender their own experiential "peace." A few tales rely on more technical scuba training, but I hope that even those unfold in a way that doesn't seem exclusionary. Kayaks, hiking boots, scuba gear—they are all tools to allow our senses a greater latitude to explore this essential energy of water. In the same way, it also doesn't hurt to rely a bit on humor as a tool to place the larger ironies in context.

As implied throughout, fashioning a true connection with this universal energy has far more to do with our capacity to *feel* than it has do with any chest-beating bravado we may drag along to place ourselves somehow above nature.

Certainly that sort of bluster was common when the world was big and scary and our sensibilities were little more than nuisances to the macho adventurer. In such times, the great soggy geography of any place was little more than what early exploiters of Florida referred to as "overflow" in need of serious mechanical intervention.

We are fortunate to have little time machines available to us that help us dial back the years to fully understand how others once saw the world. These time machines are books, of course, and in 1885 one such publication presented itself as a "guide" for potential investors to the largely unknown state of Florida. It was entitled *Florida: Its Climate, Production, and Characteristics*. And right there at the very beginning, it advised: "In Florida, the poor man becomes a Lord because nature serves him."

For the budding Lords-to-be, the guidebook gives many examples of prime terrain ripe for the taking. But it's also cautionary about that portion of the landscape that is simply too stubborn to be easily exploited as human domain. In describing the vast marsh and swamp that once ranged south from Orlando to Lake Okeechobee and east to the St. Johns, the book warns, "Because of heavy rains and defective drainage, it is subject to periodic overflow, and has therefore been found unfit for habitation." Apparently the anointment of Lords is far more problematic in marshes and swamps that remain naturally intact.

If we fast-forward barely more than a century, we find another guidebook, *The Ecosystems of Florida* (1990). In the introduction, the biologist and activist Marjorie Harris Carr wrote fondly of Florida's wondrous landscape diversity: "The ability to 'read' a landscape provides the kind of pleasure that comes from a knowledge of Bach or Shakespeare or Van Gogh. It is a pleasure that increases with your knowledge of the ecology of Florida, and it lasts a lifetime." Ironically, the poor man may metaphorically become as enriched as a Lord—but he or she will do so because of a fundamental understanding of nature—rather than a careless dominion over it.

I have often said that I've never had the conceit as a writer that my words or stories will change anyone's mind. I am not here to bear witness to the carnage of nature or to wring my hands at the insensate humans who orchestrate it. Instead, my primary goal in this work is to illustrate how a place looks and feels with the hope it might encourage the reader to envision that place, to become more aware of it—and, maybe, even to experience it or another like it for themselves.

Nestled in next to this particular goal is my desire to tell a worthy story, one that may even help the reader feel he or she is occupying that moment of time. Certainly my chronicles about diving deep into a sacred and peril-ous cenote in the Dominican Republic or participating in a six-week-long oceanographic expedition to Cuba aren't intended to motivate a reader to imitate the same behaviors. But, as with other stories that ponder both the mystery and vitality of water, I hope they do convey a bit of insight into the sometimes-cryptic dimensions of the larger aquatic-nature equation.

Although the geography here is regional in scope, I also hope the impli-cations reach far beyond the boundaries of any state, any country, extending to anywhere on earth where water exists in any form. As I've noted in one of the essays, the author Marjorie Kinnan Rawlings strongly resisted being categorized as a "regional writer" since her universal themes of the human condition far transcended that constriction. The messages in this collection are tacit and, hopefully, extend far beyond the provincial geography. The world of "blue" is woven deeply into our human lives, regardless of where we live. And it's probably not a good idea to be manipulating and otherwise abusing this water-infused world when so many mysteries are still hidden here. Surely it does offer a very real "peace." But to exploit and then to de-stroy it would be a tragedy the human heart can barely imagine.

This is certainly not an imagined fear. Right here in Florida, the flows of our freshwater springs have been diminishing at an alarming rate. Reac-tionary politicians who don't understand how water and springs—and the aquifer that feeds them—underpin our economy have carelessly allowed this to happen as a by-product of their fanatical zeal to create jobs. We can conjure up broad estimates to show how much freshwater is still available in our aquifers. But the truth is that these aquifers are hidden from sight to all but the most intrepid cave divers and explorers. Continuing to permit water withdrawals in the face of this reality is akin to writing a check without knowing the true balance remaining in the account.

Certainly it's possible that experiences suggested by these essays might even help to build a sort of critical emotional load in which individual read-ers eventually engage in advocacy for our water resources. After all, as the great nature writer Ed Abbey once warned, "Sentiment without action is the ruination of the soul." Still, I resist naming the ways in which the political process can be rendered more truly democratic, figuring that each reader has the capacity to figure that one out for themselves. Since the territory of politics these days can sometimes seem as inscrutable as the deepest cenote, activism surely takes its very own special dose of courage.

However it works, one thing is certain. Considering a great variety of ways in which we can better know our earth—and then putting those exercises into action—is not a way of keeping score. In the very best of worlds, it's an internal voyage with implications that are far more sublime. "A genuine odyssey is not about piling up experiences," the theologian Thomas Moore has written. "It is a deeply felt, risky, unpredictable tour of the soul."

Acknowledgments

I'll always be grateful to the good folks who have encouraged me as I've zigzagged about Florida and the related tropics of the Antilles for much of my adult life.

On first blush, my excursions haven't always been easy to squeeze down into a comfortable niche. I've been blessed by having the opportunity to indulge in many real adventures—but I've done so to help me more fully experience and understand some place, animal, or community in our natural landscape. In this way, my treks into swamps or dives into the ocean at night were not intended to be chest-beating demonstrations glorifying the boldness gene. The adventure, when it existed, was merely a tool that gave me rare access to a place I would not otherwise have had.

A few of these narrative-style essays were born from expeditions sponsored by the Discovery Channel ("Laberinto" and "Sacred Caves"), while others ("Saba" and "Nurse Shark") evolved out of assignments from Islands Publications. *Forum*, the Florida Humanities Council's fine quarterly magazine, has provided their own share of support ("Alph the Sacred River"), and in doing so, demonstrated more fully the powerful ways nature can shape culture and place. The very literate *Oxford American* commissioned my piece on "Solastalgia," and even hosted a literary forum at the National Archives in Washington, D.C., so authors contributing "sense of place" essays to that issue could riff about it in public. The reliving of the machinations that powered the dynamic of our PBS film *In Marjorie's Wake* found its way into the virtual *Journal of Florida Studies*. While the making of the documentary generated its own special broadcast art, the highly eclectic, behind-the-scenes energies were yet one more example of how a widely diverse assortment of skills really does embody the multidisciplinary visions needed to problem-solve in an ever-changing place like Florida.

The core of supporters who have always been there for me—as both a man, as well as a writer—continue to selflessly offer support and guidance —sometimes figurative, sometimes literal. My intrepid swamp-trekking buddy Dr. Steve Phelan, professor emeritus at Rollins College in Winter Park, remains every bit the steady and resolute seeker of natural secrets that he's always been. Certainly, I've appreciated the dauntless curiosity of my other fellow investigators of nature, including Dr. Bruce Stephenson, also of Rollins, Jane Tolbert of the Center for Earth Jurisprudence, and the filmmaker Michelle Thatcher. And I've greatly admired the innovation and courage of those real-life adventurers who have pushed the envelope in caves and on deep, night reefs, including Dr. John McCosker of the California Academy of Sciences and the cave explorer and cartographer Eric Hutcheson of Ocala, Florida.

Had it not been for the genuine and loving support from my now-departed mom and dad, the curiosity and confidence that have led me far, far beyond the safety of my computer and its keyboard would have been far, far less. And so again, I thank Kathleen Dulaney Belleville and Bill Belleville Sr. for this heartfelt and earnest caring. Thanks also to my brother, Jack, of Parsonsburg, Maryland, as well as my childhood exploring buddy, Rick Smith, of Salisbury. Thanks, too, to Dr. Kathleen Whitten of Savannah, Georgia, who generously helped me more fully refocus my energies during my tenure on Folly Island. I will always appreciate my good-hearted and deeply spirited friends, including Jen Chase of Jacksonville and Yvette Comeau of Sanford. Finally, I offer a very real and deep-seated appreciation to Bonnie Martin Church, who selflessly provided the loving support and encouragement that first landed me on a published page years ago.

Award-winning author Bill Belleville specializes in nature, conservation, and helping to define sense of place. *The Peace of Blue* is his seventh book of creative nonfiction. His earlier title, *Losing It All to Sprawl,* was named "One of the Best Books of the Year" by the *Library Journal,* while his last essay collection, *Salvaging the Real Florida,* won top honors from the National Outdoor Book Awards in the category of Natural History Literature. He has scripted and produced films for PBS and radio documentaries for NPR and has written over 1,000 articles and essays for periodicals including *Oxford American, Islands Publications,* and many more.